The Linux Problem Solver

THE
LINUX
PROBLEM
SOLVER

HANDS–ON SOLUTIONS FOR SYSTEMS ADMINISTRATORS

Brian Ward

No Starch Press

San Francisco

THE LINUX PROBLEM SOLVER ©2000 By Brian Ward

Printed in the United States of America

1 2 3 4 5 6 7 8 9 10—03 02 01 00

Trademarked names are used throughout this book. Rather than use a trademark symbol with every occurrence of a trademarked name, we are using the names only in an editorial fashion and to the benefit of the trademark owner, with no intention of infringement of the trademark.

Publisher: William Pollock
Project Editor: Karol Jurado
Assistant Editor: Nick Hoff
Technical Reviewer: Scott Schwartz
Cover and Interior Design: Derek Yee Design
Compositor: Magnolia Studio
Copyeditor: Gail Nelson
Proofreader: Suzanne Goraj
Indexer: Nancy Humphreys

Distributed to the book trade in the United States and Canada by Publishers Group West, 1700 Fourth Street, Berkeley, California 94710, phone: 800-788-3123 or 510-528-1444, fax: 510-528-3444

For information on translations or book distributors outside the United States, please contact No Starch Press directly:

No Starch Press
555 De Haro Street, Suite 250, San Francisco, CA 94107
phone: 415-863-9900, fax: 415-863-9950, info@nostarch.com, www.nostarch.com

The information in this book is distributed on an "As Is" basis, without warranty. While every precaution has been taken in the preparation of this work, neither the author nor No Starch Press shall have any liability to any person or entity with respect to any loss or damage caused or alleged to be caused directly or indirectly by the information contained in it.

Library of Congress Cataloging-in-Publication Data

Ward, Brain, 1972–
    The Linux problem solver / Brian Ward.
        p. cm.
    ISBN 1-886411-35-2
        1. Linux. 2. Operating systems (Computers) I. Title.
    QA76.76.063 W3655 2000
    005.4'469--dc21   99-049513

BRIEF CONTENTS

CONTENTS IN DETAIL

1
ABOUT THIS BOOK

2
NETWORK INSTALLATION

3

NFS, NIS, AND RDIST

4

MS-WINDOWS AND APPLETALK
NETWORKS; WEB PROXY SERVER

5
PRINTING

6
INSTALLING SOFTWARE FROM SOURCE CODE

7
KERNEL UPGRADES

8

BACKUPS AND CRASH RECOVERY

9

USER ENVIRONMENTS

LEXICON
241

PROBLEMS LIST
245

ABOUT THE CD-ROM
251

INDEX
259

PREFACE

Beneath the surface of the many graphical Unix environments that have come out in recent years is a world of diverse little programs and files. Linux is no exception to this. While it may seem overwhelming at first, you'll soon realize that anything on the system can be altered by changing a file, or maybe compiling and installing a new program.

The basic environment for systems administration in Linux is not much different than other Unix variants: it's still a shell (command-line interface). Over the years, various tweaks have appeared which make some tasks much less painful (an example is the kernel configuration that you'll see in Chapter 7).

Repeated efforts have been made to give a graphical user interface to Unix systems administration. Invariably, these tend to do a decent job of configuring a base system and getting it running, but they fall short handling complex tasks. Unix software is highly configurable, and typically designed to work as independently as possible. To get a firm grip on your system, you must get comfortable with the shell, because it is the most efficient interface to the filesystem and currently running processes.

If there's one thing that you're going to see throughout this book, it's the phrase "Try to keep it simple." I can't stress this enough, especially with regard to configuration files of any sort. The default files which come with most packages are usually reasonable places to start, although there are some notable exceptions (mostly with user environments). The larger and more complicated your configurations are, the more difficult they will be to understand and modify later. You'll also minimize the risk that a later version of a package will be slightly incompatible with the old configuration files.

Much of the material in this book takes root in traditional Unix systems administration. For example, Chapter 9 on user environments is as applicable to any Unix flavor as it is to Linux. However, this is not to say that things don't change, and unfortunately, people tend to have a tendency to stick with their old ways for a bit longer than they should. A case in point is illustrated in Chapter 5 on printing: A great number of sites still run the older lpd printing daemons instead of LPRng. But that's not to say that every new program should be embraced and the old stuff thrown out; new (and hence fairly untested) software isn't known for its stability, after all.

Much of my experience in systems administration is due to the people I met while I was an undergraduate at The Pennsylvania State University. James Duncan and Douglas N. Arnold provided excellent guidance at my first systems administration job in the Department of Mathematics. Other big influences were Bill Fenner, Ken Hornstein, Scott Dickson, Dan Ehrlich, Felix Lee, and of course, Scott Schwartz, who was the technical reviewer for this book.

Brian Ward
Chicago, Illinois
April 2000

ABOUT THIS BOOK

1.1 Fighting Fires

This book is all about solving the two basic types of Linux systems administration problems: configuration issues and ongoing maintenance problems. Roughly half of the book deals with configuration issues (that is, setting up some sort of service); the rest deals with keeping your machine up and running.

Since hardly anyone gets things right the first time, troubleshooting (or firefighting, as they call it in Unix circles) is an important part of systems administration. This book will help you solve difficult Linux snafus by integrating troubleshooting techniques with explanations and tutorials of Linux utilities. (You can't be expected to fix problems you have no knowledge of, after all.) When there's a common pitfall related to the subject under discussion, we'll flag it like this:

PROBLEM SAMPLE N

Symptom: How the problem manifests itself.

Problem: Short description of the glitch.

Fix: How to go about fixing (or peacefully ignoring) it.

Even if you're not having the problem, try not to skip over it as you're reading the book—at the very least, look at the symptom description. You'll probably run into it sooner or later.

What This Book Assumes You Know

To get the most out of this book, you need to know a little about Linux or Unix already. Specifically, we assume that you know how to navigate the filesystem, do a process listing, and kill processes. We also assume that you know all the basic file commands (cp, rm, mv, ls, chmod, chown, chgrp, and so on) and are familiar with a shell—bash, to be specific. Section 1.3 below contains a review of Linux system basics.

You also need competence with some text editor. This is a religious topic for Unix types, but for the purposes of this book it makes no difference whether you know vi, emacs, ed, pico, or whatever. But you must know how to open a file, make changes without damaging it, save it, and exit. Linux will not tolerate typos in configuration files.

Brief Outline of Contents

In addition to explaining notation, **Chapter 1** also covers the basics of how Linux starts and runs, along with a few of the core utilities such as the system logger. We intend this mostly as review, so the discussion is on the terse side.

Chapter 2 ("Network Installation") deals with the basics of network setup. It's purely about connecting to a network and the tools for diagnosing problems when they come up.

Chapter 3 ("NFS, NIS, and rdist") is about spreading information around a network. Topics include NFS (the Network File System—used for file sharing); NIS, a simple network information database system; and Rdist, a program that copies groups of files to remote machines (to keep their software sets up-to-date, for example).

Chapter 4 ("MS-Windows and AppleTalk Networks; Web Proxy Server") is about making Linux talk to other non-Linux machines on a network, specifically Windows machines and Macintoshes. The last section covers a Web proxy server that can improve your entire network's performance.

Chapter 5 ("Printing") talks about printing from a system perspective. This chapter covers how printing works on Linux and Unix machines, from the expected format down to the filters that process output before it passes to the printer.

Chapter 6 ("Installing Software from Source Code") takes you through the traditional method of installing Unix software—from source code.

Chapter 7 ("Kernel Upgrades") is all about configuring and compiling a new Linux kernel, along with the accompanying modules. The kernel is the core of the operating system.

Chapter 8 ("Backups and Crash Recovery") runs through everyone's favorite topic: disasters. If you have anything halfway valuable on your system, you're going to need some kind of backup, and this chapter tells you how to create one. It also describes how to get started with the bootable portion of the CD-ROM bundled with this book, which you can use to get your system back on track after a bad crash.

Chapter 9 ("User Environments") covers how to set up accounts for users. New accounts need *dot files* for a proper environment. Unfortunately new, inexperienced users also have a tendency to wreck their dot files. We'll talk about how to write dot files clearly (so users aren't just making a stab in the dark when they modify them) and how to optimize them.

1.2 Conventions

We'll use a monospaced typeface for text that appears on-screen or that you type into a terminal window. Punctuation will appear outside of quotation marks containing any on-screen text or commands.

Unless otherwise noted, examples in the book assume you're using bash, but we'll generally avoid the extensions that bash offers over the Bourne shell (/bin/sh). The user prompt will be the dollar sign ($). Anything a *user* types that appears outside a paragraph will be in **boldface**, so user commands will look like this:

$ **echo Hi, I am a user.**

The *superuser* (root), on the other hand, will have the pound sign (#) for a prompt:

echo Hello, I am the sysadmin, and that user complains too much.

Many Linux files and scripts have comments that begin with #, so pay attention to the context.

echo This is not a comment.
my program has a comment here

Dealing with Manual Pages

We reference manual pages that give further information as follows:

Relevant man pages: ascii (7), man (1)

This means sections 7 and 1 of the manual contain additional information for ascii and man. The command `man ascii` gives you the online manual for `ascii`, and if you happen to come across an item with entries in multiple sections, you can pick out different sections using `man` followed by the section number, then the item name (for example, `man 5 passwd`).

If you want to look at some unformatted manual page that's in a directory all by itself (not in any system man directory), such as `foo.1` in `support/ introduction` on the included CD-ROM, you can format and view it with the following:

```
$ nroff -man foo.1 | less
```

We won't dwell on manual pages, as they can range from nonexistent to sloppy to very decent. But if a program has a couple thousand options and a manual page that explains them, we'll mention the manual page as a reference.

Avoid printing manual pages if possible. Most people I've seen who print manual pages out never read them, for good reason: Manual pages are primarily references, so they aren't particularly wonderful reading material. When you're looking for a particular item, searching the on-screen version is almost always faster. But if you insist on printing manual pages, do it the proper way:

```
$ groff -Tps -man foo.1 | lpr -Pprinter
```

Unix, Linux, and Linux Distributions

Linux looks and acts like other systems that call themselves Unix, so many of the things you'll find in this book apply to other kinds of Unix. Keep in mind, though, that file and directory paths, interfaces, and commands and their arguments vary over the many flavors of Unix. When we discuss Unix in general, we're not talking about Linux in particular.

There really is no one true Linux system; only the kernel itself is standardized. The various Linux distributions occasionally put files in different places and use different scripts. In this book, we'll mention the file name and the place where you can usually expect to find the file. If you don't see it there, you can always try searching for it with find. For example,

```
$ find /usr -name '*.conf' -print
```

finds anything that ends with `.conf` under `/usr`.

1.3 Linux System Basics

One of the difficulties in writing a book like this is that every reader has a different level of experience with Linux. So that we all start on the same page, here's a quick rundown of some Linux system components you'll need to understand. If this seems like too much too soon, pick up a beginner's book (such as Bob Rankin's *The No B.S. Guide to Red Hat Linux*, No Starch Press) to familiarize yourself with your system.

Init, /etc/inittab, init.d, rc.*

The first process Linux starts up when it boots is called init. It always has a process ID (PID) of 1. Most Linux distributions use the System V–style init, which starts up services based on an inittab and a few directories containing initialization and server start-up scripts.

/etc/inittab contains basic init configuration information. The entries consist of colon-delimited fields in lines (corresponding to actions) and comments prefaced with #. Here are some sample entries:

```
# default runlevel
id:3:initdefault:
# runlevel 2 is multi-user with network
l3:3:wait:/sbin/init.d/rc 3
# what to do when CTRL-ALT-DEL is pressed
ca::ctrlaltdel:/sbin/shutdown -r -t 4 now
# getty entry
3:123:respawn:/sbin/mingetty tty3
```

Each line defines the characteristics of an action. The first field in a line is an identifier (maximum four characters), the second says in what runlevels the actions should take place, the third defines an action type, and the rest is the action (usually a program). Runlevels are 0–6 and the rarely used a–c, and they define different states of the machine. That is, each runlevel runs its own specific set of processes.

The initdefault and ctrlaltdel actions work a little differently from other action types: initdefault denotes the default runlevel, and the ctrlaltdel action type specifies what to do when a user presses CTRL-ALT-DELETE.

The l3 entry above is a typical start-up action. It runs /sbin/init.d/rc 3 and waits for it to complete. This is how most of the system services start; we'll talk about init.d and rc shortly.

The last line has a respawn type that runs a getty on a virtual terminal (in this case it's tty3, the one you get when you press ALT-F3). getty's function is to do some initialization and then run login, a program that waits for a user to log in to a terminal. login does not terminate right away, but rather does an exec—a system call which one process uses to start up another in its place.

Only after the user logs out does the original process, formerly a getty, terminate. Then the respawn type takes effect again: init runs another getty and the whole cycle starts again.

Rereading /etc/inittab

To tell init to reread /etc/inittab (for example, if you add or delete a respawn action and want the effects to take place), send it a HUP (hang-up) signal:

```
# kill -HUP 1
```

PROBLEM 1

Symptom: When you send the signal to init, your system dies.

Problem: You accidentally sent init some signal other than HUP (1).

Fix: You should accustom yourself to double-checking any kill command. An alternative form of kill -HUP is kill -1. Avoid this form of the command, because you may miss the hyphen (-) in front of the 1.

/sbin/init.d/rc 2 example

The /sbin/init.d/rc 2 action starts most of the system services for runlevel 2. Red Hat 6 systems have a directory called /etc/rc.d/rc2.d containing a bunch of symbolic links with names like S05network and S20gpm to files in /etc/rc.d/init.d. The init.d scripts, usually shell scripts and start and stop system services. The names of the links in rc2.d decide the scripts' arguments, as well as the order in which to call them.

If the name of the link starts with an S, the argument will be start; a K signifies stop. The number after this first letter determines when the program will start. Those with lower numbers are the first ones init's invocation of /sbin/init.d/rc 2 calls.

Since there are six numerical runlevels, there are six directories, rc0.d through rc6.d (rc*.d). Unfortunately, every Linux distribution puts init.d and rc*.d in a different place. We've already mentioned that Red Hat puts them in /etc/rc.d; Debian puts them right in /etc (as Solaris and other System V systems do); S.u.S.E. is similar to Red Hat, except that init.d is just a link to rc.d.

Adding or Removing a Service

Adding or removing a new service is fairly straightforward. Let's say you have some server called fooserv you want to start up at boot time, and your system has rc*.d in /etc/rc.d. Make a new script fooserv in /etc/rc.d/init.d that's similar to the scripts already in there, and test it with /etc/rc.d/init.d/fooserv start and /etc/rc.d/init.d/fooserv stop. If everything works fine, make appropriate links in the rc*.d directories. Make a link with a high number such as

```
# ln -s ../init.d/fooserv S90fooserv
```

in /etc/rc.d/rc2.d so the service will start up near the end of bootup. Similarly, in the runlevels that shut services down, you probably want to shut fooserv off early, so the link to shut the service off would get a name like K10fooserv.

To remove a service, remove its links in /etc/rc*.d. You may also opt to rename the links; for example, you could add an underscore (_) in front of the name. Be careful when removing links, because if you use the service again in the future, you'll need to put the links back. In addition, before you remove a link, see if its init.d script (the file to which the link points) has a line like this, testing a configuration variable or file:

```
[ -z "$RUN_GATED" ] || exit 0
```

Certain distributions (like S.u.S.E.) read a global configuration file that sets these variables (like $RUN_GATED), which all of the service start-up scripts read. Red Hat has a bunch in /etc/sysconfig. If your distribution uses one of these configuration files, you'll probably find it easier to turn services on or off by modifying the configuration files rather than removing links in the rc*.d directories.

Relevant man pages: inittab (5), init (1)

The Syslog Facility

The syslog facility reports system notice and error messages. The message recording daemon, syslogd, waits for messages from other programs, sorting them into different files as it receives them. The standard log directory under Linux is /var/log, but /etc/syslog.conf is the ultimate authority on where messages go.

You can configure messages to go to a file (including special devices such as a terminal), another machine, a set of users, or a named pipe. Here are a few example entries:

```
kern.warn;*.err;authpriv.*    /dev/tty10
mail.*                        @logs.example.com
*.*                           /var/log/messages
*.emerg                       root
```

The first column describes what kinds of messages to record, and the second says where to record them. The first line says that kernel, error, and authorization messages should go to /dev/tty10, the second sends mail diagnostics to the syslogd on logs.example.com, the third sends all syslog messages to the file /var/log/messages, and the last writes emergency messages to root's screen, if root happens to be logged in.

An entry for kern.warn states that the *facility* name of the message is kern and the *priority level* is warn. Valid facility names for Linux 2.2 are auth, authpriv, cron, daemon, kern, lpr, mail, news, syslog, user, uucp, and local0 through local7. Priorities are alert, crit, debug, emerg, err, info, notice, and warning. There are also a few outdated priorities (look in /usr/include/sys/syslog.h for a list of these).

As your system runs, messages continue to pile up in /var/log. If your system did nothing about them, the disk partition containing /var would eventually fill up, making it difficult to use the system. Most distributions realize this and run cron jobs to clean up the log directories so this never happens.

If you have a substantial network, it's a good idea to have a log host to which other machines can send log messages. Keeping the logs for your whole network in one place can make the process of detecting and debugging problems much quicker and easier. You may also want to maintain a local log—you could save a few minutes here and there at the expense of only a little disk space and system time.

NOTE *Some distributions don't put all message facilities in* /etc/syslog.conf *(especially the* local *facilities). If* /etc/syslog.conf *doesn't mention a facility, any program's output to that facility will be thrown away. Use the* **logger** *command to debug your configuration.*

Relevant man pages: syslog.conf (5), syslog (1), logger (1)

cron

A periodic event scheduler, cron is a useful system daemon. It reads files called *crontabs* that specify times, intervals, and the commands to run at the end of every interval. These files are usually located in /var/spool/cron, and users create, access, modify, and put them into place with the crontab command. Here's a short crontab reference:

crontab *file*	Use *file* as the crontab
crontab -e	Edit crontab (with the editor specified in the environment variable VISUAL or EDITOR)
crontab -l	Display crontab
crontab -r	Remove crontab

Here's an example crontab (for a user with a login of jamie):

```
SHELL=/bin/sh
PATH=/usr/bin:/usr/sbin:/usr/local/sbin:/usr/local/bin:/sbin:/bin
MAILTO=jamie
53 6,20 * * * /home/jamie/bin/clean-junk > /dev/null 2>&1
```

SHELL, PATH, and MAILTO are set to what you'd expect: the shell and path to use for the commands, and the user to send mail to if any commands produce output. In the fourth line, the first six fields specify the times and intervals; from first to sixth, they are minute, hour, day of month, month, and day of week. They are specified either numerically or with an asterisk (*), which includes everything—for example, * in the day of week field is the same as 0,1,2,3,4,5,6. The last line in jamie's crontab above matches every day (of the month and week) and every month when the minute is 53 and the hour is 6 or 20 (that is, 6:53 am and 8:53 pm).

When a time matches what's specified in the six fields, the action after the fields is performed. If you want to annoy a user called bob on any Friday the 13th, you could write:

```
* * 13 * 5 /bin/mail -s "Beware, Bob" bob
```

The * entries for minute and hour make this a particular nuisance for bob: Poor bob receives a message from you every minute on Friday the 13th. To give bob just one message at noon on every Friday the 13th, you could use this:

```
00 12 13 * 5 /bin/mail -s "Beware, Bob" bob
```

(We're not saying any of this tormenting of bob is a particularly good idea, mind you.)

Another version of the crontab file, /etc/crontab is a system crontab and has an additional field after the time specifications: the user running the job. In the following two entries, the users running the tasks are root and backup.

```
15 4  * * * root /usr/local/sbin/sysclean > /dev/null 2>&1
25 23 * * * backup /usr/local/sbin/do-backups
```

The version of cron that comes with Linux (Vixie Cron) is quite flexible in comparison to those on other Unix flavors; take a look at the manual pages for more information.

Relevant man pages: crontab (5), crontab (1), cron (8)

The passwd File

The principal user database under Unix is /etc/passwd. There are a number of ways to modify it. The passwd command available to users is also a maintenance tool for the systems administrator.

Because more than one process may attempt to modify the passwd file at once, you have to do some locking through the file /etc/ptmp. If available, the vipw command is the preferred way to modify /etc/passwd directly. A passwd entry looks like this:

```
bob:x:3119:100:Bob the Tormented:/home/bob:/bin/bash
```

As you can see, colons (:) separate the fields, and they are fairly straightforward. Only the second field, the encrypted password, deserves some mention. The example above shows a shadow password scheme, which puts the encrypted password into /etc/shadow, where the user can't read it. This is meant as a security measure (although its effectiveness is somewhat dubious). Most major distributions use shadow passwords or give you the option.

Unix does not keep a user's password around in its original (*plain-text* or *cleartext*) form; that would make the password too easy to steal. Instead, it encrypts the passwords on the spot and stores them in encrypted form. When the user types a password, Unix encrypts it and matches it against the one on the system.

On larger networks, it's a hassle to maintain passwd files for many users across machines. That's where systems like NIS come in (see Chapter 3).

Relevant man pages: passwd (5), passwd (1), shadow (5)

Devices

Unix programs talk to devices through *device files* found in /dev. Device file names include tty1, hda3, and audio. Interaction with the device files using regular programs like cat and dd yields different results depending on the kind of file and its permissions (these vary, since you may not want a regular user to scribble all over a raw hard disk device, for example).

If you look in /dev, you'll find a lot of *devices* there (also called *special files*). Do you really have all of this stuff on your system, and what do the device names correspond to? The answer to the first question is no; if you try to do an operation on a device that doesn't exist on your machine, either you'll get an error message like "/dev/**device**: No such device" or your command will just wait forever for the nonexistent device to become available. As far as the second question goes, the device names are up to the programmers. Here is a list of a few basic device names.

/dev/tty* Terminal devices of some sort. They all work through the same interface.

/dev/tty*n* (where *n* is a number) Linux virtual consoles.

/dev/ttyS* Serial ports.

/dev/ttyp*, /dev/ttyq*, .. Pseudo-terminals: xterm, telnet, ssh, and other shell-invoking programs use these (they emulate the rather archaic interface of a real terminal in order to provide compatibility for terminal-reliant shells and programs).

/dev/hd* ATA/IDE devices; these can include ATA hard disks, CD-ROM drives, removable media, and so on. The device without any number after it refers to the whole disk; with a number, it refers to a partition. For example, /dev/hda2 is the second partition on the master disk of the primary interface.

/dev/sd* SCSI disks; can include removable media. Partitioning is similar to that of ATA/IDE devices. However, unlike schemes on other operating systems and the ATA/IDE naming convention, the SCSI disks are assigned the names /dev/sda, /dev/sdb, and so on, in the order in which they appear to the SCSI host adapter (controller). /dev/sda is the lowest SCSI ID on the first SCSI host adapter (scsi0) with disks, /dev/sdb is the next ID up. If you have multiple SCSI host adapters in your system, the assignment follows the ordering of the host adapters; first the devices on scsi0 are assigned, then scsi1, and so on.

/dev/scd* SCSI CD-ROM drives.

/dev/sg* Generic SCSI devices. With a generic SCSI device, a user program can interact directly with any SCSI device without a special kernel driver. Scanning and CD-burning programs use the generic SCSI devices.

/dev/null Anything written to /dev/null goes into the proverbial bitbucket; it's thrown away. If read from, the result is an end of file (EOF).

/dev/zero Reads from this return null characters (every bit is zero).

/dev/fd* Floppy disks (of various geometries).

/dev/audio, /dev/dsp, /dev/midi, /dev/mixer, /dev/sequencer Various sound devices.

/dev/lp* Parallel ports.

/dev/psaux The PS2 auxiliary port. Most PCs come with these mice. These are not USB mice, which may become popular in the near future.

Examining and Creating Devices

ls -l /dev/hdb1 reveals this:

```
brw-rw----   1 root     disk      3,  65 Jul 26  1998 /dev/hdb1
```

Most of the fields appear as ls would present them for normal files, except that there is a b at the beginning of the first field, and two numbers (here, 3 and 65) have replaced the size field. The b means it is a block device (character devices have a c instead). The two numbers in place of the size are the *major* and *minor device numbers*. Each major number is assigned to one device driver, and the minor numbers go to the devices that use the driver (for example, an ATA/IDE driver, which handles disks, CD-ROMs, and other hardware). The kernel assigns the major and minor numbers.

To make a device, use the mknod command. The command to make the /dev/hda1 above would be

```
# mknod /dev/hdb1 b 3 56
```

Distributions usually come with a fairly complete /dev, but since disk crashes can wipe them out, it's good to keep the mknod command in mind.

Relevant man page: mknod (1)

NOTE *The GNU mknod manual page is unmaintained; the info page for it is current. This command hasn't changed significantly in years, though.*

Working with Disks

Linux offers a number of programs for dealing with matters such as partitions and filesystems. Some of the programs carry out the same task, the only difference being their interface.

When you are meddling with disks, check your actions carefully. Unix tradition dictates that you don't get 60 warnings about your actions—it assumes you know what you're doing. If you mistakenly execute dd if=/dev/zero of=/dev/hdb as root, the operating system will happily run off and zero out that entire disk.

Here's a rundown of the important Linux disk programs:

fdisk, cfdisk   Disk-partitioning programs. They work with ATA/IDE as well as SCSI disks. cfdisk is a full-screen curses interface to fdisk, but it can be a little cranky at times, so fdisk remains the favorite of most admins who do extensive partitioning.

mke2fs   This program creates an ext2 (second extended) filesystem, as in mke2fs /dev/hdb1. Be especially careful when doing this, since you are wiping out all previous partition information.

fsck   Examines a filesystem for errors and fixes them. We'll talk about this one in Chapter 8.

mount   Attaches a filesystem to the currently running system, otherwise known as *mounting* a filesystem.

umount   Unmounts a filesystem.

mkswap   Creates a swap space signature on a partition.

du   Shows disk usage for a directory.

df   Shows capacity statistics of filesystems.

We'll talk about disk programs in more detail in Chapter 8.

As the system boots, various instances of mount -a are executed with different arguments. After parsing those arguments, mount reads /etc/fstab, finds any filesystems that match the arguments, and attempts to mount them. Therefore, /etc/fstab is the main reference for the machine's local partitions. /etc/fstab looks like this:

```
/dev/hda1   /        ext2      defaults                1   1
/dev/hda2   swap     swap      defaults                0   0
/dev/hda4   /home    ext2      defaults                1   2
/dev/hdd    /cdrom   iso9660   ro,noauto,nosuid,user   0   0
/dev/sda4   /zip     ext2      rw,noauto,nosuid,user   0   0
```

The first and the second fields (columns) are the device and where to mount it. The third is the filesystem type, and the fourth contains options for mount. The options seen here include:

default Use default options.

ro Mount the filesystem read-only.

rw Mount the filesystem read-write.

nosuid Disable any suid (setuid) bits found on the filesystem. If you allowed users to mount a removable disk (such as a Zip disk) with some suid-root program on it, they would be able to romp all over the system—you probably don't want that.

user Any user may mount and umount this filesystem; root access is not required.

noauto Ignore this filesystem on an invocation of mount -a.

The fifth and sixth fields deal with backups and fsck ordering. Notice also that /etc/fstab mentions swap partitions, although they aren't actual filesystems. When using the /etc/fstab above, the command swapon /dev/hda2 activates /dev/hda2 as a swap partition, and swapon -a activates all swap partitions mentioned in /etc/fstab.

Relevant man pages: mount (8), fstab (5), du (1), df (1), fdisk (1), mkswap (8), mke2fs (8), swapon (8)

The /proc Filesystem

/proc is a special type of filesystem in Linux that allows flexible interaction with processes and kernel parameters.

If you try ls /proc, you get a list of files and directories pertaining to several parts of the currently running Linux system. One way to explore the contents of /proc is through experimentation. Try these two commands:

```
$ cat /proc/cpuinfo
$ cat /proc/$$/status
```

The first command returns what the kernel knows about the processor inside the machine. In the second, the $$ expands to the process ID of the current shell (if you're running bash), and the whole line returns the status of the shell process. These are examples of the two kinds of items you'll find in the Linux /proc file system: kernel and process information.

Every process on the system is represented in a directory /proc/**pid**, where **pid** is a process ID (/proc/self is always set to the ID of the process querying it). The entries under these directories tell you about how the command was called, its environment, its status, and a host of other information. Most versions of ps use the /proc filesystem to gather information.

The other stuff in /proc (such as cpuinfo) consists of kernel information. The more useful of these files include:

interrupts   *Active* interrupts. For example, if a serial port isn't in use, it won't show up in the list. Also shows the number of interrupts received since boot-up.

ioports   All I/O port assignments.

dma   DMA assignments.

devices   Available devices. The number before the device symbol is the device's major number; this corresponds to the major device number in /dev.

filesystems   All available filesystem types.

modules   Active modules.

meminfo   Memory information.

scsi/   Directory holding SCSI host adapter and device information.

version   Kernel version.

mounts   Mounted filesystems. /etc/mtab is also supposed to have this information, but the -n argument of mount prevents any writes to /etc/mtab.

net/   Network information.

You may be curious about all the stuff in /proc, but it's probably not a good idea to use cat on every item you see. A cat /proc/kcore (which you can only perform as root) dumps all sorts of binary garbage to your screen. Use a program such as less instead of cat on items you're not sure about.

Relevant man page: proc (5)

Untangling Quote Messes

A *literal* character is one that does not receive special treatment. For example, shells treat the characters such as $ and * differently than regular letters (like a and j). When you want the shell to read $ in the same way that it would treat an a, you're asking for a *literal* $.

While looking at scripts and examples on the system and in introductory books, you have probably noticed that they use an array of methods to get literal characters: single quotes, double quotes, and backslashes. Because there are so many ways to get literal characters, Unix shells sometimes cause utter confusion. Worse still, some shells have inconsistent schemes, and they're all somewhat incompatible. One factor in the choice of bash in this book is its relatively clean syntax.

To write effective scripts and commands, you need to understand how a shell parses its input and runs a command. When you type a command, you are specifying a number of arguments. Even the program you intend to run is an argument. After processing the arguments, the shell puts each argument into its own slot and runs a system call on all of the slots to execute the command. The argument slots' numbers start at zero in this system call—therefore, the actual first argument (in this case, the command), is often called the *zeroth argument*.

If you enter a command such as

```
$ echo "I'm a command" * $PATH
```

the zeroth argument is echo. The first argument is the string I'm a command (including the spaces). The rest of the arguments depend on the contents of the current working directory and what the environment variable PATH is set to.

When you type a command, your shell first parses quoted arguments and expands variables and patterns. Then it fills the argument slots with whatever the expansions yielded. Problems tend to occur when you forget that the shell expands some character in an argument before putting it into an argument slot.

Any * out on its own expands to a list of files in the current directory that do not begin with a dot (.) before the execution of the command. If the current directory holds no files, a literal * is passed as the argument; no error messages appear. This holds for all pattern matching. For example, foo* expands to all files in the current directory that start with foo except when none match, in which case it doesn't expand at all. This kind of expansion is known as *globbing*.

Any unquoted string beginning with $ expands to a shell or environment variable.

The confusion with quotes comes in when you want to prevent the shell from expanding special characters. There are three types of quotes: the double quote ("); the single quote (') or *tick*; and the back quote (`), or *backtick*. Their meanings are:

' **Literal.** Anything inside single quotes does not expand; the shell passes it straight to the command.

" **Somewhat literal.** There is no globbing, so a character such as * is sent to the command, but shell and environment variables (beginning with $) are expanded.

Command substitution. The shell executes any command inside two backticks, and passes the output of that command as an argument (for example, FOO=`ls` places the output of the ls command into the variable FOO).

To pass any of the three quotes as literal arguments, put a forward slash (/) in front of the quote *outside* any single or double quotes. There are other ways to do it in bash, though; for example, "'" passes a single quote, and """ passes a double quote. Because there are so many ways to get literal characters as arguments, users often try to use all of them at once and end up with unexpected results. The best way to debug a problem with quoting is to use echo to see what arguments follow the substitution—for example:

```
$ echo '$this should put a dollar sign before the text'
```

NOTE *Annoyingly, ISO 8859-1 defines an acute accent that looks a lot like a single quote; you might have come across it in email messages, or you may have seen it on keyboards from outside the United States.*

That's it for the basics. In the following chapters, you'll not only encounter solutions to over a hundred Linux problems, but you'll also see in-depth detail on why the solutions work. With this information in hand, you'll have everything you need to fix your Linux headaches.

2

NETWORK INSTALLATION

2.1 Introduction

Basic network configuration (configuring a network interface and adding a default route) shouldn't cause you much grief. The challenges come in if you want to set up your network to share a PPP connection to the Internet over several machines, share files, play network games (of course), and so on. Due to the increasing number of network security exploits (and people who want to use them), attention to network security is also important. Unix diagnostic tools come in handy for configuration and the occasional glitches that crop up.

This chapter is not meant to be an all-inclusive guide to setting up a Linux network; rather, it will teach you how to use some of Linux's more useful (and tricky) networking facilities.

2.2 Basic Commands and Files

Linux network devices are called *interfaces*. Device names include eth0 and ppp0, which are Ethernet and PPP interfaces, respectively, although these are only the network-layer device names. PPP, for example, runs on top of another device, usually a serial port such as ttyS0.

Device drivers are in the Linux kernel; Chapter 7 explains how to build a custom kernel with the drivers you may need to use the network.

Commands

Here is a short review of network configuration commands. We'll cover most of the diagnostic commands in the last section of this chapter.

The ifconfig Command

The command

```
ifconfig [<interface> [<addr|hostname>] [<option value> ..] <up|down>]
```

manually configures an interface and is commonly used for Ethernet. The following example sets the interface to the IP address 10.0.0.13 and the net mask to 255.255.255.0:

```
# ifconfig eth0 10.0.0.13 netmask 255.255.255.0 up
```

Although you'll rarely call ifconfig under normal operating circumstances, it and the route command (see Adding a Route in Section 2.2) come in handy for debugging.

With -a or no arguments at all, ifconfig returns the status of all interfaces, along with some other potentially useful information, such as the number of collisions. For example, we took the following excerpt from a gateway machine:

```
# ifconfig -a
...
eth1      Link encap:Ethernet  HWaddr 00:A0:CC:3B:47:66
          inet addr:10.1.2.1 Bcast:10.255.255.255  Mask:255.255.255.0
          UP BROADCAST RUNNING MULTICAST  MTU:1500  Metric:1
          RX packets:667785 errors:0 dropped:0 overruns:0 frame:0
          TX packets:504611 errors:0 dropped:0 overruns:0 carrier:0
          Collisions:177
          Interrupt:10 Base address:0x4000

ppp0      Link encap:Point-to-Point Protocol
          inet addr:192.168.69.35  P-t-P:192.168.69.1
          Mask:255.255.255.255
          UP POINTOPOINT RUNNING NOARP MULTICAST  MTU:1500  Metric:1
          RX packets:3055 errors:6 dropped:0 overruns:0 frame:6
          TX packets:2901 errors:0 dropped:0 overruns:0 carrier:0
          Collisions:0
```

NOTE *Some Unix versions (like Solaris) require the* -a *flag to get the interface configuration.*

Red Hat 6.*x*, for example, keeps its basic interface configuration in /etc/sysconfig/network-scripts. For the configuration of the interface eth0, the file with all of the values is ifcfg-eth0. At boot time, the script /etc/rc.d/init.d/network finds all the interfaces and attempts to run script ifup inter-face on the ifcfg-*devname* script (which in turn runs some other scripts).

NOTE *The networks 10.0.0.0 and 192.168.69.0 are reserved for private networks. Anyone may use them for their own network (corporations often use them for network numbers behind a firewall), but no router on the true Internet knows about them. IANA also reserves names example.com and example.net for use in examples (such as those in this book).*

The route Command

To do anything useful, network packets need a route to travel along. The route command (route [<add|del> args ..]) changes the routes that your computer knows, or the *routing table*. (Routing is a complex subject, so it's best to keep the table as simple as possible when you're starting with a small network.)

With no arguments, route returns the current routing table. The -n option turns off host name resolution and comes in particularly handy, since you usually want to look at the table when there is some sort of problem (if you have trouble with the network, the DNS server is probably having trouble as well).

Setting the Default Route

If a network packet doesn't have a specific route to follow in the kernel routing table, it goes to the *default route* (also known as the *default gateway* or *gateway*). If no default route exists and nothing in the routing table applies to a packet, the program trying to send the packet gets a "No route to host" error. Use

```
# route add default gw 10.0.0.1
```

to set the default route to 10.0.0.1.

Adding a Route

To add a route, use the command

```
# route add -net 10.0.1.0 netmask 255.255.255.0 gw 10.0.0.48
```

This adds a route to the network 10.0.1.0, with net mask 255.255.255.0 and gateway 10.0.0.48. (As explained in Section 2.4, this network consists of the hosts from 10.0.1.1 to 10.0.1.254.)

Showing the Kernel Routing Table

The command route -n (or netstat -nr) shows the kernel routing table. The -n option disables domain name resolution. If you're running this command, you're probably doing so because you can't reach the outside world, so there's a good chance you can't get to the name server to look up domain names, either.

/etc/resolv.conf

The file /etc/resolv.conf contains information for finding host names with DNS (domain name service). It usually contains the IP addresses of one or more name servers with some default domains to use as an optional suffix in searches. For example, under the setup

```
search home.example.com example.com
nameserver 10.0.0.2
nameserver 10.0.0.3
```

atlantic.home.example.com would be the first attempt at a valid host name for an attempted connection to a host called atlantic. If atlantic.home.example.com didn't exist, atlantic.example.com would be the next attempt.

/etc/nsswitch.conf

The file /etc/nsswitch.conf provides a flexible means of host name resolution and other system information. When a program wants to resolve a host name into an IP address, it makes a library call, which consults a number of files and services based on /etc/nsswitch.conf. For example, if the line

```
hosts:          files dns
```

appears in /etc/nsswitch.conf, files comes first, so initially the file /etc/hosts is consulted as a table of host names, and if nothing relevant is found there, dns becomes the active keyword and DNS is consulted. (See the subsection on /etc/resolv.conf above to see how to configure the DNS resolver.)

/etc/services

Internet services run on a machine's port, which has a numeric value. TCP examples include SMTP mailing on port 25, telnet on port 23, finger on port 79, and www (http) on port 80. However, programs don't usually refer to the ports by number, so they map ports in /etc/services and convert names to numbers. Here's an excerpt from one such file:

```
ftp             21/tcp
ssh             22/tcp    # secure shell
ssh             22/ucp    # secure shell
telnet          23/tcp
# 24 - private
smtp            25/tcp    mail
```

The first field is the name. The second is the number and the protocol it refers to, followed by any aliases or comments. In the second line, ssh is the field, 22/tcp the number and protocol classification, and # secure shell a comment.

inetd and /etc/inetd.conf

A so-called superserver, inetd is responsible for many of a machine's services. It starts up at boot time and runs for the duration of the machine's uptime, waiting for incoming connections on specified ports and forking off an appropriate program if a connection comes in.

The following are typical entries for inetd's configuration file (/etc/inetd.conf):

```
login   stream  tcp   nowait  root    /usr/sbin/tcpd  in.rlogind
# exec  stream  tcp   nowait  root    /usr/sbin/tcpd  in.rexecd


# Pop et al
pop3    stream  tcp   nowait  root    /usr/sbin/tcpd  /usr/sbin/popper -s
```

The first field is the service as specified in /etc/services, followed by the socket type, protocol, wait status, user (with optional group), server path name, and finally the server arguments. Note the server path name and arguments of the typical pop3 entry: /usr/sbin/tcpd (described below) does some filtering and logging, then hands the connection to /usr/sbin/popper -s.

To remove a service, place a pound sign (#) at the beginning of the desired line to comment it out, then send a hang-up (HUP) signal to the inetd process. Usually the process ID of inetd is in /var/run/inetd.pid, so you can run **kill -HUP `cat /var/run/inetd.pid`**.

NOTE

Since inetd *is not particularly essential to a machine's uptime, the operating system will still run pretty much as usual if you kill it, so don't be afraid to experiment on a machine that doesn't run any essential network services.* inetd *takes a* -d *option for debugging (and will complain about bad entries in* /etc/inetd.conf *in any case).*

tcpd, /etc/hosts.allow, /etc/hosts.deny

Part of the TCP wrappers package, tcpd checks an initial connection to see which remote host is attempting to connect and whether the remote host is allowed to connect as specified in /etc/hosts.allow and /etc/hosts.deny. It also logs the remote host information (via syslog) as well as the connection's success status.

The following /etc/hosts.deny configuration throws out most connections from bad-guys.com and finger requests from cant-finger.com:

```
ALL: .bad-guys.com
in.fingerd: .cant-finger.com
portmap: ALL
```

The format of /etc/hosts.allow is much the same as in /etc/hosts.deny.
Adding this portmap line turns access on for hosts barred in /etc/hosts.deny:

```
portmap: .example.com
```

This gives access to the hosts in the domain example.com.

PROBLEM 2

Symptom: Changes in hosts.allow and hosts.deny have no effect.

Problem: Service doesn't use tcpd or the libwrap library.

Fix: To set up more general rules that work at the kernel level, look at the discussion of IP filters in Section 2.4.

Relevant man pages: tcpd (8), hosts_access (5)

2.3 PPP Configuration

Due to the large variety of ISPs and dial-out devices, successful PPP configuration can be elusive. To complicate matters, the PPP setup of every Linux distribution is somewhat different. This section explains the PPP programs, what they do, and which files they use.

pppd

The pppd system daemon is at the heart of Linux PPP. It takes raw data from a device (usually a serial port connected to a modem), decodes the data stream, and talks to a network interface (ppp0, for example), which then acts like an Ethernet interface on the other side. (For the rest of this section, assume the device we're talking about is a serial port attached to a modem.)

The difficulty with pppd usually comes in setting up the initial connection to the ISP. Before pppd can even start its negotiation, your system must connect to the device, initialize the modem, dial the number, detect a connection, and then perhaps chat with the server on the other side. By itself, pppd doesn't do any of this. Instead, it calls another program, usually chat, to keep the modem and connection busy until the actual PPP protocol starts streaming out at the other end. Then chat terminates and pppd takes over.

NOTE
If you can get PPP to work with the configuration tool that came with your distribution, you can skip to the next section.

Starting pppd

Most pppd invocations come in the form

```
# pppd call isp
```

Here, *isp* is the name of a remote system; /etc/ppp/peers/*isp* sets its options (see the pppd Options section). The name you give a remote system isn't usually relevant. It must simply match the name of the configuration file in /etc/ppp/peers—unless you plan to use CHAP (see page 29). If you don't know the name of the remote system, don't worry—you can either figure it out from debug messages or just override it with a remotename option (see page 27).

Options to pppd have a somewhat nonstandard form—for example:

```
# pppd noauth defaultroute connect '/usr/sbin/chat -v -f /etc/ppp/chat-foo'
```

These options are quite verbose and vary from system to system—you'll usually find pppd call *system* easier than writing long scripts.

Starting pppd: A Simple Example

The dial-up to our organization is a fairly standard Cisco box. The command

```
# pppd call compsci
```

connects a home machine to this dial-up. The /etc/ppp/peers/compsci file contains the following:

```
ttyS1 57600 crtscts
connect '/usr/sbin/chat -v -f /etc/ppp/chat-compsci'
noauth
defaultroute
mru 1500
```

(Note: This file specifies the serial device, ttyS1 [that is, /dev/ttyS1], and the connection speed, 57600 baud).
    The chat file /etc/ppp/chat-compsci is:

```
ABORT "NO CARRIER"
ABORT BUSY
"" ATZ OK
ATDTnumber CONNECT
"" ername:
```

```
login ssword:
\qpass
> ppp
```

In this file, *number* is the phone number to dial, *login* is the login name, and *pass* is the password. The greater-than sign (>) is a prompt that appears after a successful login. Keep in mind that this prompts varies widely between dial-ups.

To start up pppd, type the following:

```
$ /usr/sbin/pppd call compsci
```

The user invoking pppd must be able to read the /etc/ppp/chat-compsci file. This brings up some difficulties, since normally only root can read /etc/ppp, but using PAP or CHAP (see page 28) eliminates this problem, since the passwords aren't in the chat script. (However, you may not be thrilled with the idea of putting your chat script in a directory that's not on the system— and if you want to make it accessible to multiple users, they must be able to read it as well, further reducing security.)

To kill the pppd and hang up (assuming the interface came up at ppp0, which is usually the case), run

```
$ kill `cat /var/run/ppp0.pid`
```

PROBLEM 3

Symptom: pppd cannot open files in /etc/ppp or devices as a user other than root. No one but root can run pppd.

Problem: pppd not setuid (suid) root, or unreadable by user.

Fix: Some distributions figure that pppd is either inherently insecure or that allowing everyone to execute it is too dangerous, so they either don't set the suid bit of the file permissions or they don't set the world-execute bit. You can add specific users to a group and make the program group-executable (better for decent-size networks), or you can just make pppd world-executable and suid root:

```
# chmod u+s /usr/sbin/pppd
```

```
# chmod o+x /usr/sbin/pppd
```

pppd Options

If you peruse the pppd manual page, you'll notice quite a few options you can put into the files in /etc/ppp/peers (or specify on the command line). This section is an outline of the most important ones. The first two should be the device and serial port speed.

Device

Choosing the device (that is, ttyS1 or /dev/ttyS1), unless you're using call to specify a configuration file, is the first option in pppd. Although you can just use something like ttyS1 and have pppd prepend /dev/ to it, it's best to use the full path name, as it makes the device path completely clear.

Serial Port Speed

With modern modems, you want a speed higher than your modem's connection speed. For 56-kbps modems, your serial ports should probably be set to at least 115200 baud unless they just can't support that rate. In general, the higher the baud rate, the better, but if you set it too high, the modem and/or the serial port may drop characters, resulting in a much slower (or even nonexistent) connection.

Other Options

Besides the device and serial port, there are a number of other pppd options.

defaultroute Sets the default route for the PPP interface. If you don't use it (for example, if you're dialing up a leaf site somewhere), you'll need to set your own route with the route command to get to hosts beyond the remote PPP server.

noauth Disables authentication on the other end of the connection. Since your remote server may not support authentication, you might need this. This refers to authentication over the PPP protocol, so if you use a chat script to dial *and login to the server*, it's likely that you don't need this.

PROBLEM 4

Symptom: pppd runs, but you can't reach anything except the remote server.

Problem: No default route.

Fix: If you have only one ISP and you dial up to it with PPP, you need the defaultroute option.

connect *command* With a *command*, initializes the connection before PPP initiates on the remote side. Usually an invocation of the chat command—for example, connect '/usr/sbin/chat -v -f /etc/ppp/chat-isp'.

nodetach Normally, pppd acts as a real daemon and forks off into a background process while running. The nodetach option disables this forking off—handy for debugging, as it makes pppd interruptible immediately with CTRL-C.

mru *number* Defines the maximum receive unit (mru), which tells the remote server not to send any chunks of data larger than *number* bytes. The size you set depends on how fast your connection is; the default of 1500 bytes is fine for modem speeds such as 33.6k baud.

mtu *number* pppd won't transmit chunks of data higher than the *number* bytes you set here. (The default is 1500 bytes.) Tweak this value (usually by lowering it) when you're having difficulty uploading data onto a remote machine or when your connection seems slow (even if it's only via modem). (Note that the quality of phone lines and switches often limits the capacity for sending data back through the line.)

PROBLEM 5

Symptom: Some programs cannot send or receive data at all.

Problem: mtu and mru too low.

Fix: You need to set the mtu and mru higher. In general, settings of lower than 1300 bytes will cause problems with many applications (like scp).

PROBLEM 6

Symptom: Connection often hangs or drops. ARQ light on modem often blinks.

Problem: Poor switch or telephone line.

Fix: If you can't find a problem with the wiring in your building, you'll have to work with the phone company. Sometimes the problem is a poor connection to the building, but often the company's overloading the phone switch. If you notice a lot of static when you're using the voice phone, see if you can get the phone company to put you on a better switch.

name *name* Forces pppd to use *name* as the username for CHAP or PAP (see the sections on PAP and CHAP).

remotename *name* Forces pppd to recognize the remote server as the *name* you enter here (see the sections on PAP and CHAP).

debug Turns on connection logging with the syslog. The facility will be daemon and the level will be debug. (See Section 1.3 for more information on syslog.)

PROBLEM 7

Symptom: No pppd messages in any log files.

Problem: /etc/syslog.conf not configured to log messages from daemon.debug.

Fix: Some distributions (like Red Hat) don't log many services. Add a line like

daemon.debug: /var/log/daemon

to your /etc/syslog.conf file, and send a hang-up signal to syslogd:

```
# kill -HUP `cat /var/run/syslogd.pid`
```

Serial Devices

One way to find information on your serial ports in /dev is to look at the names; the files with names that start with ttyS are your serial ports. What DOS calls COM1: (IRQ4, port 0x3f8) is /dev/ttyS0; COM2 (IRQ3, port 0x2f8) is /dev/ttyS1. (The command cat /proc/ioports is another way to view their current configuration, but /proc/interrupts shows only the active devices; if a serial port isn't in use, it will not show up there.)

Machines with fewer than two serial ports are prone to misconfiguration; similarly, machines with more than two ports can have problems if ports share interrupts. If on bootup dmesg gives incorrect IRQs and reconfiguring your serial ports fails, set up your ports manually with setserial (usually in /bin). Here's an example:

```
# setserial /dev/ttyS3 irq 5
```

In addition to the other options (such as those pertaining to I/O ports), the setserial manual page includes a good overall explanation of serial ports.

NOTE *The devices* /dev/tty1, /dev/tty2, *and so on are the virtual consoles of your Linux machine. Don't mistake them for serial ports.*

PROBLEM 8

Symptom: Device files beginning with cua not found. Warning messages about old interfaces.

Problem: Device name confusion.

Fix: Traditional Unix flavors used names like /dev/cua for call-out and /dev/ttya for dial-in and direct terminal connections. Linux followed this convention at one time, but abandoned it. Therefore, you may find devices such as /dev/cua0 on your Linux system, but they are obsolete as of kernel version 2.2, and you shouldn't use them.

PPP Configuration Files

The directory /etc/ppp contains the configuration data for pppd. You'll find at least some of these files and directories:

peers A directory containing configuration files for each ISP you dial up to. The files contain pppd options (some of which the next section explains).

options A text file containing generic pppd options. This file must exist, even if it's empty.

chat-*server* Often contains the scripts chat uses to speak to the modem as it dials and logs in to the remote server.

chap-secrets, pap-secrets See the next section.

PAP

Many dial-ups require logins that use PAP (Password Authentication Protocol). The /etc/ppp/pap-secrets file contains the PAP passwords. This file contains up to four fields: the client, server, secret, and IP address.

Setting the Fields in pap-secrets

When connecting to a dial-up, you should in theory set the first field to the remote system name, the second to your system name, the third to your password (use double quotes if you have spaces in it), and the fourth to the remote IP address:

```
your_hostname    remote_hostname    password    ipaddr
```

Unfortunately, most users don't run a gateway or server but simply have a user name and a dynamically allocated address. In such cases, have your pap-secrets file read as follows:

```
username              *                password
```

This forces `pppd` to accept any remote host and IP address. To tell `pppd` what user name to use, put

```
name username
```

in your ISP's options file (that is, a file in `/etc/ppp/peers`), or in `/etc/ppp/options` if you don't plan on using more than one ISP.

Multiple ISPs

If you have more than one ISP with the same user name, you can distinguish between them in `/etc/ppp/pap-secrets` by changing the asterisk (*) to a name, then forcing the remote name to *name* in that ISP's options file (in `/etc/ppp/peers`) with

```
remotename name
```

Doing so allows you to add more lines to `/etc/ppp/pap-secrets` for additional ISPs.

When adding ISPs, make the appropriate changes to the files in `/etc/ppp/peers`.

PROBLEM 9

Symptom: `pppd` successfully begins negotiation, but authentication times out or fails (even though the server accepted your password).

Problem: Using the `require-pap` option.

Fix: When using PAP as a normal dial-up user, don't put `require-pap` in your options files, or your `pppd` will ask the dial-up server to prove its identity. Even if your dial-up tries to prove its identity, you most likely won't have an entry in your `pap-secrets` file to back it up.

If you configured Red Hat 6 for PPP and PAP with `linuxconf`, *you may notice that it never puts an asterisk in the* `/etc/ppp/pap-secrets` *file.* `linuxconf` *forces everything into the* `/etc/sysconfig/network-scripts/ifcfg-ppp*` *files by setting the variables* `DEVICE` *to the interface and* `PAPNAME` *to the user (they get passed to* `pppd` *as the options* `remotename` *and* name*).*

CHAP

CHAP (Challenge Handshake Authentication Protocol) is similar to PAP, but requires that both sides give user names and passwords. It is usually used for connecting to Windows NT servers.

CHAP's secrets file is `/etc/ppp/chap-secrets`. You may need to force the names in this file with the `name` and `remotename` options (see the Multiple ISPs subsection above). Your finished `/etc/ppp/chap-secrets` file should look like this:

```
username    remote      our_password
remote      username     their_password
```

PPP and Red Hat 6.x

Red Hat doesn't really use the `/etc/ppp/peers` directory. The `linuxconf` tools in Red Hat 6.x store the configuration files in `/etc/sysconfig/network-scripts`. The options for the interface `ppp0` are in `ifcfg-ppp0` and the chat scripts are in `chat-ppp0`. The PPP daemon runs with the `ifup-ppp` script, which Red Hat integrates with other network interfaces at boot time.

Adding more than one ISP requires configuring an additional PPP interface and doesn't allow for all possible `pppd` options. In the end, since configuring PPP for Red Hat 6.x with the `linuxconf` tool involves about the same number of steps as adding files to `/etc/ppp` does, you may just find yourself doing the latter: Editing files is faster than running through a maze of menus.

Verifying a Correct Login

If you're having trouble connecting, first make sure you can actually connect to the remote server and successfully start PPP there. To do this, use a terminal program on your Linux machine (it probably won't be a real terminal program, just an interface to the serial port—xterm and the Linux console are terminal emulators). You have a couple of terminal programs to choose from, including `minicom`, `tip`, `cu`, and `kermit`. Since `tip` and `cu` are somewhat archaic and `kermit` has a restrictive license, `minicom` is what you'll most likely find on your system.

To begin, log in as root and configure `minicom` with **minicom -s**. Change the modem device under the serial port setup if necessary. Then exit, and `minicom` will connect to the serial port. If it's the right one, you'll be able to enter the usual modem commands, like at, atdt, and atm.

Reset your modem with **atz** and dial your ISP with **atdt***number*. When your ISP connects, log in and take careful notes on everything you see on screen. Keep going until you start up the PPP server on the other end. You'll recognize it as a short string of random-looking characters, like the following:

```
~ÿ}#À!}!}!} }.}%}&} } ÿ
```

Once you've reached your PPP server, you have all the information you need to run chat properly. Exit `minicom` by pressing CTRL-A, then x. Finally, edit your chat script according to the session you just had.

> ## PROBLEM 10
>
> **Symptom:** `minicom` hangs when trying to exit.
>
> **Problem:** `minicom` blocks trying to read an incorrect serial device.
>
> **Fix:** Open up another window and kill the `minicom` process with `kill` `-KILL`. Unfortunately, this happens more when you're trying to use `setserial` to configure the port. Try to use x to exit instead of q, as resetting the port before you close often tells the kernel to give up trying to talk to it.

Relevant man pages: pppd (8), minicom (1), setserial (8)

2.4 Routing, IP Filters, Firewalls, and IP Masquerading

After you're familiar with network configuration on single hosts, you may need to use Linux to bind networks, filter out traffic, and act as a gateway to the Internet. The first step is to learn about subnets and routing. Then you can use `ipchains` to add more sophistication.

Basic Routing and Subnets

A router is basically a computer that passes traffic between *subnets* (chunks of Internet address space assigned to a local network) through network ports. For a router to work, the subnets must have assigned, static IP addresses (in the case of leaf networks, your ISP assigns them).

The router will have at least two network interfaces, one linking to the ISP and the other linking to the rest of the world.

Subnets

Version 4 Internet addresses consist of 4 bytes, usually written in decimal form (as in 10.4.5.6). A host's subnet is the part of the address identical on all hosts on the immediately surrounding local area networks. In one of the most common subnet configurations, only the address's last byte varies (see the example below).

The *subnet mask* (also called a *net mask*) determines which parts of an address belong to the local network. The number 0 in the subnet mask's binary representation means that the corresponding address bit varies over the local subnet; a 1 means that it does not.

Let's take the example address 10.4.5.6 and say that we have a subnet mask of 255.255.255.0. The binary representations of the address, the subnet mask, and the network 10.4.5.0 (where the fourth digit changes) are as follows:

```
00001010.00000100.00000101.00000110 (address)
11111111.11111111.11111111.00000000 (subnet mask)
00001010.00000100.00000101.xxxxxxxx (10.4.5.N, N = {1, .., 254}, network)
```

The *xxxxxxxx* can be any eight-character string of 0s and 1s.

When converted into binary, the first number in the subnet mask, 255, yields eight 1s. Since 1 in the subnet mask means the corresponding binary digit in the IP address does not change, the number 255 (or eight 1s in binary) means the number on the address of an incoming packet must be the same as the corresponding number in the host's address. Therefore, the subnet mask 255.255.255.0 stipulates that the first three numbers on the address of the incoming packet must be the same as the first three numbers of the host's address, and that the last number can vary. The last number refers to a machine or network connected to the host. The subnet mask 255.255.255.0 is easy to work with, because you never have to do any binary conversion to figure out whether an address is local. Either the first three bytes (numbers) are the same, meaning that the host is part of the local network, or the host is somewhere else.

NOTE *For simple routers, this is more or less all you need to know for the moment. Skip to another section if you don't want to see more complex examples.*

Part of a router's work may be to distribute packets bound for different subnets. Let's say you have one address space, 10.4.5.0, with the subnet mask 255.255.255.0. For some physical reason (such as different types of network interfaces), you have to split your address space into four subnets.

The four new networks you propose are 10.4.5.0, 10.4.5.64, 10.4.5.128, and 10.4.5.192, which you get by taking all combinations of two bits in the last byte (you control the last byte, so you can do anything you want with it):

```
00001010.00000100.00000101.00xxxxxx (10.4.5.N, N = {1, .., 62})
00001010.00000100.00000101.01xxxxxx (10.4.5.N, N = {65, .., 126})
00001010.00000100.00000101.10xxxxxx (10.4.5.N, N = {129, .., 190})
00001010.00000100.00000101.11xxxxxx (10.4.5.N, N = {193, .., 254})
```

The underlined bits are the ones that you've chosen to define the four new networks. Your router now must do a little extra work to figure out where to send packets based on their destination address. Of course, if the address doesn't match 10.4.5, the router still knows that it should send the packet off to the outside world. But if the address does match, the router must also look at two more bits of the address—the first two in the last byte. Hosts on this subnet use a subnet mask of 255.255.255.192, which in binary is

```
11111111.11111111.11111111.11000000
```

You may also see networks specified in a form such as 10.4.2.0/24. The 24 is a shortcut for a net mask of 255.255.255.0; 24 is the number of leading 1s in the net mask.

IP Forwarding

Say you want to enable simple *IP forwarding* (sometimes known as *gatewaying*, a feature that allows network traffic to pass through your machine from one network to another) on your Linux machine. First set up all your network interfaces on the machine (with the proper subnet masks) so that it can reach everything it needs to (including any outside network accessible through the default gateway). Then tell the kernel you want to turn forwarding on:

```
# echo 1 > /proc/sys/net/ipv4/ip_forward
```

Firewalls

A *firewall* is a router that looks at a packet (usually the network address and port part of the packet) and decides whether to let it pass. A firewall alone won't make your network particularly secure, and it can hinder throughput to the outside world, but at least it can hamper annoying things such as port scans.

IP Chains

An *IP chain* is a list of rules the kernel uses to decide if it should let a packet pass, and in some cases how to route it. The three chains built into a kernel—input, output, and forward—come into play at different stages of packet routing.

The kernel looks at the input chain when a packet comes in from the outside world and the output chain just before transmission of a packet to the outside world. The forward chain goes to work when a packet passes through the input chain and the kernel determines that its ultimate destination is not the local machine (that is, the kernel should route the packet back out again).

Each rule in a chain has a *target*—the decision the kernel makes if the packet matches the rule. The rules follow one of these six targets:

ACCEPT   Pass the packet through.

DENY   Drop the packet.

REJECT   Drop the packet and try to inform the host that created it.

REDIRECT   On the input chain, intercept a packet and send it to a port on the local machine regardless of its original destination.

RETURN   Stop trying to match rules and use the default (chain policy).

MASQ   Use masquerading on the packet.

The *policy* of a chain is the default target, and its values are limited to ACCEPT, DENY, REJECT, and MASQ. This combination of chains, rules, and targets is fundamental to firewalls, IP masquerading, and IP filters. If you're running a firewall, you'll use the forward chain to either throw out most general traffic or redirect it through a proxy server with the input chain. You may also use the forward chain for masquerading, and the input chain to filter IP packets bound for the local machine.

Here is a brief list of some important ipchains options. Capital letters signal the start of a *command;* lowercase letters, the beginning of a *rule.*

-L [*chain*]	List *chain* and the rules under it. With no additional parameters, show all chains and all rules.
-I *chain*	Insert a chain rule.
-A *chain*	Append a chain rule.
-D *chain* [*num*]	Delete a chain rule number *num* (1 by default).
-P *chain target*	Set the policy of *chain* to *target*.
-F [*chain*]	Delete all rules in *chain* (with no argument, in all chains).
-R *chain num*	Replace rule *num* in *chain*.
-s *source*	Specify the source network or address and optional ports.
-d *dest*	Specify the destination network or address and optional ports.
-j *target*	Jump to *target* if this rule matches.
-b	Create two rules; the second will be the same as the one stated, but will swap the destination (-d) and source (-s).
-v	Ask for verbose mode.

Example 1: IP Filters

Unlike firewalls, IP filters allow some or all machines to do the filtering themselves instead of making one machine look at all the packets passing through. Before incoming network packets are passed off to user programs, a machine with an IP filter has the kernel look at the packets and decide if it should throw them out. If configured to throw out incoming packets from most of the world on insecure ports (a large majority of them are), an IP filter can defend against a variety of attacks.

Suppose you want to share a bunch of services with a group of machines on a local network, and these services are particularly vulnerable to denial-of-service attacks (or worse). You'd like to make all services but ssh unavailable to the outside world. We'll go through each ipchains command you need to run, explaining them along the way.

Let's say that you want to allow any packet from your local network to pass to any of your host's ports. If your host is at 10.1.1.2 and your local network is 10.1.1.0, with a net mask of 255.255.255.0, the following would let everything from your network through:

```
# ipchains -A input -s 10.1.1.0/255.255.255.0 -d 10.1.1.2 -j ACCEPT
```

Yet you also want to allow connections from your host to the outside world. The rule

```
# ipchains -A input -j ACCEPT -p tcp '!' -y
```

says to let response packets through.

This rule allows use of ICMP tools like ping and traceroute (among others):

```
# ipchains -A input -j ACCEPT -p icmp
```

Some parts of Linux tend to break if the machine can't talk to itself:

```
# ipchains -A input -j ACCEPT -d localhost
```

Since we have some trust in ssh, we allow connections on that port.

```
# ipchains -A input -j ACCEPT -p tcp -d 10.1.1.2 ssh
```

Everything's now in place, with one exception that isn't necessary if you use FTP proxy. Due to its design, FTP connects back to the FTP client's machine. The next line provides direct FTP connections to the outside world:

```
# ipchains -A input -j ACCEPT -p tcp -s any/0 ftp-data -d 10.1.1.2 1024:
```

Since you want to deny stuff in general, set the default policy to DENY. You probably want to do this after putting your other rules in place, since the kernel just throws everything out after you state it, and you may need DNS for a few other rules.

```
# ipchains -P input DENY
```

However, if you're feeling *really* paranoid, you'll want to set this first and specify everything in IP addresses or in some way that doesn't require DNS.

Example 2: IP Firewall

Now let's modify the example above to make it into a firewall for the network 10.1.20.0/255.255.255.0. Assume that you already have the interface working.

Turn forwarding on if you haven't done so already (you may want to do this last):

```
# echo 1 > /proc/sys/net/ipv4/ip_forward
```

Set a default policy of DENY for forwarding:

```
# ipchains -P forward DENY
```

Accept any input (including that for the firewall machine) and forwarding from 10.1.20.0 to the outside world:

```
# ipchains -A input -s 10.1.20.0/255.255.255.0 -d any -j ACCEPT
# ipchains -A forward -s 10.1.20.0/255.255.255.0 -d any -j ACCEPT
# ipchains -A forward -j ACCEPT -p tcp '!' -y
```

Then allow ssh connections to within the firewall from anywhere:

```
# ipchains -A input -s any ssh -d 10.1.20.0/255.255.255.0 -j ACCEPT
# ipchains -A forward -s any ssh -d 10.1.20.0/255.255.255.0 -j ACCEPT
```

PROBLEM 11

Symptom: Your firewall machine is vulnerable to attack.

Problem: False feeling of security.

Fix: Don't let the firewall machine accept connections on just *any* port from absolutely *anything* in the outside world. If the firewall machine can reach any part of the network with no problem, then intruders need only break into the firewall to get to the "secure" network. Don't expect perfect security in your firewall (from attacks from the outside or the *inside*); keep all of your machines up to date on the latest security fixes.

Example 3: IP Masquerading

IP masquerading is a handy feature for small networks, such as home networks that share one dial-up without a dedicated IP subnet. Other systems refer to it as NAT (Network Address Translation). In *IP masquerading*, one Internet-connected machine acts as the default Internet gateway for the other machines on the local network (even when they're using dynamic address allocation from an ISP). When combined with proxy services (such as squid, a Web proxy server—see Chapter 4), IP masquerading can even improve performance through efficient caching. However, it doesn't work with all protocols; it's best at TCP.

Take a typical home network, for example. Its first local subnet is 10.1.1.0 and the subnet mask is set to 255.255.255.0. Its primary network hardware is a 100BaseT Ethernet hub to which a Linux workstation, notebook, Power Mac G3, and the Linux router/gateway are connected. The gateway's Ethernet interface (eth0) is set for the address 10.1.1.1 and configured for PPP on the ppp0 interface.

The commands

```
# ipchains -P forward DENY
# ipchains -A forward -i ppp0 -j MASQ
# echo 1 > /proc/sys/net/ipv4/ip_forward
```

set the masquerading in motion—the first command denies generic routing, the second says all packets normally routed though the ppp0 interface should masquerade instead, and the last enables IP forwarding in the kernel.

To finish off the job, we set the default gateway address to 10.1.1.1 for the rest of the machines on the network (which have addresses such as 10.1.1.4).

Adding Kernel Support

In addition to the ipchains command, your system needs to add kernel support for IP masquerading, which you'll find buried beneath a few items in the kernel configuration (at least for version 2.2—see Chapter 7 for details on how to build a kernel). When you're configuring the kernel, remember to go through these steps in the configuration menu:

1. Under Networking options, choose Network firewalls.

2. Go down a couple of lines and choose IP: Firewalling (this appears only after you choose Network firewalls).

3. Go down a few lines and pick IP: Always defragment (required for masquerading).

4. Choose IP: Masquerading (this should pop up along with IP: Firewalling).

5. Include IP: ICMP masquerading among your options—it enables a few diagnostic tools such as ping and traceroute.

The above procedure works fine for one local subnet, but let's say that we have two. To get our ancient NeXT and some other toys connected—and because we're too cheap to buy a dual-speed hub—we have a 10BaseT Ethernet hub for subnet 10.1.2.0 (net mask 255.255.255.0). The gateway has an additional Ethernet interface, eth1, plugged into the slower hub and running at the address 10.1.2.1. After setting the default gateway to this address for the machines on this other subnet, we use the ipchains command:

```
# ipchains -I forward -b -s 10.1.1.0/255.255.255.0 -d 10.1.2.0/255.255.255.0 -j ACCEPT
```

This command allows traffic between the two local subnets without any extra frills. The -b option adds two rules; we could have done the same thing with

```
# ipchains -I forward -s 10.1.1.0/255.255.255.0 -d 10.1.2.0/255.255.255.0 -j ACCEPT
# ipchains -I forward -s 10.1.2.0/255.255.255.0 -d 10.1.1.0/255.255.255.0 -j ACCEPT
```

The end result has this listing (24 as a net mask is the same as 255.255.255.0; it's the number of leading bits in the subnet mask set to 1). We'll use -L (list) as described with the other ipchains arguments on page 34.

```
# ipchains -L
...
Chain forward (policy DENY):
target   prot    opt      source        destination    ports
ACCEPT   all     ------   10.1.2.0/24   10.1.1.0/24    n/a
ACCEPT   all     ------   10.1.1.0/24   10.1.2.0/24    n/a
MASQ     all     ------   anywhere      anywhere       n/a
...
```

PROBLEM 12

Symptoms: The gateway doesn't pass packets between certain hosts on the network. Excess traffic on all subnets.

Problem: Incorrect net masks.

Fix: Make sure to specify the correct net mask. Net masks are optional in the -s argument, but the default values are almost always wrong.

2.5 Network Security

Quite a few unsavory types play out there on the Internet, and it's generally to your advantage not to let your Linux box become their playground. Whether they deface your Web site, run IRC bots, or remove all of your files, they invariably cost you two things: time and irritation. Don't wait for a break-in to occur before securing your system.

NOTE *This section isn't an all-encompassing guide to network security, but aims to solve some common security problems. A good place to start for in-depth security information (including topical information) is http://www.sans.org/.*

Keep Things Simple

Don't run excess or questionable services on your Linux machine. (Unfortunately, some distributions do a pretty good job of starting as many services as possible by default.) Also, if only some remote hosts require certain services, limit the services to those hosts.

Since most Internet services launch from inetd, the first place to look for excess services is /etc/inetd.conf (see Section 2.2 for a discussion on inetd). If inetd does not start a network service, probably init is starting it. Have a look at the section on the `init.d` and `rc.d` directories in Chapter 1 to see how to manipulate those.

Restricting Access

You can restrict access to services with either TCP wrappers (`tcpd`, see Section 2.2) or with firewalls (see Section 2.4). The following services are common candidates for removal or restriction, either because they pose security risks or because they're simply unnecessary.

telnetd If someone uses telnet to access your machine, he or she types a password and conducts an entire session over the network in plain text (cleartext; no encryption). Anyone with a packet sniffer can pull passwords off the network at whim if your users are ingrained with telnet. Turn it off and force the users to use an encrypted alternative such as `ssh`, the Secure Shell (see below).

rlogind The same problems for `telnetd` also exist for `rlogind`, except that you can circumvent the use of a password with a `.rhosts` file. However, this opens you to the additional problem of intruders gaining access to your system without a password.

rexecd This sometimes provides a way for software on non-Unix hosts to access certain programs, such as X Window System clients, on Unix or Linux machines. It uses a cleartext password and its traffic is unencrypted.

ftpd If you have no use for `ftpd`, don't run it, because it transmits the session (including passwords) in the clear over the network. A better alternative to nonanonymous FTP is `scp` (which comes with `ssh`). Numerous security problems have cropped up with the various `ftpd`s in the past.

fingerd While seemingly harmless, this service has had buffer overflow problems. Intruders can also obtain user lists with it. Turning it off is never a bad idea.

talkd, ntalkd Seriously consider restricting the number of hosts with access to these.

sendmail or other mailer services If your machine doesn't handle mail, don't run any mail services. If you're a dial-up home user, you may be using POP or imap anyway. Alternatives to the typically exploitable `sendmail` are `qmail` and `postfix`.

chargen, echo, discard, daytime, time These are internal to `inetd`; originally meant for debugging, they are useless.

The Secure Shell (ssh)

To protect yourself and your users from attacks through telnet as well as packet snooping and password sniffing while you access machines remotely, you must use an access system that encrypts everything that passes through it. The most popular encryption package is ssh, which offers:

- Encryption of everything that goes over the network, from passwords to the session itself.

- Key verification to identify hosts.

- Automatic X Window System client tunneling of client packets (in encrypted X packets), so you never have to do another xauth or xhost again.

- Clients for a wide variety of operating systems.

- Commercial support.

The principal client program is ssh, and the Unix server is sshd (ssh daemon). The daemon can either run stand-alone and accept connections on its own, or run from inetd. The ssh package also provides two other clients: scp (an argument-compatible replacement for rcp) and slogin (a similar replacement for rlogin). You can obtain ssh from its principal distribution site (ftp://ftp.cs.hut.fi/pub/ssh) or Web site (http://www.ssh.fi); it does not come with Red Hat. More implementations of ssh can be found at http://www.freessh.org/.

Don't hesitate to install ssh. Try to get all of your users on it; the sooner you turn telnet, rlogin, and their pals off, the better. Installing this package on a new machine is the first action you should take after putting the operating system in place.

Relevant man pages: ssh (1), scp (1), sshd (8), ssh-keygen (1)

Installing and Configuring ssh

The autoconf system (see Chapter 6) configures and installs ssh. Make sure the configure script knows where to find the xauth program so the X tunneling can work. When you install, ssh generates public and private host keys for your machine. The public key (/etc/ssh_host_key.pub) is considered common knowledge and will spread to any machine that wishes to connect. The private key (/etc/ssh_host_key) must remain secret.

To generate a 1024-bit host key on a machine, enter the command

```
# ssh-keygen -N '' -b 1024 -f /etc/ssh_host_key
```

and fill the file /etc/ssh_known_hosts with the public host keys of the rest of the machines on your network. The host key will resemble this:

```
broadway,broadway.example.com 1024 33149914395573812422526576910023704307
35304532793202455851463444618610244719198805271650346934799195377060242
7...
...
```

   If you're installing ssh for the first time, make install generates and
installs the host keys for you. All you need to do is start up sshd at boot time.
Chapter 1 covers the init.d and rc*.d directories, which control the processes
that start at bootup.

   If you connect to another machine with ssh, and its public host key isn't
in /etc/ssh_known_hosts, ssh (depending on how it was configured) either
asks if you want to continue connecting and add the host key to your personal
.ssh/known_hosts file, or simply adds the key without asking. If ssh's host key
verification fails upon connecting (due to different keys), you'll get an ugly
and somewhat unsettling message:

```
@@@@@@@@@@@@@@@@@@@@@@@@@@@@@@@@@@@@@@@@@@@@@@@@@@@@@@@@@@@@@
@        WARNING: HOST IDENTIFICATION HAS CHANGED!         @
@@@@@@@@@@@@@@@@@@@@@@@@@@@@@@@@@@@@@@@@@@@@@@@@@@@@@@@@@@@@@
IT IS POSSIBLE THAT SOMEONE IS DOING SOMETHING NASTY!
Someone could be eavesdropping on you right now (man-in-the-
middle attack)!
It is also possible that the host key has just been changed.
Please contact your system administrator.
...
```

   (This message usually results from an administrator's host key change or
a machine upgrade, but it never hurts to ask.)

   The systemwide configuration files for ssh and sshd are /etc/ssh_config
and /etc/sshd_config, respectively. The defaults for ssh_config on a normal
system include the following (along with their relevant command-line counterparts).

Configuration File Option	Command-line Option
ForwardAgent yes	(-a disables this)
ForwardX11 yes	(-x disables this)
RhostsAuthentication yes	(none)
RhostsRSAAuthentication yes	(none)
RSAAuthentication yes	(none)
TISAuthentication no	(none)
PasswordAuthentication yes	(none)

```
FallBackToRsh yes              (none)

UseRsh no                      (none)

BatchMode no                   (none)

StrictHostKeyChecking no       (none)

IdentityFile ~/.ssh/identity   (-i $HOME/.ssh/identity)

Port 22                        (-p 22)

Cipher idea                    (-c idea)

EscapeChar ~                   (-e ~)
```

Once installed, ssh behaves more or less like rlogin. If you want to ssh to another host with a different login name, the command line is ssh -l *name hostname*, just like rlogin.

scp

Another important service ssh provides is scp, a secure way of copying files to and from remote hosts. It takes options like those of rcp:

```
$ scp user@remotehost local-pathname
$ scp local-file user@remotehost
```

The *user@* part is optional if your user name is the same on the remote host. The *local-pathname* can be either a file name or a directory on your local machine; *local-file* must be a file on your local machine.

ssh Clients for Other Operating Systems

TeraTerm is a very popular and free ssh client for Windows.

```
http://www.zip.com.au/~roca/ttssh.html
```

NiftyTelnet-ssh for the Macintosh, also free, includes ssh support; unfortunately, software patent issues make it illegal to use in the United States until the patent runs out.

```
http://www.lysator.liu.se/~jonasw/freeware/niftyssh/
```

SecureCRT, a commercial ssh client, is the ssh-compatible version of the popular CRT terminal emulator for Windows.

```
http://www.vandyke.com/products/securecrt
```

Data Fellows offers commercial ssh clients for Macintosh and Windows.

```
http://www.datafellows.com
```

PROBLEM 13

Symptom: You get a log message like this:

```
...
...
Sep 1 19:48:18 baldy syslogd: Cannot glue message parts together
Sep 1 19:48:18 baldy 27>Sep 1 19:48:18 amd[398]: amq requested
mount of <90><90><90><90><90><90><90><90><90><90><90><90><90>
<90><90><90><90><90><90><90><90><90><90><90><90><90> [ .. ]
[ ... ... ... ] <90><90><90><90><90><90><90><90><90><90><90>
<90><90><90><90><90><90><90><90><90><90><90><90><90><90><90>
<90><90><90><90><90><90><90><90><90><90><90><90><90><90><90>
<90><90><90><90><90><90><90><90><90><90><90><90><90><90><90>
<90><90><90><90><90><90><90><90><90><90><90><90><90><90><90>
<90><90><90><90><90><90><90><90><90><90><90><90><90><90><90>
<90><90><90><90><90><90><90><90><90><90><90><90><90><90><90>
<90><90><90><90><90><90><90><90><90><90><90><90><90><90><90>
<90><90><90><90><90><90><90><90><90><90><90><EB>^P1<C0>1<DB>
1<C9>1<D2><C3>1<C0><B0>^A<CD><80><C3><E8><EB><FF><FF><FF><B0>
^F<CD><80><B0>^F<FE><C3><CD><80><B0>^F<FE><C3><CD><80><B0>^B
<CD><80>9<C1>u<DC><E8><CE><FF><FF><FF><B0>^B<B1>^A<B2>^FRQP
<B3>^A<B0>f<89><E1><CD><80><89><C6><E8><B6><FF><FF><FF><83>
<C4>^RP<B9>^B<FF>^H<AE>O<ED>Q<89><E2><83><EC>^F<B0>^PP<B3>
^BRV<B0>f<89><E1><CD><80><B0>^PPV<B0>f<B3>^D<89><E1><CD><80>
<E8><87><FF><FF><FF>PPV<B0>f<B3>^!
E<89><E1><CD><80>1<C9><88><C3><B0>)<CD><80><B0>?<CD><80><EB>
^V^<88>N^G<89>v^H<89>N^L<B0>^K<89><F3><8D>N^H<8D>V^L<CD><80>
<E8><E5><FF><FF><FF>/bin/sh<90><D2><F2><FF><BF><D2><F2><FF>
<BF><D2><F2><FF><BF><D2><F2><FF><BF><D2><F2><FF><BF><D2><F2>
<FF><BF><D2><F2><FF><BF><D2><F2><FF><BF><D2><F2><FF><BF><D2>
<F2><FF><BF><D2><F2><FF><BF><D2>
Sep 1 19:48:18 baldy <FF><BF><D2><F2><FF><BF><D2><F2><FF><BF>
<D2><F2><FF><BF>
<D2><F2><FF><BF><D2><F2><FF><BF><D2><F2><FF><BF><D2><F2><FF>
<BF><D2><F2><FF><BF>
<D2><F2><FF><BF>^C
Sep 1 20:01:01 baldy PAM_pwdb[5938]: (su) session opened for
user news by (uid =0)
Sep 1 20:01:01 baldy PAM_pwdb[5938]: (su) session closed for
user news
```

PROBLEM 13 (CONTINUED)

Problem: Buffer overflow exploit.

Fix: See the next section.

Explanation: Someone has attempted a break-in and has probably succeeded. The above example indicates a buffer overflow attack, which feeds a server with continuous input in an attempt to overload it to the breaking point. While many buffer overflow problems have been corrected, inevitably more lurk out there.

Detecting Break-Ins

If you've experienced a break-in (and it's not always obvious), a program called tripwire can find so-called Trojan horses and altered files. After creating a catalog of all system files, it periodically checks your system's integrity (it's useless unless you initially run it on a clean system to get a "snapshot" of a healthy configuration, so don't wait to do so).

Keep on the lookout for extra inetd processes running. A favorite attack method is to exploit a buffer overflow hole, then create a file in a place such as /tmp with a single inetd.conf line:

```
8080 stream tcp nowait root /bin/sh -s -i
```

The attack then runs another inetd on that file. A telnet to port 8080 on the compromised machine yields a root shell, enabling the attacker to do whatever they wish to the machine.

What to Do if Someone Breaks In

If someone breaks into your machine, there's really no telling what your attacker did. To prevent the individual from coming back, you need to reinstall at least the core part of the operating system (and any custom services) on your machine. First, though, try to find out how the intruder got in, because if you put the system on the machine exactly as before, chances are whoever broke in will return.

Of course, you should also back up your data first.

2.6 Diagnostics

We all know networks don't always behave the way they're supposed to. Fortunately, many tools available for Linux can help you find problems. Most distributions come with a large set of tools installed in /usr/sbin. Here's a list of the good stuff and their basic functions.

ping The most basic of all network probing commands, `ping` sends roundtrip packets to remote hosts and reports how long they took to get there and back. Start it with

$ **ping** *remote-host*

CTRL-C stops it. When terminated, `ping` reports average the times and the percentage of packets lost. Not all remote hosts respond to a `ping`.

The `-f` (flood `ping`) option to `ping` sends at least 100 packets per second. Normally loaded local Ethernet connections should have no trouble handling a flood `ping`, but when you have a flaky or underperforming connection, a significant number of flood `ping` packets get lost. With most versions of `ping`, you can only use the flood option when logged in as `root`.

netstat This command shows network connection status. If you're having network problems, it's important to know what you have connected to your machine. Typical usage is with an option or two to filter output: `-t` displays TCP connections only (usually what you're looking for), and `-n` disables host name lookup (for those times when the network is so slow that the lookup hangs). The `-a` option lists every active port. An example of `netstat` in action is shown below.

PROBLEM 14

Symptom: When using `ping -f`, many packets on the network get lost and excessive collisions occur.

Problem: Older, poorly optimized network or bad wiring.

Fix: Try to eliminate hardware such as thin Ethernet and cascaded hubs on 10Mbps networks. An Ethernet switch can help matters at certain bottlenecks, but even a 100Mbps shared hub can help. Also, look out for bad wiring, especially Category 5 twisted-pair cable that doesn't have the pairs aligned properly.

```
$ netstat -t -u
Active Internet connections (w/o servers)
Proto Recv-Q Send-Q Local Address       Foreign Address       State
tcp        0      0 10.1.2.1:3128       mikado:4310           FIN_WAIT2
tcp        0    109 dialup-s229-8:1020  broadway.example.co:ssh ESTABLISHED
tcp        0      0 dialup-s229-8:1023  broadway.example.co:ssh ESTABLISHED
tcp        0    438 dialup-s229-8:2787  209.207.224.222:www   ESTABLISHED
tcp        0      0 dialup-s229-8:2786  209.207.224.222:www   ESTABLISHED
```

```
tcp       0     0 10.1.2.1:3128       mikado:2872       FIN_WAIT2
tcp       0     0 10.1.2.1:1912       mikado:6000       ESTABLISHED
udp       0     0 10.1.2.1:ntp        *:*
udp       0     0 localhost:ntp       *:*
```

The first line shows that netstat is listing TCP (-t option) and UDP (-u option) connections (netstat by itself shows Unix domain sockets—due to syslogd and a few other items, this can yield quite a long list). The above listing is from a gateway machine at home. This listing includes connections from one of the Ethernet interfaces (10.1.2.1)—a PPP dial-up. The machine also runs a Web proxy server on port 3128. A Web browser on the machine mikado has asked for a Web page, so mikado connects to us at port 3128, and we in turn have gone to the port www (80) of 209.207.224.222 for the page. We also have two ssh connections open to a machine called broadway. The second-to-last line shows an NTP (network time protocol) daemon running, using UDP instead of TCP.

Note that the service name (such as ssh, www, and ntp in this example) is the corresponding port in the file /etc/services.

traceroute This command traces the route to a remote host and reports the time between connections. Try it with www.userfriendly.org—the output looks like this:

```
$ traceroute www.userfriendly.org
traceroute to www.userfriendly.org (207.6.140.17), 30 hops max, 40 byte
packets
1  rsm-ryerson-v11 (128.135.11.210)  0.658 ms  0.731 ms  0.599 ms
2  vipernet-gw-a30-4.uchicago.edu (128.135.253.1)  2.382 ms  1.366 ms 1.281 ms
3  NChicago1-core0.nap.net (207.227.0.209)  32.673 ms  119.314 ms  18.613 ms
4  NChicago2-core0.nap.net (207.112.247.181)  8.337 ms  9.396 ms  8.287 ms
5  NSeattle1-core0.nap.net (207.112.247.169)  62.974 ms  62.059 ms  54.506 ms
6  * sea0-oc3.bctel.net (207.227.3.154)  48.438 ms  50.563 ms
7  inetgw4-s1.bctel.net (209.53.75.93)  59.654 ms  *  59.62 ms
8  204.239.129.205 (204.239.129.205)  55.683 ms  60.692 ms  61.28 ms
9  www.userfriendly.org (207.6.140.17)  59.601 ms  63.771 ms  67.636 ms
```

Notice the large latency gaps between NChicago2-core0.nap.net and NSeattle1-core0.nap.net. The hop between the host and the first gateway is a fast one, and the numbers reflect the speed of the network. Between 1 and 2, the gap expands a little. Then things start to get busy. At hops 6 and 7, asterisks (*) indicate this router is fairly busy and didn't have time to return one of the ICMP TIME_EXCEEDED messages that traceroute relies on.

If traceroute gives you the result 23 * * *, either the gateway is unreachable (which shouldn't be a surprise if the remote host is also unreachable) or it just doesn't want to return messages. You will occasionally get other messages such as !H (host unreachable); the traceroute (8) manual page outlines the different traceroute messages.

As with many of the other diagnostic programs, -n disables host name resolution, often speeding up the process quite a bit.

arp This command lets you look at and play with your system's ARP (address resolution protocol) cache. The ARP cache is a table that pairs hardware interface (such as Ethernet) addresses with Internet addresses. You'll need to use arp if you switched Ethernet interfaces on a machine, or if a machine on your network is sending bad ARP data.

The -a option shows the table; the -d hostname option deletes an ARP entry—for those times when you switch an Ethernet card on another machine and your cache is still out in left field; -s *hostname hardware-address* manually sets an entry in the cache. And -n disables name resolution, as in many other network diagnostic tools.

tcpdump Use this command with discretion, since it is a packet sniffer that can look at any unencrypted data going across your network and may seriously invade privacy. It sets an interface to what is called *promiscuous mode,* and prints out any traffic it sees on the interface after application of a user-specified filter. It can find the origin of stray packets or make a general collection of statistics if your network is saturated. This mode also slows the machine's network interface.

Here's an example run on the host 10.1.1.100:

```
# tcpdump port '!telnet'
Kernel filter, protocol ALL, datagram packet socket
tcpdump: listening on all devices
15:23:11.915995 eth0 < atlantic.6000 > 10.1.1.100.1025:
P2912965341:2912965373(32) ack 1334232813 win 32120 <nop,nop,timestamp
29867825
551877> (DF)
15:23:11.916444 eth0 < atlantic.6000 > 10.1.1.100.1025: P 32:64(32) ack
1 win
32120 <nop,nop,timestamp 29867825 551877> (DF)
15:23:11.916969 eth0 > 10.1.1.100.1025 > atlantic.6000: P 1:93(92) ack
128 win
31856 <nop,nop,timestamp 552798 29867825> (DF)
15:23:11.922532 eth0 > 10.1.1.100.1024 >
alexandria.cs.uchicago.edu.domain:
39700+ PTR? 100.1.1.10.in-addr.arpa. (41)
15:23:11.933808 eth0 < atlantic.6000 > 10.1.1.100.1025: . 128:128(0) ack
93 win
32120 <nop,nop,timestamp 29867827 552798> (DF)
15:23:12.126738 eth0 < alexandria.cs.uchicago.edu.domain > 10.1.1.100.1024:
39700 NXDomain* 0/1/0 (118) (DF)
...
```

The port !telnet argument tells tcpdump not to print anything related to the telnet port. The first line of real output tells us that port 6000 on atlantic is talking to our port 1025. The X Window System uses port 6000; we sent an xterm from 10.1.1.100 to atlantic and moved the mouse over the window to generate the packet corresponding to that line. Just below, you'll see something interesting: our machine asks alexandria.cs.uchicago.edu for the PTR record for 10.1.1.100. Here tcpdump itself tried to find out the name of the machine it's running on! (To make this work, we didn't put 10.1.1.100's name in its own /etc/hosts file).

If you're on a shared network, tcpdump allows you to look at the packets of anyone else on that network, but it's generally in bad taste to do so. You can only use tcpdump as root.

host The host command is a quick way to look up host names and their IP addresses with DNS. Unlike most similar programs, host makes a guess as to what kind of record you desire. Here are some examples:

```
$ host atlantic
atlantic.example.com has address 10.1.1.1
```

```
$ host 207.6.140.17
17.140.6.207.IN-ADDR.ARPA domain name pointer www.userfriendly.org
```

```
$ host printserver
printserver.example.com is a nickname for atlantic.example.com
atlantic.example.com has address 10.1.1.1
atlantic.example.com mail is handled (pri=10) by postfix.example.com
```

dig A more powerful tool than host, dig produces the same kind of output that the name server expects as input. You use this tool on the command line; it's very straightforward but somewhat strict about its arguments, and can yield hard-to-parse results. Try these examples on your machine:

```
$ dig mx flonk.net @ns1.netaxs.com
$ dig any slashdot.org
```

The second example gives you an "Answer Section" that lists some name servers (they're after the IN NS part). If you want more specific information on a record, you have to ask one of those servers. Pick the first one and try

```
$ dig any slashdot.org @nameserver
```

nslookup This is the traditional DNS query program, and it's almost sure to appear on any system you come across. You can use nslookup directly on the command line or in a more interactive mode. You usually have to know what kind of record you're looking for to use nslookup (see the examples below).

```
$ nslookup www.userfriendly.org
Server:    alexandria.cs.uchicago.edu
Address:   128.135.11.87

Non-authoritative answer:
Name:      www.userfriendly.org
Address:   207.6.140.17

$ nslookup
> set q=ptr
> 207.6.140.17
Server:    alexandria.cs.uchicago.edu
Address:   128.135.11.87

Non-authoritative answer:
17.140.6.207.in-addr.arpa          name = www.userfriendly.org

Authoritative answers can be found from:
140.6.207.in-addr.arpa  nameserver = dewey.mindlink.net
140.6.207.in-addr.arpa  nameserver = giant.mindlink.net
dewey.mindlink.net      internet address = 204.174.16.4
giant.mindlink.net      internet address = 204.174.18.2
> ^D
```

For a more detailed explanation of the above examples, see *DNS and BIND, 3rd Edition* (O'Reilly & Associates).

3

NFS, NIS, AND RDIST

3.1 Introduction

NFS and NIS are often bunched together in many books. Functionally, they don't have much to do with each other; they perform different tasks and for the most part work independently. Sure, you can use NIS maps in your NFS configuration, but you can use NIS maps almost anywhere. Still, they both send information from one machine to another, which makes it useful to discuss them together.

NFS (Network File System) is a means of mounting one machine's filesystem on another. NIS (Network Information Service) performs a variety of mostly user-based stuff—centralized user accounting (passwd and group files) is its biggest function.

NFS and NIS are not perfect. NFS suffers from a variety of performance and design shortcomings, and both have an annoying habit of sending their information unencrypted over the network. Furthermore, if configured incorrectly, they can perform horribly and have deleterious effects on system stability. They are widely used in spite of their faults because you can find free implementations everywhere.

We present rdist as an alternative to NFS in some cases. NFS was once used for any filesystem of substantial size, including parts of the system installation, since disk space was far too expensive to keep a complete local copy of the system on every machine on the network. Since average hard disk capacity has grown substantially, it makes more sense to keep this load off the network and put as much local software as possible on local disks. That's where rdist comes in—as a tool for copying directory trees to remote machines.

3.2 NFS Clients

Client configuration with NFS is initially straightforward. First, your kernel must support the NFS filesystem (or have a module that supports it). Of course, your machine must also have the server's permission to mount its filesystems.

Mounting a Filesystem

To mount a filesystem manually, use

```
# mount -t nfs server:/remote-filesystem /mount-point
```

where *server* is the remote server, */remote-filesystem* is the filesystem's location on the server, and */mount-point* is where you want to put the filesystem on your machine.

To make such a mount available at system boot time, add this entry to your system's /etc/fstab:

```
server:/remote-filesystem        /mount-point   nfs   defaults   0   0
```

NOTE *The last two fields are set to 0 because they are irrelevant with NFS clients. When the system boots, these will be among the last filesystems mounted.*

PROBLEM 15

Symptom: Noncritical NFS server often crashes, freezing user processes for the duration of the server's downtime.

Problem: Unreliable server.

Fix: Use the intr option to mount. When an NFS client's kernel can no longer communicate with a server, any programs attempting to access that server freeze, and you can't kill them until the server responds. Here is an example for /etc/fstab:

```
server:/remote-filesystem   /mount-point   nfs   intr   0   0
```

With the intr option, you can interrupt the process with a CTRL-C or kill.

Fixed Mounts

NFS mounts in /etc/fstab or attached by hand are sometimes called *fixed mounts*. Once the mount is in place, it stays there until it is manually unmounted or the system shuts down. But in most situations, fixed mounts are undesirable, since they tend to cause system instability on reboot.

PROBLEM 16

Symptom: One machine, acting as both an NFS client and a server, reboots, and the rest of the network hangs. When that machine reboots, it hangs.

Problem: Fixed NFS mounts tend to create cross-dependencies and lead to system instability.

Fix: Use the Automounter. If machine 1 gets files from machine 2, and machine 2 gets files from machine 1, you have the following problem: If both machines are down at one time, the first one that boots will time out trying to talk to the second. When the second machine eventually boots, it will be missing filesystems from the other server.

This is a trap of cross-dependencies that tends to catch inexperienced systems administrators.

PROBLEM 17

Symptom: Computer hangs at boot time.

Problem: Files needed for system bootup are on NFS-mounted filesystems.

Fix: Try to eliminate network dependencies on bootup by putting essential configuration data files on the local disk. (Using the Automounter won't help if a bootup script in one of the rc*.d directories tries to get a configuration file from one of the automounted directories.) To verify proper bootup on a machine, disconnect the network cable to see if it still hangs on reboot; if not, the hang probably stems from a network dependency problem.

The Automounting Daemon

The *automounting daemon* (or *Automounter*) follows the principle of on-demand filesystems and is a way to control file dependencies that cause boot problems.

The Automounter monitors a directory and freezes attempted accesses until it mounts a filesystem at that directory. Once the filesystem is mounted, access is allowed to continue as usual.

Because the Automounter only mounts the filesystem as needed, machines that share data on a network can all go down at the same time and can boot at will. As long as nothing in the bootup process needs to look at any NFS-mounted filesystems, the machine will boot as fast as a stand-alone.

NOTE *Even the Automounter won't prevent delays if a file server crashes. If server X is down, and you try to look at /foo/bar on X, the Automounter will freeze your access, and while attempting a mount it will probably time out and give you an I/O error. However, this will not affect currently running processes; as long as they don't attempt to access an unavailable filesystem, they should continue normally.*

There are two automounting daemons in common use: the native Linux automount, and amd, which runs on a number of platforms. We'll focus on automount because it's fairly small and simple to use.

automount

automount takes a (preferably empty) directory as its base and attaches the remote directories to it. (The most common example of this is /home. A user's home directory is usually /home/*user*, since users generally like their home directory to be in the same place over an entire network.)

The Automounter Map File

To configure the Automounter, use a map (a file) to determine what directories automount will handle and where it will get them when requested. Place the map somewhere on the network and make it available using NIS, NIS+, or arbitrary program execution, or simply as a plain text file. Whatever method you choose, the format for accessing the map is more or less the same. An example map for /home follows:

```
sue     mikado.example.com:/u25/sue
bob     atlantic.example.com:/u1/bob
```

Say you have the map in a file called /etc/auto.home. To start the Automounter on it, use this command:

```
# automount /home file /etc/auto.home
```

Now entering **cd /home/bob** takes you to bob's home directory.

For automount *to work, you must configure the autofs filesystem into the kernel either directly or as a module. In contrast,* amd *doesn't particularly need an autofs filesystem, but it's better to use autofs in order to keep bizarre path names like* /a/mikado.example. com/u25/sue *from popping up—if they exist, your users will discover them and ask you about them, and you won't want to bother explaining. In short,* amd *doesn't mount the directories at their given names, but rather in another part of the system, putting symbolic links from the "right" place to where the directories actually are located.*

The automount map format (as in the example above) is compatible with Sun Microsystems' Automounter, providing good integration with Sun networks. In addition to the file formats, Linux can also share Sun's /etc/auto.master, which contains all of the automount points (such as /home referenced above) and the map locations.

autofs

Linux provides a script called autofs that should run out of one of the rc*.d directories. autofs start reads /etc/auto.master and starts up an automount process for each entry. Here is an example of auto.master:

```
/home        auto.home              -rw,intr,noquota
/scratch     /etc/auto.scratch
```

The first entry instructs automount to look in the NIS map auto.home for the /home data, and the second starts with a forward slash (/), so automount consults the file /etc/auto.scratch. In other words, autofs start on this example above is equivalent to running these commands:

```
# automount /home nis auto.home
# automount /scratch file /etc/auto.scratch
```

Options to mount are placed in an optional middle field in the maps. Let's modify the /home map above:

```
sue      -r                      mikado.example.com:/u25/sue
bob      -nolock                 atlantic.example.com:/u1/bob
cdrom    -ro,fstype=iso9660      /dev/hdb
```

This code says set read-only access at /home/sue, and don't lock the mounts from atlantic.example.com (presumably because locking doesn't work very well on that server). The last entry isn't for an NFS filesystem at all; it's provided here to show how one may use the Automounter to handle removable media.

PROBLEM 18

Symptom: Stale NFS file handle errors. I/O errors. Empty directories.

Problem: Lingering processes, a moved directory, or a stale file handle.

Fix: When you move a directory or change the source of a mount point, there's always a risk that a user will be using a file or directory underneath that mount point when you make the change. Fix it by trial and error. First make sure the Automounter is not running for this mount point. Then try to umount the directory at the mount point by hand. If umount complains that the directory is busy, you probably need to kill some process (most likely a user process) that's accessing it. Usually it's pretty simple to hunt these down with a process listing, but sometimes you have to use lsof.

Often the Automounter refuses to start backing up because the automount point itself is hung up on something. You can also try to umount that (for example, in our /home example, you'd try **umount /home**). In rare cases, rebooting is the only fix.

Relevant man pages: autofs (5), automount (8), autofs (8)

NFS Mount Options

There are a few (sometimes) useful options to an NFS mount. You can invoke them with the -o option, placing a comma between multiple options:

```
# mount -obg,soft foo.example.com:/scratch /mnt
```

rsize=*n*, **wsize**=*n* Set the read and write buffer sizes to *n* bytes. Before Linux kernel version 2.2, the default NFS buffer size was 1024 bytes. However, this small size significantly slowed throughput, so version 2.2 raised the defaults— you shouldn't have to worry too much if you're running that kernel or higher. You can usually take the limits up to 8192 bytes.

intr For hard mounts, allows interruption of processes hung on an NFS access.

soft Gives an I/O error to any program hung on an access due to a server that's not responding. Useful when some *really* nonessential server has a habit of crashing.

bg If there's a timeout on the first mount attempt, keep trying in the background.

Relevant man pages: nfs (5), mount (8)

3.3 NFS Servers

An NFS server allows you to share files on a Linux machine across a network of Unix machines. While its performance is mediocre (and Linux NFS servers tend to lag behind those in other Unix variants), an NFS server comes in handy for spreading files over the network, especially if the files are small. There is no restriction on what you may share with NFS—you can even export a floppy disk if you like.

Essentials

The essential programs for NFS servers are portmap, mountd, and nfsd; /etc/exports is the main configuration file.

portmap maps RPC (remote procedure call) programs to regular network ports. RPC is a communications system that NFS, NIS, and a few other services use. mountd (or rpc.mountd) handles incoming mount requests—it is the only program that reads /etc/exports. Finally, the program that does the actual file transfers is nfsd (or rpc.nfsd).

To start an NFS server, you'll first need an appropriate /etc/exports file. If portmap isn't running, start it (as root), then start mountd and nfsd. If you make changes to /etc/exports, you'll need to send mountd a HUP (hang-up) signal:

```
# kill -HUP `cat /var/run/mountd.pid`
```

Here is an example of the /etc/exports file on the machine called mikado.example.com (used as a server in the client section above):

```
/u25          *.example.com
/u40          *.example.com(rw) @other_hosts(ro)
/data2        pacific.example.com(ro)
```

We're assuming that example.com is the local domain. When mountd starts up, it allows all hosts in example.com to read and write to /u25 and /u40; /data2 is only available to pacific.example.com, and then with read-only access. In addition, the hosts in the netgroup other_hosts have read-only access to /u40 (netgroups are an NIS concept, and we'll talk about them in Section 3.4).

The rw and ro in this example are options that apply to mountd and nfsd. Other options include the following:

noaccess Removes access for a directory. In the previous example, if we didn't want /data2/foo available to anyone, we'd put

```
/data2/foo        (noaccess)
```

at the end of the exports file.

no_root_squash By default, root's userid is set to that of an unprivileged user (usually nobody). This is a security consideration; no_root_squash turns this mapping off.

PROBLEM 19

Symptom: You can't change NFS-mounted items, even though you're root.

Problem: The NFS server maps the root userid to an unprivileged user.

Fix: You can add no_root_squash to the export options as described above. Keep in mind that such a mapping has its limits in terms of how much security it provides. For example, in order to modify any file root doesn't own, you must become that user, which you can do as root with su. Only systems like Kerberos can prevent this.

> **squash_uids=*list*** You can give the unprivileged mapping to users other than root by specifying a *list* of uids (such as 3-22,67,3235).
>
> **all_squash** Use squash_uids for all userids. Also consider using ro for read-only access.
>
> **anon_uid=*num*** Set the unprivileged userid for the squash options to *num*.
>
> **anon_gid=*num*** Set the unprivileged group for the squash options to *num*.

Unless you've explicitly turned off access with the noaccess option, any host with access to a given directory can mount a subdirectory of that one instead. This is particularly handy for use with the Automounter. (We didn't put /u25/sue in mikado's /etc/exports file; only /u25 is necessary to make the Automounter example in the previous section work.)

NOTE *Unlike the* nfsd *on other Unix variants, the Linux* nfsd *doesn't allow multiple copies. If you try it, the* nfsd *processes operate in read-only mode.*

Security Considerations

Don't expect NFS to be the most secure system in the world. It doesn't encrypt data, for one thing, and its default client authentication leaves a lot to be desired. If you're planning to use it, make certain to export filesystems, especially those for which you're allowing write access, to as small a subset of machines as possible. Don't let portmap out of your sight, either. The versions that come with most Linux distributions have tcp wrapper support built in, so you can use /etc/hosts.allow and /etc/hosts.deny with it. (See Chapter 2 for more information on these files.)

NFS Alternatives

Alternatives to NFS include AFS, DFS, and Coda, but if you want to use any of these, you'll either pay a lot of money or deal with lingering bugs in the free versions. Coda shows promise as a free network filesystem, but until it is in widespread use, you'll just have to deal with NFS.

3.4 NIS

NIS (Network Information Service) is a quick way to grab a bunch of keyed information from a server without worrying too much about who the server is. It can be handy for small networks, because it comes standard with Linux distributions. For larger networks, though, you should definitely consider alternatives like LDAP and Hesoid.

NIS is one of the simplest ways of distributing user information such as `passwd` and `group` files across a network, and it is in wide use on many multi-platform networks. But like NFS, it isn't terribly secure, mainly because it doesn't encrypt its transmissions.

Definitions

NIS databases are made up of a bunch of records consisting of key and data sections. The databases are dbm (under Linux, gdbm) files, usually made from plain text files.

An *NIS domain* is basically a network of machines bound to the same set of information. Each NIS domain has an *NIS domain name*.

NOTE *Don't confuse the NIS domain with DNS domains. DNS is a system used primarily for looking up Internet names, numbers, and closely related information. (Although you could replace NIS with an authenticated DNS, it isn't usually used that way.)*

Two kinds of NIS servers may serve the information to the clients in the NIS domain: master and slave servers. The master holds the original information about the network, and the slaves, if any, hold copies of the master's information.

NIS runs on top of RPC, so you'll need to have the portmapper running (`rpc.portmap` or just plain `portmap`) if you plan to use NIS servers and clients.

NIS Clients

The main programs associated with an NIS client are `rpc.portmap`, `domainname`, `ypbind`, `ypmatch`, `ypcat`, and `ypmatch`. Of these, `rpc.portmap`, `domainname`, and `ypbind` set up the communication with the server, and the rest are query programs.

Setting Up an NIS Client

1. Set the NIS domain name with the `domainname` command (here, the NIS domain name is *mydomain*):

domainname *mydomain*

2. Make sure `portmap` is running and start up `ypbind`, which broadcasts over the network in an attempt to find an appropriate NIS server. If your subnet has an NIS server with your NIS domain name, the server should respond and `ypbind` on the client will *bind* to that server.

3. Check the server with the `ypwhich` command. If everything looks right, use `ypcat` to dump a map (for example, if there's a group map, use a `ypcat group`).

    If everything goes well, set up your files to get the information from `ypbind` like so:

/etc/passwd
The code

```
+::::::
```

at the end of the `passwd` file allows all users in the `passwd` map to log in. If you want to limit access to only one *user* in the NIS `passwd` map, use

+*user*::::::

netgroups
To allow access to users in an NIS netgroup *ng*, add the line

+@*ng*::::::

The netgroup is particularly useful when you want to deny general user access to servers, which you would typically do with this type of `passwd` file:

```
root:x:0:0:root:/root:/bin/bash
daemon:*:1:1:daemon:/usr/sbin:/bin/sh
bin:*:2:2:bin:/bin:/bin/sh
..
.. (other passwd entries)
..
+@sysadmins::::::
+:::::::/usr/local/bin/noaccess
```

Here, sysadmins is a netgroup containing the user names of all systems administrators. The last line serves as a catchall so that the users are not unknown on the server. Failure to use proper user names will confuse or break many server daemons (Web servers, for instance).

PROBLEM 20

Symptom: You can use ypcat netgroup, but your netgroup entries to /etc/passwd don't actually seem to do anything.

Problem: Wrong /etc/nsswitch.conf.

Fix: If you're going to use the netgroup at all, /etc/nsswitch.conf must have a line like this:

```
netgroup:       nis
```

NOTE *If you're configuring Solaris NIS clients alongside your Linux clients,* netgroup *in* /etc/nsswitch.conf *is only valid with* nis.

PROBLEM 21

Symptom: Users can log in, even though you disallowed them with

+@*ng*::::::/bin/noaccess

in /etc/passwd.

Problem: Wrong /etc/nsswitch.conf.

Fix: /etc/nsswitch must have this line:

```
passwd:         compat
```

On the other hand, the following will not work with the +/+@ convention in /etc/passwd:

```
passwd:         files nis
```

The fastest way to verify a user's shell is with finger or with an ugly perl command such as

```
$ perl -e 'print join(" ",getpwnam(username)) . "\n"'
```

Debugging with ypcat, ypmatch, and ypwhich

Part of debugging NIS clients is figuring out whether you're actually getting the data you're supposed to. The ypcat and ypmatch programs can help with this. ypcat simply dumps an NIS map to the standard output:

```
$ ypcat group
```

Use the -k option to ypcat to see the map's keys in addition to its values.

REMEMBER *NIS is based on dbm files, so the output you get is in no particular order.*

If you know exactly what key you're looking for and in which map to find it, use ypmatch:

```
$ ypmatch key map
```

This prints the value for *key* in *map*.

If you don't know which NIS server your machine is bound to (if any), use ypwhich:

```
$ ypwhich
```

NIS Servers

The server side of NIS consists of a collection of prototype files, dbm files generated from those files (these dbm files are the NIS maps when put on the network), some programs that perform the conversion, and the NIS server itself (ypserv). The NIS master server has all of these components, and they come with most Linux distributions. Slave servers only need ypserv, which looks at dbm files, usually located in /var/yp. Inside this directory, you'll find a Makefile, your guide to how all the files fit together.

Before going through how to start up the NIS server (in the next subsection, Setting Up the NIS Master Server), let's explore how a file gets into NIS map format with /var/yp/Makefile. We'll look at passwd because it leads to the creation of more than one map.

Look in /var/yp/Makefile for the all: target (it's about the 98th line in some distributions), and you'll see passwd mentioned there. Ignore the passwd.adjunct for now. Now find the passwd: target (around line 123)—you'll see that it actually references two more targets, passwd.byname and passwd.byuid, so go ahead and look for these (line 257). Skip past the MERGE_PASSWD stuff to this target:

```
passwd.byname: $(PASSWD) $(YPDIR)/Makefile
        @echo "Updating $@..."
        @$(UMASK); \
        $(AWK) -F: '!/^[-+#]/ { if ($$1 != "" && $$3 >= $(MINUID) ) \
            print $$1"\t"$$0 }' $(PASSWD) | $(DBLOAD) -i $(PASSWD) \
                -o $(YPMAPDIR)/$@ - $@
        -@$(NOPUSH) || $(YPPUSH) -d $(DOMAIN) $@
```

The above looks ugly, but it's mostly a bunch of awk commands that throw out comments and blank lines. We can tell that the $(PASSWD) file is processed with an awk script. The first part of the awk script is -F:, which sets the field marker to a colon (:), which in turn tells awk that colons separate the fields. The next portion, !/^[-+#]/, removes any comment lines (even though you're not likely to have a comment in a password file). Then the if statement looks for what it considers valid passwd entries: here, the entries with a UID greater than or equal to whatever $(MINUID) is. If all of this checks out, the script prints field 1 (the user name), followed by a tab, then the whole line. So if you have the following file, and the $(MINUID) is set to 500 (the default in many distributions), here is what you'd see:

```
root:x:0:0:root:/root:/bin/bash
bin:x:1:1:bin:/bin:
daemon:x:2:2:daemon:/sbin:
adm:x:3:4:adm:/var/adm:
bri:.ASF.P//O83Ck:500:50:Brian Ward:/home/bri:/bin/bash
dave:fdsaf.DSAFdmm:501:50:David Beazley:/home/dave:/bin/bash
jjohnson:kgfsd7Rnn./4T:502:50:John Johnson:/home/jjohnson:/bin/bash
```

The result of the awk in the Makefile target is:

```
bri bri:.ASF.P//O83Ck:500:50:Brian Ward:/home/bri:/bin/bash
dave dave:fdsaf.DSAFdmm:501:50:David Beazley:/home/dave:/bin/bash
jjohnson jjohnson:kgfsd7Rnn./4T:502:50:John
Johnson:/home/jjohnson:/bin/bash
```

All of this gets piped to:

```
$(DBLOAD) -i $(PASSWD) -o $(YPMAPDIR)/$@ - $@
```

The $(DBLOAD) command is usually /usr/lib/yp/makedbm with a couple of arguments (the definition should be around line 107 in /var/yp/Makefile). The entire pipeline produces the binary maps in $(YPMAPDIR) (normally /var/yp/domain), and ypserv looks at these files. The final step in the Makefile rule for the target passwd.byname: pushes the map to slave servers.

Setting Up the NIS Master Server

Fortunately, you don't have to write the /var/yp/Makefile by yourself. To initialize the NIS master server, first make sure portmap (or rpc.portmap) is running. Then set the NIS domain name with the domainname command, as described in the NIS Clients section. Finally, do this:

```
# ypserv
# cat >> /etc/netgroup
foo bar
bar baz
^D
# /usr/lib/yp/ypinit -m
```

An interactive session will start, asking you for the next host in the list of NIS servers to add—it wants you to specify any slave servers. Don't worry about slave servers for now; press CTRL-D and confirm that the information is correct. After the verification, ypinit sets up /var/yp/*domain* for you (where *domain* is the NIS domain name), and attempts to run make on the newly created /var/yp/Makefile. (Note that ypinit isn't in any of the sbin directories.)

Don't panic if make fails with this:

```
gmake[1]: *** No rule to make target `/etc/netgroup', needed by `net-
group'. Stop.
gmake[1]: Leaving directory `/var/yp/domain'
```

This just means Makefile wants to build a file from /etc/netgroup, but there isn't any file there—we put cat >> /etc/netgroup in the example above, because it's the only file in the default NIS configuration that doesn't come with many distributions.

The more general fix is to remove unnecessary targets from Makefile if you don't need them. The listing of all targets is another target called all around line 98 in many systems:

```
all:  passwd group hosts rpc services netid protocols netgrp mail \
      #shadow publickey # networks ethers bootparams amd.home \
      auto.master auto.home passwd.adjunct
```

Here, netgrp is the target for the netgroup maps. Notice the comment on the second line—it means the all target uses only the first line.

NOTE   *If you remove a target and do a* make *in* /var/yp, make *won't remove the map files for that target if they were previously there. You'll need to either wipe them out by hand or do another* ypinit -m.

Concentrate on getting your NIS master server working reasonably well before you set up any NIS slave servers (we'll get to slave servers shortly).

When You Update a File

If you modify a file on your NIS master server, one that NIS has spread out on the network, you must cd /var/yp on your master server and make to build new maps and push them out to any slave servers. Some programs do this automatically—yppasswdd, for example, allows users to change their password over NIS.

Depending on how the Makefile is written, make may regenerate all of the maps, or it may just work on files changed since the last make. This was once a big deal because old machines weren't terribly quick at making maps and spreading them through the network, but it really doesn't matter anymore.

Slave Servers

If you have more than one subnet with NIS clients, you must set up at least one server for each subnet, which means you'll need a minimum of one slave server. A slave server is easy to set up. On the machine you want to act as a slave, first make sure portmap is running and the domainname is set. Then do

/usr/lib/yp/ypinit -s *master_server*

where *master_server* is the name of your master server. The ypinit program will now set up a /var/yp/domain directory and transfer all of the information from the master. You're not done yet—go back to your NIS master server and run

/usr/lib/yp/ypinit -m

again. This time, when it asks for the next server to add, include your new slave server's name.

PROBLEM 22

Symptom: Lookups on small maps never return. High load average on NIS server with many busy ypserv processes running.

Problem: Buggy ypserv.

Fix: NIS maps must have at least two entries. If a map has nothing in it, or if it has only one entry, when you try to access that map ypserv spawns a process on the server, which runs until you kill it.

Netgroup Maps

You won't run into netgroups in anything but NIS. It groups machines and users together; while this is not the most elegant system around, it is compatible with most other Unix variants. Here is a sample netgroup file that can generate the NIS netgroup map:

```
goodusers       (-,bri,) (-,jjohnson,) (-,dave,)
localmachines   (atlantic.example.com,-,) (pacific.example.com,-,)
remoteservers   (www.example.com,-,)
allmachines     localnet remotestuff
```

Each line consists of a key with three field entries within parentheses, separated by commas. If the field is a *user entry*, the user name is the second field and the first field is a hyphen (-). The opposite is true for *host entries*. The third field should be the NIS domain, but you're usually best off leaving this blank because that makes the file a bit more readable. You can combine netgroup entries by picking a new key and including other key names as the entries, as on the last line of the example above.

PROBLEM 23

Symptom: Some users or hosts are excluded from the netgroup map. The map builder program fails.

Problem: Netgroup lines are too long.

Fix: Netgroup entries, especially those for users, have a tendency to get too long for the dbm format. To fit everyone in, create a series of users as follows:

```
goodusers     goodusers1 goodusers2 goodusers3
goodusers1    (...) (...) \
    ...
goodusers2    (...) (...) \
    ...
goodusers3    (...) (...) \
    ...
```

NOTE *You can use the* expn-netgroup *program on the included CD-ROM in* support/nfs-nisrdist *to expand a netgroup entry.*

PROBLEM 24

Symptom: Solaris NIS clients miss the netgroup or have outdated data, although ypcat netgroup works fine.

Problem: The Solaris machines are looking at two additional netgroups.

Fix: When you run make in /var/yp, you create three netgroup maps: netgroup, netgroup.byuser, and netgroup.byhost. Some operating systems (including Linux and FreeBSD) just use netgroup map, but Solaris clients use the others, so make sure you synchronize them (usually the default).

3.5 rdist

Keeping software up to date over a bunch of machines is a simple matter of copying files from one machine to the rest and deleting outdated files as you go. The traditional Unix approach to this problem (before larger disks became more affordable) was to put the central distribution on a big server and make the rest of the clients mount them with NFS.

However, this strategy has two disadvantages that make it unsuitable for modern machines. First and foremost, accessing files with NFS is much slower than with a filesystem on a local disk. Second, it places too much importance on the reliability of the big server. Network filesystems like Coda address the problems of speed and reliability, but as previously mentioned, these are either very expensive or buggy.

The rdist (remote distribution) package copies a bunch of files around without asking too many questions, and it's been around for years. It consists of two programs, rdist and rdistd (the client and the server). You can connect to the rdistd on a remote server in a couple of different ways, but the safest way is to have rdist use ssh or rsh to connect instead of rdistd's network authentication mechanism. rdist consults a Distfile for its configuration (much like Makefile).

We will assume you're using rdist6. It's standard on most Linux distributions, and in addition to various versions on the CD-ROM in support/nfsnisrdist, you can get the latest version from

http://www.magnicomp.com/rdist/rdist.shtml

Let's start with a basic example of a Distfile.

```
STUFF = ( www src )
MACHINES = ( mikado atlantic )
${STUFF} -> ${MACHINES}
```

This just says you want to mirror the directories www and src on the hosts mikado and atlantic. Try this as your personal user before executing it as root. If you run

$ **rdist**

it tries to connect to mikado and atlantic with rsh to dump the directories www and src onto those hosts. By default, rdist will not delete files and directories on a remote host.

In order for rdist to function properly, it is essential that you have the ability to login to the remote host without a password.

PROBLEM 25

Symptom: Can't rsh to remote hosts.

Problem: You turned off rshd.

Fix: For now, you can do one of two things while you get used to rdist.

You can temporarily turn rsh back on by making the appropriate changes to /etc/inetd.conf (see Chapter 2), and adding this to your /etc/hosts.deny file:

in.rshd: ALL except *servername*

where *servername* is the machine on which you're running rdist. (Don't forget that you'll need a .rhosts or hosts.equiv on the remote host because .rhosts in particular can create a security hole.)

If, however, you can ssh to the remote host without a password (this requires matching host keys and authorized keys or hosts.equiv), just put the following code into a script called (for example) srsh:

```
#!/bin/sh
ssh -q $@
```

Then (assuming srsh is in the current directory), you can use rdist as follows:

```
$ rdist -P ./srsh
```

(We'll get into more details on how to use ssh with rdist later.)

Options

We've now introduced one of rdist's options, -P. rdist has two kinds of options: *normal* (*regular*) and *dist* options. Regular options are the same as in other programs: path names, configuration files, flags, and so on. Dist options control the remote distribution, and are specified with -o on the command line, as in this example:

```
$ rdist -oremove,younger,verify
```

This line tells rdist to remove files that are present on the remote host, but aren't in the local directory. It also instructs rdist to ignore files on the remote that have a newer modification time than those of the local copy, and to verify only (that is, to say what rdist needs to do) without actually doing it. A dist option in a Distfile looks like this:

```
( www src ) -> ( mikado atlantic )
    install -oremove,younger ;
```

The second line is a *command*. In addition to specifying dist options, commands allow even tighter distribution control by comparing certain file parameters (such as the date).

Here's more about commands.

Commands

except, except_pat

Ignore files and directories (don't update them). except_pat takes regular expressions as arguments and ignores files or directories that match.

Examples:

```
except lib ;
except_pat ^/usr/local/etc/.*\.conf$ ;
```

PROBLEM 26

Symptom: Some files mysteriously don't get updated.

Problem: Going overboard with except_pat.

Fix: Use the -overify dist option and examine the output. Try to start all expressions with a caret (^) and end them with a dollar sign ($). The regular expression in

```
    except_pat etc/.*\\.conf ;
```

matches files in /etc, /usr/etc, and /usr/local/etc (that is, if those directories are among those specified for the dist in the first place).

---

install

Specify options or alternate installation directories. We've already seen dist options in examples such as

```
install -oremove,ignlinks ;
```

For alternate installation directories, rdist behaves differently, depending on the source files. For the Distfile

```
( stuff ) -> ( atlantic pacific )
    install -oremove newstuff ;
```

the file or directory stuff is distributed as newstuff on the remote hosts. However, the following Distfile demonstrates a different scenario:

```
( morestuff/one morestuff/two morestuff/3/4 stuff ) -> ( atlantic pacific )
    install -oremove newstuff ;
```

In this case, rdist puts morestuff/one and morestuff/two into newstuff/one and newstuff/two on the remote hosts, but morestuff/3/4 becomes newstuff/4, and stuff goes into newstuff/stuff!

Why does rdist do this? It's trying to match items up, replacing as much of the base directory as possible. If rdist knows for certain that the source path name is a directory (in the case of morestuff and morestuff/3), it replaces all of the path name with the argument to install (here, with newstuff). But in our example, rdist doesn't know right away if stuff is a directory. If stuff is just a file, trying to put its contents into newstuff would be pointless.

PROBLEM 27

Symptom: rdist behaves differently with a single argument.

Problem: Design of rdist.

Fix: If your needs are fairly simple, use the whole dist option (described below) to force items to appear in the target directory without any path mangling. Try not to use the directory option to an rdist command with any complex arguments, because the resulting directory structure can be unpredictable. Split things up in the Distfile if you need to.

---

notify

Send the results of the rdist to a user, for example:

```
notify foo@example.com ;
```

This option is really useful only if you want to notify different people of specific changes within the same Distfile. Otherwise, you can just log rdist's output to a file and mail it to the user(s).

cmdspecial, special

When a certain file is distributed to a machine, special instructs rdist to run a program on that machine immediately. Here's an example for a syslogd and its configuration file:

```
special /etc/syslog.conf "/bin/kill -HUP `cat /var/run/syslogd.pid`"
```

On the other hand, cmdspecial waits until the distribution has finished before executing the program.

Dist Options

As mentioned above, you can specify a global dist option on the command line with -o, as in this example using the compare option:

```
$ rdist -ocompare
```

or in the Distfile with the install command:

```
( stuff ) -> ( machine )
      install -ocompare ;
```

There are a lot of dist options, and not all are terribly useful—for example, a better file system structure has largely superseded the need for a noexec option. We'll only describe the more commonplace, useful options. For the full list, see the manual page.

compare

Normally, rdist looks at the date and the size of a file or directory to determine if it's different on the remote host. The compare dist option tells rdist to go all the way and compare the file data itself.

PROBLEM 28

Symptoms: rdist is too slow. Machines and network are slow during the rdist run.

Problem: -ocompare is slow.

Fix: If you use -ocompare, remember that you're transferring all of your files across the network because they have to get from one host to the other for comparison. It's good to use it every now and then for a sanity check on your machines, but if you rdist on a regular basis, using -ocompare is extreme.

remove

Eliminate all files on the remote machines that aren't on the local machine.

younger

If a file you're distributing has a newer modification date on the remote host, this command makes sure that you don't touch the file on the remote host. This is particularly useful for debugging purposes when combined with the verify dist option, because it tells you what files have been customized on a remote host, then leaves them untouched.

nodescend

Don't go into subdirectories and examine their contents.

nochkowner, nochkgroup, nochkmode

Ignore owner, group, and mode (permission) differences, respectively.

follow

Resolve symbolic links and treat them as if they were real files or directories.

Using ssh with rdist

Since rsh isn't very secure, many systems administrators opt to turn it off. If they do use it, they don't allow root access through it. It is, however, possible to configure ssh to perform the same thing as rsh, through either configuration or authorized keys. (For more information on ssh, consult Chapter 2.) The process is different for ssh versions 1 and 2, so we'll first go over version 1 and then talk about the next version.

PROBLEM 29

Symptoms: Accidental transfer of large amounts of data. rdist gets into infinite loops, filling up the disk.

Problem: follow is a dangerous dist option.

Fix: Only use follow when you're absolutely sure what it is you intend to copy—such as a single directory. You can, however, use nodescend in combination with follow to get a flat directory free of symbolic links. Because rdist will only install the first level of directories it sees when given the nodescend dist option, your Distfile needs to reflect all files in a directory (here, for a directory *dir*):

```
( dir/* ) -> ( machines )

install -ofollow,nodescend ;
```

ssh Version 1

To configure sshd to accept root logins without any questions, place this in the sshd_config file:

PermitRootLogin yes

(This is the default value for sshd, but ought to be pointed out in any case.) Then you'll need the trusted host in root's .shosts (or /etc/hosts.equiv) file, because rdist will not work if it gets any output other than that of rdistd.

If you want to use authorized keys, first make sure the following is in the sshd_config file on the remote host:

PermitRootLogin nopwd

Now, on the machine where you'll run rdist place

 # ssh-keygen -N '' -b 1024

to create two key files in root's .ssh directory, identity and identity.pub. Copy the identity.pub file from that machine to the target machine in root's .ssh/authorized_keys file, inserting **from="*hostname*"** at the beginning, where *hostname* is the name of the machine running rdist. The authorized_keys file should look like this (one long line):

from="*hostname*" 1024 NN *<big long string of numbers>* root@hostname

Also, make sure the host key (not the one you just created) for *hostname* is in ssh's known_hosts file.

ssh Version 2

For ssh version 2, do this instead:

 # ssh-keygen -P -b 1024

You get the public and private keys in .ssh2 as the files id_dsa_1024_a and id_dsa_1024_a.pub (or similar). On the server, have both files present in root's .ssh2 directory, and put this in a file called identification:

IdKey id_dsa_1024_a

Then, on the remote hosts, place *only* the id_dsa_1024_a.pub file into root's .ssh2 directory. Add an additional file, authorization:

Key id_dsa_1024_a.pub

Verify that you can now `ssh` from one host to the other as root:

```
# ssh remote_host whoami
```

You should get `root` as a response.

To put it all together, make a script (as described above) called `distssh` with this content:

```
#!/bin/sh
ssh -q $@
```

You may want to give the full path name to `ssh` in this script, and you may also need to specify an extra option or two (we'll get to that in a moment).
To invoke `rdist` with this script instead of `rsh`, use the -P option:

```
# rdist -P ./distssh
```

PROBLEM 30

Symptom: Error message:

```
machine: LOCAL ERROR: Unexpected input from server: ...
```

Problem: Interference from `ssh` diagnostic warnings.

Fix: Use the -q option to `ssh`, which attempts to turn off all warning messages—though it does not turn everything off. For example, if you use -c arcfour and `ssh` decides it wants to use blowfish instead, it tells you (and causes `rdist` to abort, if `rdist` is running `ssh`). Still, this is useful for failed xauth commands and other noncritical warnings.

PROBLEM 31

Symptom: `rdist` takes much longer with `ssh` than it does with `rsh`.

Problem: Encryption can be CPU-intensive.

Fix: Count on a performance penalty with `ssh` no matter what you do (the overhead can get up to a factor of three or so), but for older, slower machines, try a different cipher option to `ssh`. Most support blowfish, which is faster than the default of idea. Try adding **-c blowfish** to the arguments in your `distssh` script.

Make sure the identity *(or* id_dsa_1024_a*) file never leaves the server. If someone breaks into the server, change the keys immediately; if you don't, you risk a very serious intrusion. Setting up IP filters to block out most of the world is a good idea for* rdist *servers.*

Larger-Scale Distributions

If you've got a large network, keeping things uniform across your machines is important. All of your machines should have the same software set, and ideally you should be able to set it up without a large time commitment. A good practice is to set up one machine as a prototype for the rest. What's important (and what many systems administrators forget) is not to lose touch with the programs your users really depend on.

You basically have two choices with regard to which machine will run rdist. Either the prototype can run the dist itself, or a more powerful server can do the task (the prototype does an rdist to the server first). If you have the resources, the latter option is preferable for two reasons. The first is that you can load this so-called rdist server with fast disks, which you wouldn't typically put into a desktop machine. The second, more significant reason is that you can put a distribution set onto a disk other than the system disk. If you make the prototype run an rdist from its own system disk, a conflict will arise when the prototype accesses the system and files for distribution, slowing the process down considerably.

Try to make your prototype machine one that gets fairly heavy use from an experienced user. If you have a staff of systems administrators, have one of them use it. Furthermore, when you are about to do a large rdist, test it on your own machine first. It's much better to break only your own machine rather than your entire network!

Next come the questions of what to distribute and when to perform rdist. In general, it's fine to put items in /usr on all hosts. Only distribute /bin, /sbin, and /lib when you need to—for libc upgrades, base Linux utility fixes, and such tasks.

/etc is a different story. If you plan to rdist stuff into /etc, run rdist with -overify first and make sure you aren't walking over anything important like /etc/fstab.

Relevant man pages: rdist (1), rsh (1), ssh (1)

4

MS-WINDOWS AND APPLETALK
NETWORKS; WEB PROXY SERVER

4.1 Introduction

If you are running a fairly typical network, you probably have other computers
on it that don't run Unix but still need to communicate with Unix machines
on the local network. The traditional Unix approach to the problem of inter-
operability is to make the foreign machines speak the Unix protocols, but
people with non-Unix machines tend to resist this solution because it requires
installing more software.

Fortunately, other computers no longer have to speak Unix protocols to get
along with Unix. In this chapter, we'll see how to make Linux talk to Windows
machines over SMB (or CIFS) with the SAMBA package, and to Macs with
Netatalk. Both packages are stable and relatively easy to set up, and perform
fairly well. We'll also discuss how to improve the performance of networks, especially those with a slow link to the outside world, by setting up a Web proxy
server called squid.

4.2 SAMBA

Among the various communications protocols for Windows, the SMB (CIFS)
share is probably the most common because it comes with the operating system.

This section talks about SAMBA server basics. SAMBA is a remarkably complete package for talking to Windows machines with NetBIOS running over TCP/IP. This large package contains support for all sorts of services like network logins and login path mappings, but we'll stick to printing and filesharing for starters. You'll find a fairly good reference to all of the options in the online documentation at http://www.samba.org/ (as well as in the manual pages).

SMB Shares and NetBIOS

We could write quite a lot about how SMB shares over NetBIOS are supposed to work, but the basic idea is that you associate server names with IP addresses and a service path name. Here's an example SMB share name:

```
PRINTSERVER\\MYPRINTER
```

These shares may have a password, and they may also be *browseable*, meaning that you can use Windows' Network Neighborhood to look through shared services.

SAMBA Daemons

The two main daemons in SAMBA are nmbd and smbd. nmbd is a NetBIOS name server, and smbd provides SMB server functions. There is one main configuration file called smb.conf, which looks like a PC file. Here is a very simple example:

```
[global]
    guest account = nobody
    invalid users = root
    browseable = yes
    workgroup = HOME
    socket options = TCP_NODELAY
    security = share

[homes]
    comment = Home Directories
    writeable = false
    guest ok = false
    path = /home/%S

[printers]
    guest ok = true
    guest only = true
    printable = true
    path = /tmp
```

This configuration file sets up some standard SMB services, including read-only home directories and printers for smbd's use.

There are three sections in the example smb.conf file above: [global], [homes], and [printers]. These three are called *special sections*. The purpose of the [global] section is to set defaults for the rest of the file; [homes] and [printers] control access to home directories and printers.

Here are some of the [global] section parameters you should be aware of. You can override most of them in individual sections.

guest account = *username*

username should be an unprivileged user who can't do much (other than print and access public directories). The default is nobody.

browseable = true|false

If set to true, remote hosts can access a list of SMB shares.

security = *type*

Set the *type* of access control. The default value is user, which only allows registered logins to access the server. Other options are share (appropriate for public servers), server, and domain. (See Problem 35 about encrypted passwords later in this chapter for information on why you may not be able to log in to the SAMBA server from a Windows machine.)

netbios name = *name*

Make the server known as *name* on the network instead of by the Unix host name.

While the example smb.conf file specifies that the SAMBA server should belong to the HOME workgroup, it doesn't say anything about how the machines around it will identify the SAMBA server. The server is not running any *browse masters*, so if it shows up in any Network Neighborhood browsers, a Windows machine on the network is probably acting as browse master.

To begin working with SAMBA, start with a simple smb.conf file, like the above example. After you've got a file that at least allows you to list the shares available on the server (with smbclient -L *servername*), start tailoring smb.conf to your own needs.

Start the SAMBA daemons with

```
# nmbd -D -s configfile
# smbd -D -s configfile
```

where *configfile* is the full path name to your smb.conf file.

Debugging

You'll find debugging information in log files named `log.nmb` and `log.smb`, in whatever directory you configured to store SAMBA's `var` (the default is *prefix*/`var`, where *prefix* is the installation prefix).

PROBLEM 32

Symptom: Too little or too much access control.

Problem: Confusion as to what security you need.

Fix: If you're just starting out, use `security=share`, which asks the client for a password once per connection to a share. The default (`security=user`) requires a login to the SAMBA server (we won't discuss this). The `security=server` setting tries to pass the login to a different server, while `security=domain` says SAMBA should act like it's on a real Windows NT network (that is, it should ask the Windows NT primary domain controller if the client has access). You'll find details of each setting in the smb.conf (5) manual page.

Workgroup and Network Browser Options

To use the Network Neighborhood browser on a Windows machine, you must run a browse server of some sort on a networked machine. This server collects a list of SMB servers on the network and gives the list to clients that ask for it. There are two ways to do this: with a Windows workgroup or with a Windows NT domain.

Browse Servers

If you'd like the Network Neighborhood to function and you have no Windows machines on your network, you need to set up SAMBA as a browse server. As with most SAMBA options, you'll find the configuration in the `smb.conf` file. Note that if you want to set up browsing for a Windows NT domain, you can set it up in the same manner as a workgroup. However, to make your Windows NT logins and passwords the same as on your Unix network, you'll need to set up SAMBA as a domain master. That subject goes beyond the scope of this book, however.

When running browse servers, you'll use a combination of *domain master* and *local master* browsers. Each workgroup needs one domain master, and if you have multiple subnets you'll need a local master on each subnet outside the domain master.

The most relevant smb.conf options for browse servers are these:

```
workgroup = name
```

Set the workgroup to *name*.

```
domain master = true|false|auto
```

Setting domain master to true makes nmbd (the NetBIOS name server) attempt to become the domain browse master for your workgroup. If another service has already claimed itself as the master, nmbd won't attempt to run a master browser. If you start up nmbd with this option by mistake prior to starting a Windows NT Primary Domain Controller with the same NT domain name as your workgroup, you may have browsing problems (machines missing from the Network Neighborhood browser, unusually slow response).

```
local master = true|false
```

This parameter, when set to true, asks nmbd to attempt to become the local master for a subnet. If you want to use this parameter, take a look at the WINS server parameters as well (wins server and wins support); you may need to set up a WINS server on your domain master browser and make the local browsers point to it.

PROBLEM 33

Symptom: Although you want nmbd to become the local master browser on your subnet, another machine seems to be filling that role, so the host mappings you set up in the lmhosts file aren't showing up in network browsers.

Problem: Your nmbd loses a local master browser election with a Windows machine.

Fix: Use the OS level parameter in smb.conf. If you specify OS level = 65, you'll defeat an NT server every time. This can come in useful if you're dealing with a bunch of machines you don't control and their users have a bad habit of turning all the services on.

Name Resolution and the lmhosts File

lmhosts is a simple file that maps IP addresses to NetBIOS names. It looks like this:

```
10.1.1.37 CRUMMYNTBOX
10.1.1.4 SPIFFYLINUX
```

SAMBA uses lmhosts for direct name lookups so it doesn't have to waste time asking for IP addresses over the network. By default, SAMBA first looks in lmhosts for the IP address. If it doesn't find what it wants in lmhosts, it performs standard host resolution (using whatever is set in /etc/nsswitch.conf—usually /etc/hosts and DNS, in that order). The next method SAMBA tries is WINS (see the WINS section below). If all of these fail, it broadcasts the request all over the subnet.

To change this default behavior, set the name resolve order parameter. For example, if you only want it to search with lmhosts and WINS, and not broadcast or use standard Internet host lookups, use this:

```
name resolve order = lmhosts wins
```

(The parameter values for broadcast and standard host lookups are bcast and host.)

NOTE *By default, the* lmhosts *file is in the* etc *directory of your SAMBA installation. You can use the* -H file *option to* nmbd *to set the location, but as of this writing there is no equivalent option for* smbclient. *If you're planning to put* lmhosts *in a location other than the default, put a symbolic link to that place in its default location. Otherwise, you may run into difficulty when you're debugging.*

WINS

Due to shortcomings in NetBIOS, you'll need a WINS server to resolve host names from one subnet to another (if you have more than one subnet, that is). This server is like a DNS server, but it's limited to small NetBIOS-style names, and you should use it only with a local Windows network. You should have just one WINS server for all of your subnets. These are the smb.conf parameters relating to WINS:

```
wins server = name|ip
```

name or *ip* is a WINS server. If SAMBA needs to look up a name with WINS, it queries this server.

```
wins support = true|false
```

This parameter causes nmbd to act as a WINS server.

```
dns proxy = yes|no
```

If you set this parameter to yes, nmbd attempts to look up unknown NetBIOS names over DNS when nmbd acts as a WINS server.

More Access Control Options

Sometimes you need better control over who has access to a share. Most of the following parameters are set on a per-share basis—that is, you normally specify them in sections other than [global].

```
allow hosts = list
```

This parameter allows connections to *list*. The format resembles that of /etc/hosts.allow (see Chapter 2 and the hosts_access(5) manual page). Here is an example:

```
allow hosts = @goodguys, 10.1.1.0/255.255.255.0 EXCEPT 10.1.1.37
```

@goodguys is an NIS netgroup.

```
deny hosts = list
```

This parameter rejects connections from *list*.

PROBLEM 34

Symptom: Although you used deny hosts, an undesired host still seems to have access.

Problem: allow hosts has the final word on specifically allowed hosts.

Fix: Use the EXCEPT keyword in the allow hosts setting.

```
available = yes|no
```

A no setting disables the share.

```
guest ok = yes|no
```

A value of yes allows access to the share as a guest (that is, no password is required for access).

```
guest only = yes|no
```

When this parameter is set to yes, only guest logins are allowed. This requires guest ok = yes.

```
invalid users = list
```

This denies users access; you specify it as *list* of users, *@group* (which expands to a netgroup or group), *+group* (expands only to a group), or *&group* (netgroup only). Keeping root out is a good idea.

```
valid users = list
```

Only *list* may access the share. The format is the same as that of the invalid users parameter above.

PROBLEM 35

Symptom: Guest logins work, but user logins don't.

Problem: Windows NT Service Pack 3, Windows 98, and later versions enforce encrypted passwords.

Fix: You have two choices: Tell SAMBA to recognize encrypted passwords, or make Windows send clear-text passwords by altering the Registry. For encrypted passwords, set the following in smb.conf:

```
encrypt passwords = yes
```

Get the mksmbpasswd.sh file that's in the SAMBA distribution and run it on your passwd file. Put the result of mksmbpasswd.sh into *prefix*/private/smbpasswd (*prefix* is your SAMBA installation prefix), then run the following:

 # chmod go -rwx *prefix*/private/smbpasswd

You should probably put this in a cron job to ensure that the password information gets updated on a regular basis (see Chapter 1 for more information on cron).

The other fix is to change the Windows Registry to make it accept clear-text passwords. This is generally not a good idea, but if you wish to do so, have a look at the SAMBA FAQ under the heading "Windows 98 Passwords."

Printing

The [printers] section of smf.conf is straightforward. The following is a sample section that works on many systems:

```
[printers]
  comment = Network Printers
  browseable = true
```

```
printable = true
guest ok = true
guest only = true
path = /tmp

printing = BSD
load printers = yes
print command = /usr/bin/lpr -r -P%p %s
lpq command = /usr/bin/lpq -P%p
lprm command = /usr/bin/lprm -P%p %j
printcap name = /etc/printcap
```

The first six lines after [printers] describe general access control. The browseable parameter allows clients to browse the list of printers. The lines containing guest specify that the users should only print files as guests. path specifies a place for temporary files (when you issue a print request, it goes to this location before going to the printer). Using /tmp makes it easier to debug problems (for example, if lpq requests fail and pile up). In any case, you should specify a place where your anonymous user (usually the default, nobody) can write.

The second set of lines in the example above illustrates how SAMBA handles print commands. The commands are the default values with the printing = BSD setting. If you're using LPRng (which we recommend), change BSD to LPRNG. LPRng commands work like their BSD counterparts, but the output from lpq is different (see the problem below for information on what happens in this case).

The printer list in this example comes straight out of /etc/printcap (using the printcap name parameter in the last line). This is usually appropriate, but you may wish to limit the list of printers. Copy your existing /etc/printcap file, cut out any unwanted printers in the copy, and set printcap name to this newly modified file.

PROBLEM 36

Symptoms: The printer queue doesn't show up on the Windows client. Temporary files beginning with lpq pile up.

Problem: SAMBA doesn't parse lpq output correctly.

Fix: Make sure you have the lpq command set to the correct syntax, and verify the printing parameter value. Linux has three main possible values: LPRNG, PLP, and BSD. The manual pages for the print utilities (lpr, lpd, and so forth) should say which one of these print spoolers you have installed on your system.

Symptom: After a while, several files named lpd.* appear in /tmp (or whatever you have path set to).

Problem: Sometimes SAMBA doesn't clean up after itself.

Fix: From time to time, the queue checker may malfunction and drop a file. You should keep a cron job around to run a find and get rid of any of these old files. For example, if smb.conf specifies path = /tmp, put this command in the system crontab:

```
find /tmp -name 'lpq.*' -ctime 1 -exec rm '{}' ';' > /dev/null 2>&1
```

Symptoms: Print jobs get mangled or fail. PostScript source prints as text.

Problem: Garbage appears at the beginning of print jobs.

Fix: Some Windows print drivers put a ^D in front of the job in an attempt to clear printer memory. But in the case of a Unix print queue, if the first two characters of the job are not %!, the print filter may get confused. First try adding

postscript = yes

to your smb.conf file. This does *not* get rid of the ^D, but rather sends a %! before every job. This may not be appropriate for your printer—in that case you'll want to come up with another filter that looks at the first character before it sends any job to the printer.

Single Printer Sections

For a single printer outside the [printers] section, add a section such as the following:

```
[myprinter]
 guest ok = true
 guest only = true
 printable = yes
```

```
print command = send_job_command -Pmyprinter %s
lpq command = /usr/bin/lpq –Pmyprinter
lprm command = /usr/bin/lprm -Pmyprinter %j
path = /tmp
```

Here, whatever you specify as *send_job_command* sends jobs to the printer. You may want to do this in order to bypass a print filter or add a different filter.

Relevant man pages: lpr (1), lpq (1), lprm (1), lpd (8)

Filesharing

You can export directories to Windows clients in SAMBA's smb.conf file in two ways. One is with a regular section, and the other involves the special [homes] section. Here is a very simple single-path share in a regular section:

```
[projects]
 path = /stage/projects
 valid users = +staff
 writeable = yes
```

Here, we're allowing read-write access to /stage/projects for the users in the group staff. To use /stage/projects as a network drive on a Windows machine, you can enter the following at an MS-DOS command prompt:

net use g: \\SERVER\PROJECTS /user:*username*

Here, *SERVER* is the NetBIOS name of the SAMBA server and *username* is a user in the group staff. We're also assuming that g: isn't currently in use. Similarly, you can attach a network drive by right-clicking on the My Computer icon on a Windows machine, then selecting Map Network Drive on the menu.

Name Alterations

Because of the limitations of DOS-style file names, SAMBA presents file names differently than they actually appear in the Unix filesystem. By no coincidence, SAMBA calls this *name mangling*. You end up with a name like XINIT~3L.193 because Windows can't handle a really long name.

In order to do this kind of name mapping, you would use the mangled map setting in the smb.conf file. There's not a lot you can do about really long file names, but you can avoid some ugly names with certain extensions. The syntax of the mangled map parameter is as follows:

```
mangled map = (*.jpeg *.jpg)
```

Many servers use (*.html *.htm) here because that's one of the few four-letter extensions that will cause serious problems if mangled.

You can read all about further mangling options in the "Name Mangling" section of smb.conf (5), but the three most important are as follows:

```
mangling char = c
```

Change the marker character for mangled names from ~ to c. The XINIT~3L.193 file mentioned above would become XINIT!3L.193 if you set c to an exclamation point (!).

```
default case = upper|lower
```

When creating new files on the Unix filesystem, make the names in either all uppercase or all lowercase letters.

```
mangle case = yes|no
```

If a name isn't in the default case (above), mangle it. This option is present because a file such as README is different from a file named readme on a Unix machine (but not on a DOS machine), and you may want some consistent way to distinguish them.

PROBLEM 39

Symptoms: Clients can get to files outside the shared path.

Problem: Symbolic links may lead to a completely different place on the system.

Fix: Put the following:

wide links = no

in smb.conf to make SAMBA act more like a Web server. This is probably only really useful if you're sharing a directory as read-only to guests, since real users can probably just log in to the SAMBA server and see all files on the system that way.

[homes] Special Section

To deal with a potentially large and constantly changing number of user home directories, the [homes] section with special substitution properties is available in the smb.conf file. Instead of asking for a share implicitly by providing your user name and password, you may also supply the name of a different user's home directory.

There are two ways to ask for a home directory from a SAMBA server. The first is explicit, as in this DOS command:

```
net use g: \\SERVER\username1 /user:username2
```

When you make this request, the SAMBA server on *SERVER* first looks at the *username1* part of *SERVER**username1* as it normally would in any other section in smb.conf. If *username1* matches any other section, this matching section is used. However, if it does not match and there is a [homes] section, SAMBA makes one more attempt before returning an error: It looks up the home directory of *username1*, which becomes the share if that *username1* is a user on the SAMBA server. *username2* is the Linux user to connect as (usually the same as *username1*).

The other way to ask for a home directory share is implicit:

```
net use g: \\SERVER\homes /user:username
```

Here, you're telling SAMBA straight away that you want your home directory and that your login is *username*.

A fairly safe example for a [homes] section is:

```
[homes]
 guest ok = no
 browseable = no
```

It's up to you whether you want users to be able to write to the directories (using the writeable parameter). The file permissions go down to the underlying Unix filesystem on the SAMBA server; the SMB client can only write to the files and directories that the connecting user can write to.

Once you look at a user's share, it shows up in the shares list.

If you don't like the way the [homes] section works, you can set up a simpler one, like this:

```
[u]
 guest ok = no
 path = /home/%u
```

Any access to *SERVER*\%u results in the home directory of the account used to connect (this example assumes that all of your home directories are in /home).

SAMBA Clients

SAMBA comes with a program called smbclient. It's useful for occasional remote access purposes, as well as for debugging your own SAMBA server's smb.conf file. Use it as follows:

```
$ smbclient '\\SERVER\share'
```

You can employ -U *user* to change the user (the default is your log-in name). It asks you for a password unless you specify the -P *passwd* option. If you're trying to access a guest share, you can specify an empty password or just press ENTER at the password prompt. Upon success, smbclient gives you a prompt like this:

```
Domain=[MYWRKGRP] OS=[Unix] Server=[Samba 2.0.6]
smb: \>
```

From there, you can use commands similar to ftp's put, mput, get, mget, and so on. Use help to get a full list.

If you want to use shares on Windows machines on a regular basis, you should consider the SMB filesystem available in the Linux kernel. To use it, first get your kernel to support smbfs by either compiling it into the kernel or building and loading it as a module (the latter option is preferable—see Chapter 7). Then look in your SAMBA package for an smbmount program that combines the smbclient and mount programs:

```
# smbmount '\\SERVER\SHARE' -c 'mount /mnt' -U user -P password
```

Relevant man pages: smbclient (1), smbmount (8)

4.3 Netatalk

To get your Linux machine to speak AppleTalk, you need two things: kernel support for AppleTalk low-level protocols, and the server programs that provide services (such as filesharing and printing) to clients. AppleTalk has a number of low-level protocols (transport mechanisms), but the most common on local networks is DDP running over Ethernet. There's a kernel configuration option for this under "Networking options"; it's called AppleTalk DDP, and you should configure it as a module as described in Chapter 7.

The Netatalk package deals with the services. Its main facilities are filesharing and printing for servers and clients, but it also includes a few utilities for looking up names and converting Macintosh-style files. The original Netatalk package has not been modified for some time, but a new version with many enhancements called Netatalk+asun is now available. This book assumes you have the enhanced package. In addition to the version on the included CD-ROM in support/atalksamba, you'll find it (at least at the time we wrote this book) at ftp://ftp.u.washington.edu/public/asun/.

Unfortunately, Netatalk's included documentation is on the skimpy side; the manual pages only describe command-line options, with very little description of configuration files.

After you've built the AppleTalk kernel module (appletalk.o), use insmod on it. The kernel generates a message such as this:

```
NET4: AppleTalk 0.18 for Linux NET4.0
```

Now let's turn to the core daemon of the Netatalk package, atalkd, which handles basic AppleTalk communications services such as name lookups and service registration. atalk's configuration file is atalkd.conf, which usually consists of just the interface name, as in this one for Linux Ethernet drivers:

```
eth0
```

The atalkd.conf file included with the Netatalk distribution has a large section of comments outlining options for complex installations. The atalk (8) manual page details these options. The most significant is the -zone option to set the default AppleTalk zone.

PROBLEM 40

Symptom: Your changes don't seem to take effect.

Problem: atalkd can't find its atalkd.conf configuration file.

Fix: If you don't know where atalkd expects to find atalkd.conf, start it with

```
# atalkd -f fullpath
```

where *fullpath* is the full pathname of the configuration file, such as

```
/usr/local/etc/atalk.conf.
```

---

atalkd takes some time to start, so if you're putting it in a boot script, you should place the whole AppleTalk start-up in the background—you're not likely to miss it when it comes up just after your machine boots.

Start up a test atalk like this (remember to run insmod appletalk.o first):

```
# atalkd
# nbprgstr -p 4 hostname:Workstation
# nbprgstr -p 4 hostname:netatalk
```

where *hostname* is the name of your machine. Verify that atalkd is running with a process listing. If it's running, try this:

```
$ nbplkup
```

If atalkd is functioning properly, you should get a listing like this:

```
deskprint:LaserWriter          65280.166:128
 atlantic:AFPServer            65280.166:130
```

```
atlantic:    netatalk          65280.166:4
atlantic:    Workstation       65280.166:4
     fur:    ARA - Client-Only 41201.173:2
     fur:    Power Macintosh   41201.173:252
     fur:    Workstation       41201.173:4
```

This output comes from a network with only two machines that speak AppleTalk: atlantic and fur. In a name such as fur:Workstation, fur is the *nbp object* and Workstation is the *nbp type*. As the listing suggests, atlantic is a Linux machine running Netatalk, and is offering a filesharing service (that's what the AFPServer part of the second line means). It's also running a deskprint printer client for the printer. Notice that the dotted numbers in the second column are the same for the deskprint and atlantic lines. You might guess that fur is a Mac because it advertises itself as a Power Macintosh type on the next-to-last line.

Netatalk provides a utility similar to ping called aecho, which uses the AppleTalk Echo Protocol to see if a remote host is alive. You may specify the remote host as an *object:type* pair, an *object* (the nbp type defaults to Workstation), or a number. That means all of the following do the same thing:

```
$ aecho fur:Workstation
$ aecho fur
$ aecho 41201.173
```

The response is very similar to a ping command:

```
14 bytes from 41201.173: aep_seq=0. time=0. ms
14 bytes from 41201.173: aep_seq=1. time=0. ms
14 bytes from 41201.173: aep_seq=2. time=0. ms

—41201.173 AEP Statistics—
3 packets sent, 3 packets received, 0% packet loss
round-trip (ms)  min/avg/max = 0/0/0
```

You have to use CTRL-C to interrupt aecho.

Netatalk Startup Script

The Netatalk distribution comes with a rc.atalk script that is a good start for writing a bootup script. It includes the NBP string initialization, as well as papd and afpd (AppleTalk printing and fileservice daemons; we'll talk about those in Sections 4.3.1 and 4.3.2 below). On the included CD-ROM, you'll also find a sample init.d script in support/atalksamba. This script looks for configuration files before starting the AppleTalk daemons so that you can distribute it to a number of hosts.

PROBLEM 41

Symptom: Daemons and applications die with "Unknown service" messages.

Problem: Lines are missing from /etc/services.

Fix: Add the following lines to /etc/services:

```
rtmp        1/ddp        # Routing Table Maintenance Protocol
nbp         2/ddp        # Name Binding Protocol
echo        4/ddp        # AppleTalk Echo Protocol
zip         6/ddp        # Zone Information Protocol
```

PROBLEM 42

Symptom: Your AppleTalk boot script takes too long, so your Linux machine takes forever to boot.

Problem: atalkd and related daemons take too long to start up.

Fix: Make your AppleTalk init.d script similar to the following (where *netatalk* is your installation prefix):

```
( netatalk/atalkd ;
    netatalk/nbpstr hostname:Workstation ;
    netatalk/nbpstr hostname:netatalk ;
    netatalk/afpd ;
    netatalk/papd ) &
```

There is one small disadvantage to this approach: If any print jobs get caught in a queue for an AppleTalk printer when the machine boots, the print filters will probably silently fail on the print jobs and send them to the bitbucket because atalkd hasn't started up yet.

Relevant man pages: atalkd (8), nbplkup (1), nbp_name (3)

Printing

This section details the process of setting up a printer that's already accessible from Unix for a Macintosh to use over the network. To go in the other direction (printing to an AppleTalk printer from Linux), have a look at Section 5.3.

The papd daemon that waits for a print request from a Mac is an odd program; its default behavior assumes certain things about the lpd to which it sends print jobs. This book recommends LPRng as a print daemon. The default configuration files need some changes to allow papd to interact properly with LPRng's lpd.

papd has two configuration files: papd.conf and your system's /etc/printcap file (described in Chapter 5). The papd.conf file has entries such as the following:

```
printername:\
    :pr=name_or_command:\
    :pd=ppd_filename:\
    :op=operator_username:
```

printername is what the printer shows up as on the AppleTalk network; that is, how you see it in the Macintosh Chooser. A PPD file (PostScript Printer Description) specified with *ppd_filename* helps the Mac's printer driver adapt to the printer. *operator_username* owns print jobs sent to *printername*. But the :pr=*name_or_command*: setting is the one you should pay most attention to when using LPRng's lpd.

Under the defaults (without a :pr=..: setting), papd looks through /etc/printcap and tries to find the printer (specified by *printername*, as in the example above). If papd finds it upon receiving a print job, it looks for the printer's spool directory parameter (specified with :sd=*dir*:), and attempts to insert the job directly into the spool directory at the correct queue position. If you're running just the old Berkeley lpd, this might actually work. Usually it won't, and you'll wonder where the job went.

Therefore, you should use a command to spool the job instead of relying on papd to do it all for you. You can accomplish this with the :pr=*name_or_command*: parameter in papd.conf. Here's an example:

```
printername:\
    :pr=|/usr/bin/lpr -Pprintername:\
    ..
    ..
```

where *printername* is the printer name in /etc/printcap. Using the :pr=|..: parameter means you won't be able to use any additional queuing features from the Mac side (such as canceling a job), but that's better than not being able to print at all.

Filesharing

The Netatalk filesharing daemon, afpd, allows guest and user logins, as well as automatic access to user home directories. When a user accesses a directory from a Mac, a new afpd runs as that user on the Unix, meaning that the user has read and write privileges identical to those on their Unix account. afpd's main configuration file is afpd.conf, but an AppleVolumes file allows you to control which directories (*volumes*) are available over AppleTalk (this setup is similar to the /etc/exports file on NFS servers).

PROBLEM 43

Symptoms: No afpd options mentioned in this section seem to work. afpd.conf is ignored. Dancing icons appear under MacOS 8.

Problem: You have Netatalk, not the enhanced Netatalk+asun package.

Fix: Use Netatalk+asun (that is, until and if it merges with Netatalk). Obtain Netatalk+asun as mentioned above, or look in support/atalksamba on this book's CD-ROM. Among Netatalk+asun's extra features is a TCP/IP AppleShare server.

You don't absolutely *have* to have an afpd.conf file, but the defaults aren't terribly appealing for two reasons. First, guest access is turned on by default, so any visitor can access any volume other than a user one. The other reason is that you may want to use a server name other than the Linux host name and make it act like multiple servers.

Here's a relatively simple afpd.conf file:

```
"Private AppleTalk Server" -noguest -nouservol
"Public Software" -nocleartxt -defaultvol /etc/AppleVolumes.public
```

The first line sets up a server for users only, and the second sets up a guest-only server with volumes specified in /etc/AppleVolumes.public.

PROBLEM 44

Symptom: Some users cannot log in (but the systems administrators can).

Problem: The file /etc/shells doesn't contain the users' shells.

Fix: Just as with ftpd, a user must have a shell listed in /etc/shells to gain access to an afpd volume. Either the shell isn't listed there, or you've denied the user access to the machine with an entry in /etc/passwd such as this one:

```
+@normal_users:::::::/usr/local/bin/noaccess
```

If you add /usr/local/bin/noaccess to /etc/shells, it may come into conflict with your desire to keep FTP users off of the machine. If that concerns you, you'll just have to turn ftpd off or reconfigure it to your liking.

PROBLEM 45

Symptom: You can't have more than five Macs accessing the Netatalk server simultaneously.

Problem: You have the compiled-in maximum connection limit set too low.

Fix: Start afpd with -c *num*, where *num* is the maximum number of simultaneous connections you want to allow.

afpd Options

These are the most important afpd options. The full list is in the afpd (8) manual page.

-C	Don't allow clear-text passwords.
-c *num*	Allow at most *num* connections at once.
-d	Debug mode (don't run as a daemon; log to standard output).
-f *defvolfile*	Use *defvolfile* as the AppleVolumes.default file.
-G	Don't let guests log in (you can also set this on a per-server basis in the *afpd.conf* file).
-g *username*	Set *username* as the guest user (default: nobody).

-n *name*	Use *name* as the nbp name. The default is *hostname*: AFPServer, where *hostname* is the Linux host name. Chances are, though, if you want to do this, you should use the afpd.conf file.
-s *sysvolfile*	Use *sysvolfile* as the AppleVolumes.system file.

Quick Reference to Other afpd.conf Options

-address *addr*	Set the network address of the TCP server.
-afskrb, -noafskrb	Enable AFS Kerberos authentication (you'll know if you need it).
-authall, -noauthall	Enable all authentication except randnum and rand2num.
-ddp, -noddp	Run a DDP server.
-cleartxt, -nocleartxt	Enable clear-text passwords.
-defaultvol *file*	Set the AppleVolumes.default to *file*.
-guest, -noguest	Allow guest access.
-guestname *user*	Set the guest user to *user*.
-krbiv, -nokrbiv	Enable Kerberos IV authentication.
-loginmesg *text*	Display *text* upon access to a volume.
-nlspath *path*	Set Native Language Support path.
-nodebug	Disable debugging for this server.
-port *num*	Set TCP port for the TCP server.
-randnum, -norandnum	Enable one-way randomized password authentication with a $HOME/.passwd file. This isn't very secure, since afpd expects that file to be clear text.
-rand2num, -norand2num	Enable two-way randomized password support; works as above.
-setpasswd, -nosetpasswd	Enable setting of passwords.
-savepasswd, -nosavepasswd	Enable saving of passwords.
-systemvol *file*	Set the AppleVolumes.system to *file*.
-tickleval *num*	Set the so-called *tickle interval* to *num* seconds (for TCP connections).
-tcp, -notcp	Enable AppleShare support over TCP.

`-transall, -notransall`	Enable all transport mechanisms (at the moment there are two: TCP and DDP).
`-passwd, -nopasswd`	Enforce entering of passwords.
`-uampath` *path*	In the current implementation, this does nothing.
`-uservolfirst, nouservolfirst`	If you have a `$HOME/.AppleVolumes` file, present volumes listed there first.
`-uservol, -nouservol`	Enable use of a `$HOME/.AppleVolumes` file (see above).

AppleVolumes Files

Moving on to the AppleVolumes files, let's give an example of an AppleVolumes. default file for the Public AppleTalk Server line in the afpd.conf file earlier in this chapter:

```
~
/stage/projects Projects access=@staff
```

The first line—the tilde (~)—enables users to log in. Upon login, their home directory appears as an available volume. Since we said -nouservol in the afpd.conf file, we aren't allowing an .AppleVolumes file in users' home directories. (You should use these options only for cosmetic purposes. If users want to look at a place other than their home directory, they can make a symbolic link—you can't really do much about it unless you want to hack Netatalk to act more like a Web server and examine symbolic links.)

The second line presents a specific directory (/stage/projects) as the volume Projects, allowing access only for members of the staff group.

Relevant man page: apfd (8)

4.4 Web Proxy Service

The disk cache in most Web browsers has a tendency to run against the grain of shared resources. It's stored in a user's home directory with the browser's own caching scheme. This presents a number of problems:

- There's no sharing of users' caches—if many users access the same page, each user must pull the information through the network.

- The network connection to the outside world suffers when all users try to use it at once.

- If you have a large number of users, you have to waste a great deal of disk space on cache directories.

- The built-in caches to Web browsers are not particularly fast. In fact, they are very slow when the user's home directory is not on a local disk (for example, if you mount the cache directory with NFS).

One solution is to install a *Web proxy server* that maintains a large shared cache for all users on the network. The most popular free server is squid. It comes with most Linux distributions and has a home page at http://www.squid-cache.org/.

Once you install squid, you need to decide what to do about the configuration file, squid.conf. Because this file is enormous, you may have trouble finding the important parameters inside it.

When setting squid up, you need first of all to decide where on the disk to put the cache. The option for this in squid.conf is cache_dir:

```
cache_dir /var/spool/squid/cache 1000 16 256
```

The default is a directory called cache under the prefix where you installed squid. If you configured squid with the defaults, it attempts to use /usr/local/cache—not a good place from the perspective of clean software distribution.

The 1000 in the line above is the total number of megabytes to use for the cache (the default is 100); 16 and 256 specify the numbers of subdirectories for the cache database. This example uses 16 subdirectories in /var/spool/squid/cache, with 256 more subdirectories in each of those original directories. You need to create the base directory (/var/spool/squid/cache here) by hand. After that, run

```
# squid -z
```

to create the rest of the hierarchy. You can have as many cache_dir lines in the squid.conf file as you like; this allows you to use multiple disks for the cache (you won't need to do this unless you're running a very large proxy for hundreds of machines).

PROBLEM 46

Symptom: squid dies with access errors when it's trying to start.

Problem: You don't have the cache directory set up.

Fix: The cache directory must be writeable by the user that squid is running as. The squid.conf file defines this as cache_effective_user. Use chown to change the ownership of the cache directory (and don't forget squid -z, above).

After you've got the cache directory set up, you'll probably need to configure the log files (they're usually misconfigured by default). You set three basic log file names in squid.conf: with cache_access_log, cache_log, and cache_store_log.

Next, search the squid.conf file for the pid_filename line and change it to the following:

pid_filename /var/run/squid.pid

Now you need to test squid. To detect any remaining problems, run it with the -N option to prevent it from running in daemon mode:

 # squid -N -d 1

You may also need to specify -f *file* if you've put the squid.conf file in a place other than the default. If there are no errors, squid prints a bunch of debugging information:

```
1999/11/13 17:19:46| Starting Squid Cache version 2.2.STABLE5 for i586-pclinux-gnu...
1999/11/13 17:19:46| Process ID 10231
1999/11/13 17:19:46| With 256 file descriptors available
1999/11/13 17:19:46| Performing DNS Tests...
1999/11/13 17:19:46| Successful DNS name lookup tests...
1999/11/13 17:19:46| helperOpenServers: Starting 5 'dnsserver' processes
1999/11/13 17:19:46| Unlinkd pipe opened on FD 13
1999/11/13 17:19:46| Swap maxSize 51200 KB, estimated 3938 objects
1999/11/13 17:19:46| Target number of buckets: 78
1999/11/13 17:19:46| Using 8192 Store buckets, replacement runs every 10 seconds
1999/11/13 17:19:46| Max Mem  size: 8192 KB
1999/11/13 17:19:46| Max Swap size: 51200 KB
1999/11/13 17:19:46| Rebuilding storage in Cache Dir #0 (CLEAN)
1999/11/13 17:19:46| Set Current Directory to ..
..
```

You'll get your prompt back if an error occurred. If everything appears to be running properly, press CTRL-C; you'll need to do one more thing before you set up the clients.

Client Access Lists in squid.conf

Nothing can connect to your proxy server unless you set up access control. You'll find a few lines in the squid.conf setting up the access control lists; they start with acl. You'll find this in the default:

```
acl all src 0.0.0.0/0.0.0.0
```

This line groups all hosts on the Internet into the name `all`. To create a new access list, add a line such as the following:

```
acl mynetwork src 10.1.1.0/255.255.255.0
```

This refers to the hosts 10.1.1.1-10.1.1.254 as *mynetwork* (Chapter 2 provides a more detailed explanation of subnets). To allow hosts on *mynetwork* access to the server, insert

http_access allow *mynetwork*

into the `squid.conf` file just before the line that reads

```
http_access deny all
```

PROBLEM 47

Symptom: Access is denied even though you've included `http_access allow`.

Problem: You have an incorrect `http_access` order.

Fix: The line that denies everything (`http_access deny all`) must be the *last* `http_access` line in `squid.conf`. As with the `ipchains` rules in Chapter 2, Section 2.4, the first `http_access` line that applies to an incoming request is the one `squid` uses. In general, you'll want to put the `http_access` deny lines last unless you're doing something like this to allow access to everyone on the network `mynetwork` except those defined by `eviltwits`:

```
acl all src 0.0.0.0/0.0.0.0
acl mynetwork src 10.1.1.37/255.255.255.255
acl eviltwits src 10.1.1.0/255.255.255.0


http_access deny eviltwits
http_access allow mynetwork
http_access deny all
```

Start up `squid` as before, but without the `-N` option. It detaches itself from the terminal and runs in daemon mode. Verify that you can see it in a process listing. If it doesn't show up, use the `-N` option again (as above) to see what the problem is. Otherwise, proceed to client configuration (below).

After you've determined that everything's working correctly (including client tests), put `squid` in your boot-time scripts as described in Chapter 1.

PROBLEM 48

Symptoms: The proxy server delivers old versions of Web pages. The server doesn't seem to cache.

Problem: You have a system time mismatch.

Fix: Make sure the server containing `squid` is also running some ntp daemon. If there is a major time skew, `squid`'s behavior may seem erratic.

Client (Web Browser) Configuration

Most Web browsers keep their Web proxy configuration in its own section of whatever file you use to configure the browser (with menu options such as Preferences and Options). In these options, you need to set the HTTP proxy host to the hostname of whatever server `squid` is running on, with the port at 3128 (unless you changed it in the server's `squid.conf` with `http_port`). You can also set the FTP and gopher proxies to be the same as the http proxy, although you probably don't care about this unless you're doing the proxy because of a network firewall.

In Netscape, you'll find this information in Preferences. After you've clicked on Proxies under Advanced in the Category box, select Manual proxy configuration, then press the View button. A window pops up; fill out the relevant portions, click on OK, and you should be ready to connect through the proxy server.

It's also essential that you change your browser's cache settings to reflect that you're using a Web proxy. Clear your disk cache, then set the disk cache size to 0. Set the memory cache size to a small number (1000KB or so), then clear it. Now load a Web page.

PROBLEM 49

Symptom: You changed a page, but it doesn't reload properly.

Problem: The memory cache on your Web browser is too aggressive.

Fix: Although you may think it's squid's fault, a memory cache on a Web browser often steps in when you don't want it to. A quick fix in Netscape is to press the SHIFT button when reloading. Clear the memory cache and keep it as small as possible (making it *too* small may interfere with animations, though). As we've mentioned before, make sure all the system times on your systems are identical.

You may have noticed an automatic proxy configuration option in your browser's Preferences. squid doesn't support this option by default. To get this to work, you'll need to install a proxy configuration script on your Web server (this isn't necessarily your proxy server). Automatic configuration doesn't really make configuration much easier because you still have to enter a location, but it can make widespread distribution of some settings easier (for example, Web pages the browser should bypass the proxy server for). You'll find details of how to do this in the documentation at the squid Web site.

5

PRINTING

5.1 Introduction

Few tasks are as messy as printing under Unix, and Linux is no exception. Let's face it, printers aren't much fun—almost every model is unique in some way, and you run into an overwhelming number of different protocols and dialects.

That said, few problems will anger your users more than not being able to print when they want to. We'll try to cover as much about printing as possible in this chapter, from dealing with font problems to networked printing.

Printer drivers, as other operating systems like Windows call them, do not exist as such under Linux and Unix. Other operating systems define a common meeting place for applications and printer drivers, ensuring uniform output. In stark contrast, practically every Linux application that prints graphics has its own built-in printer driver, which generates output right down to code for the printer. Some use auxiliary programs to generate printer output—an example is xfig, which requires the fig2dev package to print.

Rather than attempt to make every program talk to a wide variety of printers, Unix programmers tend to support only PostScript, a page description language from Adobe. You can get most printers to support PostScript, but it takes time—not just to get the printer to work, but also to make the output look halfway decent. (If you have a Mac, good news—you can use the LaserWriter 8 driver to talk to a printer on a Linux machine.)

While a user can sometimes talk to a print device directly, print jobs under Linux generally run through a printer daemon. When a user sends a job to the printer daemon, the daemon *spools* it to a queue directory, where it waits its turn to go to the printer. Next, it passes through a *print filter*, and finally goes to the device itself. The filter turns the printer's various bells and whistles (tray selection, duplex mode, and so on) on or off, and may also convert the job into a format the printer can understand—if your printer doesn't have native Post-Script support, the filter will probably include a rasterizer that interprets PostScript.

In practice, setting up a printer involves three main steps:

1. Installing the print filter software.

2. Making sure the computer can talk to the printer.

3. Putting it all together for the print daemon, lpd, in /etc/printcap.

Step 1 is the time-consuming part. (Sections 5.3 and 5.4 below deal with the two main kinds of filters.) At one time, Step 2 was problematic because many printers connected to the serial port, and the various port settings had to be just right (not to mention that for Step 3, you had to code all of the ioctl settings in one hexadecimal stream). Not only has this become more uniform, but serial printers are no longer common.

Before we can do much work with printers, we need to talk about the system that oversees print requests: the print daemon.

5.2 Print Daemons

Unfortunately, Unix has a messy set of *three* main print daemons, and we have to mention all of them.

lpsched

Most System V–based machines include this. The less said about this system, the better (it has awkward queuing and obfuscated filters). However, it gets a mention because some programs try to print using its queuing programs.

Berkeley lpd

BSD systems use this, and it's standard on most Linux distributions. It's an older program, but it works.

LPRng

This new system resembles lpd, but has many enhancements and filters.

Because they're the ones found on most Linux distributions, we'll cover only lpd and LPRng. Some distributions include a system called PLP, which you can think of as a predecessor to LPRng. Which one you choose depends mostly on the printers you have and the size of your installation.

Which Daemon?

Here are the reasons to use one or the other daemon, in a nutshell:

Use lpd when:

- Your setup isn't very large.

- Everything already works.

Use LPRng when:

- You have a decent-size network.

- You have a laser printer that supports PostScript.

- You need lpsched programs like lp or lpstat (some programs expect to print to System V commands, and LPRng emulates them).

- You need the extra features.

Here is a short review of five lpd programs:

lpr   Sends a job to a printer.

lprm   Removes a job from the print queue.

lpq   Shows the printer status queue.

lpd   Printer daemon handles print requests.

lpc   Controls lpd.

/etc/printcap

In order to start lpd and enable print queuing, you must identify the available printers and how output goes to them. You maintain this information in the /etc/printcap file. Its entries look like this:

```
lp|PostScript|ps|st800|Epson Stylus Color 800 on my Desk:\
        :lp=/dev/lp0:sd=/var/spool/lpd/st800:\
        :lf=/var/spool/lpd/st800/log:af=/var/spool/lpd/st800/acct:\
        :mx#0:sf:sh:\
        :if=/usr/local/lib/filters/psif:\
        :of=/usr/local/lib/filters/psof:
```

As in many Unix configuration files, colons (:) separate the fields, and an entry continues until the end of the line, unless a backslash (\) at the end of the line signifies that the entry continues on the next line. The first field contains the name definitions of the printer; you give one of these to the -P option of the lpr commands. That is, to send a job to this printer, you might use

$ **lpr -Pst800** *file*

where *file* is a PostScript file; in this example, you could use lp, PostScript, and ps as alternatives to st800. Each entry in /etc/printcap corresponds to one printer; the example above pertains to one Epson Stylus Color 800 printer.

PROBLEM 50

Symptoms: lpd behaves oddly for one printer (jobs dropped, incorrect filtering, outright failure, and so on). Part of entry ignored.

Problem: Missing colon or backslash in /etc/printcap file.

Fixes: A colon must start and end all lines in a printcap entry (except the first line, which should *not* have a *leading* colon), and all lines but the last in an entry must end with a backslash. This entry is wrong because it lacks backslashes and leading colons:

```
lp|PostScript|ps|st800|My Printer:
        lp=/dev/lp0:sd=/var/spool/lpd/st800:
  ..

        of=/usr/local/lib/filters/psof:
```

This entry is correct—the backslashes and colons are underlined:

```
lp|PostScript|ps|st800|My Printer:\
        :lp=/dev/lp0:sd=/var/spool/lpd/st800:\
  ..

        :of=/usr/local/lib/filters/psof:
```

A Typical Remote Printer Entry with lpd or LPRng

A *remote printer* is one for which Linux does not do any queuing. When lpd gets a job for a remote printer, it simply passes the job along to another machine. This typical remote printer entry works with lpd or LPRng:

```
remote|Printer on another Desk:\
        :lp=:sd=/var/spool/lpd/lj:\
        :mx#0:rm=mikado.example.com:rp=lp:
```

The remote host that receives the print jobs is mikado.example.com and the name of the printer on that host is lp (usually defined in the remote host's /etc/printcap).

Common /etc/printcap Components

Here are some common /etc/printcap parameters:

:sd=/some_directory:

The spool directory: Files go into a queue here while they wait to print. This directory must exist, and the print daemon (which usually runs as user daemon) must be able to write to it. The spool directory for our first printcap example was /var/spool/lpd/st800.

PROBLEM 51

Symptom: Print jobs cause errors or simply disappear.

Problem: Spool directory doesn't exist or lpd can't write to it.

Fix: If you specified :sd=*dirname*: in /etc/printcap, make sure that the directory exists and that lpd, which usually runs as daemon, can write to it. This directory can cause a major hassle on larger networks where printers frequently come and go—you can create them automatically with the printcap generation system described in Section 5.5. A simple

```
# chmod -R daemon.daemon dirname
```

usually takes care of most of these problems for small networks and print servers.

:lf=/some_directory/file:

The log file: This is usually a file called log in the printer's spool directory. The print daemon must be able to write to it.

:af=/some_directory/file:

The accounting file: If your printer supports it, you can keep track of printer use with this file.

:if=/ *some_directory*/*file*:

Print (input) filter: This is the generic filter through which all jobs pass before going to the printer. In addition to converting any plain text to PostScript, this filter also prepares the device for printing and in many cases actually sends the output to the device (for example, if it's a network printer). If a printer doesn't directly support PostScript, this filter converts PostScript to the printer's native format.

:of=/ *some_directory*/*file*:

Output filter: This filter runs after a print job processes. The output filter is useful for cleanup or other between-job tasks, such as creating banner pages.

:mx#0:

This sets the maximum file size. When set to 0 (as in this example), there is no limit on the file size. Because PostScript file size doesn't bear much relation to the physical size of the job, it doesn't make sense to keep this at anything but 0.

:sh:

Suppress header page: The printing system defaults to printing a header (also known as a banner or burst) page, which identifies the user and job name. This flag turns the header page off, which is entirely inappropriate for most modern applications.

:rm=*some_printer*: and :rp=*some_host*:

These signify the remote printer name and host. These options tell lpd that the printer isn't attached locally and that it should send the job to *some_host* for printing on *some_printer*. (LPRng offers a much cleaner alternative—see LPRng Enhancements below.)

Relevant man pages: printcap (5), lpd (8), lpq (1), lpr (1)

Network Printer Access

To allow other machines on your network (Linux, Unix, or otherwise) to access a printer on your computer, you'll need to enable access control. Berkeley `lpd` has a very simple system that allows any host listed in `/etc/hosts.lpd` or `/etc/hosts.equiv` to print. (Remember that `/etc/hosts.equiv` is a more general-purpose file for hosts that can use `rlogin` without a password.)

LPRng Enhancements

Berkeley `lpd` is old software that has survived simply because no one had much motivation to improve it. Times change, though, and so do printers and especially networks, which is why Patrick Powell developed LPRng. Its license is similar to `perl`'s—a GNU-style General Public License and Artistic License. In addition to the versions included on the CD-ROM, you can get it at http://www.astart.com/ (AStart also provides commercial support). In this section, we'll see some of LPRng's more noteworthy improvements over `lpd`.

:lp=some_printer@some_host: in /etc/printcap

This is an easy way to refer to remote printers.

Better User Control over Printer Options

When you set different printer options with Berkeley `lpd`, each option requires an additional entry in `/etc/printcap`. For example, duplex printers have two `/etc/printcap` entries (and two different spool directories), with the name of one ending in `-simplex` (for single-sided output). Multiple entries for different print options are unnecessary with LPRng; instead, the user may specify options with `-Z` (as in `-Zsimplex`).

System V lpsched Emulation

Certain programs are written to print with System V's `lp` command, and you may find it hard to adapt them to BSD-style programs. LPRng provides `lp`, `lpstat`, and `cancel` programs, which behave much like the System V programs but queue with LPRng.

Flexible Configuration

An `/etc/lpd.conf` in LPRng allows a number of configuration options, including where to find the printer database (instead of placing it in `/etc/printcap`).

Better Authentication and Security

LPRng allows the use of Kerberos, and can support selective print permissions based on the user group and netgroup maps.

Using lpc to Control lpd

Once you have your print spooling system up and running, you'll periodically need to kill jobs, disable printing and spooling, and so on. The `lpc` program, usually meant to run as root, does the job, though it only manipulates the queue and spool. For diagnostics, look at the log files.

You can run `lpc` interactively or in command-line mode. To enter interactive mode, run `lpc` without any arguments, then type in commands like `status all` at the prompt. You can also run certain commands by adding the command as an argument to the shell. Thus, if you enter **lpc status all** at your shell prompt, you'll get the same result as by entering `lpc` first and then `status all`, but `lpc` will terminate immediately and you'll get your shell back.

lpc Commands

Some of the more useful `lpc` commands include:

`clean all|printer` Removes all files in the queue for local printers. This can come in very handy when a printer has been down for some time and jobs have stacked up in its queue. When you use LPRng, the `clean` command is not available for `lpc`; use the `clean` argument to `lprm` instead.

`disable all|printer` Disables the queue for a printer, making it impossible to send files to it.

`abort all|printer` Disables printing, but allows users to queue jobs. Useful if you're doing a quick fix to a printer.

Relevant man page: lpc (1)

PROBLEM 53

Symptoms: If printing is disabled, jobs will queue but won't go to the printer. When queuing is disabled, `lpd` refuses to accept jobs.

Problem: Printing or queuing is disabled.

Fix: `lpc`'s up command enables queuing and printing. To enable all printers, try `up all`.

5.3 PostScript Printers

If your printer supports PostScript, to print a PostScript job you just send it to the printer. However, some complications may arise.

HP, HP-Like Printers, and Other PostScript Printers

HP's laser printers are very popular, and many others on the market (such as those from Lexmark) work like them. The ifhp filter for LPRng is a good one to use with such printers, whether you connect to them directly through a parallel port, through a network, or by some other means. One excellent ifhp feature is the generation of appropriate PCL commands to the printer for options, such as alternative paper trays or duplex printing.

NOTE *All of the* printcap *examples here relate to LPRng only. With a little effort, you can get them to work with regular* lpd*; see below for a simple wrapper to help you do so.*

ifhp offers many different ways to specify options—through files, on the command line, and through the printcap—but you don't need to use them all. Remember, the best configuration works predictably, and that's often the simplest one.

Install the ifhp package with whatever prefix you like (it's on the CD-ROM in support/printing; see Chapter 6 for information on installation from source code). We'll use /usr/local for our examples, so the filter will end up in /usr/local/lib/filters.

LPRng ifhp printcap

Let's get right to an LPRng printcap example for ifhp—this one is for an HP network printer:

```
myprinter|MyPrinter|Printer on my desk:\
        :lp=myprinter.mydomain.com%9100:sd=/var/spool/lpd/myprinter:\
        :lf=/var/spool/lpd/myprinter/log:\
        :mx#0:sf:sh:\
        :if=/usr/local/lib/filters/ifhp:\
        :of=/usr/local/lib/filters/ofhp:
```

Here, `myprinter.mydomain.com` is the printer's network host name and 9100 is the TCP port to connect on. We've completely suppressed the header page (with `:sh:`).

PROBLEM 55

Symptom: `lpd` complains that *myprinter.example.com*%9100 is not a device.

Problem: You're using `ifhp` with Berkeley `lpd`, and the device isn't supported.

Fix: The recommended fix is to ditch the old `lpd` and install LPRng. Barring that, you can fake a device and write a shell script wrapper for `ifhp`. To do this, first change the device to a null device with `:lp=/var/spool/lpd/`*name*`/null:` (see the section on AppleTalk printers later in the chapter for instructions on how to create the null device). Then write a `/var/spool/lpd/`*name*`/ifhp.wrapper` script that looks like this:

```
#!/bin/sh
/usr/local/lib/filters/ifhp -Tdev=myprinter.example.com%9100 $@
```

Now change the `printcap` to reflect the new filter with

```
:if=/var/spool/lpd/name/ifhp.wrapper:
```

If you don't have a host name for the printer, you can use an IP address; if you haven't set one, you'll need to. You have several options for doing so—either by hand through the printer's control panel, or with RARP/ARP, bootp, DHCP, tftp, or another method. Your best bet is to look at the printer manual, since printers can have very different requirements.

Chances are if you have a network printer, you have some other machines on the network as well. If just one of those machines is a Linux or Unix machine, designate it as a print server with an `/etc/printcap` like the one above, and have the other machines treat the printer as a remote device; in other words, they send their jobs to the print server for queuing and processing. (For the print server, take a look at the earlier section called Network Printer Access on remote printer access; the other machines will have entries that look like the remote printer example in Section 5.2.)

Here's another example, this one for an HP duplex printer attached locally to a parallel port:

```
myprinter|MyPrinter|Printer on my desk:\
        :lp=/dev/lp0:sd=/var/spool/lpd/myprinter:\
        :lf=/var/spool/lpd/myprinter/log:\
        :mx#0:sf:sh:\
        :ifhp=duplex,status@:\
        :if=/usr/local/lib/filters/ifhp:\
        :of=/usr/local/lib/filters/ofhp:\
        :vf=/usr/local/lib/filters/ifhp -c:
```

As the example above shows, the special `ifhp=` part of the `printcap` specifies various filter options. To turn an option off, put an "at" sign (@) at the end. In this example, note the `status@` filter setting due to the parallel port connection. The device is `/dev/lp0`, the parallel port on most PCs (as of Linux kernel version 2.2).

There are two kinds of options: administrator options (also called `-T` options), and user options, which any user can access through the command line using `-Z` (also known as `-Z` options). For example, `lpr -Zduplex` allows two-sided printing if the printer supports it.

The following options also provide language support. (We're most interested in PostScript, but the others come in handy for selecting paper trays, turning modes on, and printing text.) You can enable any available language support options:

`PS` or `ps`   PostScript

`pjl`   PJL, Printer Job Language

`pcl`   PCL, Printer Control Language

Separate multiple options with commas, as in `:ifhp=duplex,status@:\`. *To turn off both PJL and PCL, use* `:ifhp=pjl@,pcl@:` *in* `/etc/printcap`.

Other filter options include:

model=*name*

`ifhp` predefines a number of printer models with their various capabilities and limitations. See the `ifhp.conf` file for a list.

status

This fetches the printer status. Since this requires a bidirectional connection and a printer that supports status in the first place, sometimes you must turn it off.

pagecount

In order to do accounting, you need to get page counts.

no_ps_eoj, no_pcl_eoj

Some printers don't like the end-of-job code, which the ifhp filter sends at the beginning of each job to clear any lingering errors. Use these options to turn the code off for PostScript or PCL, as appropriate.

Selecting Other Options with ifhp.conf

The options described above are the basic ones to start with, and they may be all you need. But what about selecting other options, such as duplex for double-sided printing? This is where a new file, ifhp.conf, comes into play.

As it turns out, the default ifhp.conf contains a large number of prebuilt option definitions for various printers, including default settings for most HPs. Type **less /etc/ifhp.conf** (or wherever you installed ifhp.conf), then type **/ps_user_opts** to jump to a line of user options that ifhp can make available. As the first line in the file, this should also include the default settings. Look them over to get an idea of what's available, keeping in mind that your printer may not support all of them.

Two Parts to the ifhp.conf File

The ifhp.conf file is very large and contains a tremendous amount of information, but you can divide it into two parts:

Part 1: *Default options and definitions.* Each option is defined as a printer code for each language. For example, the ps_duplex definition tells you what the filter will hand to the printer when PostScript is the active language. The pcl_duplex definition performs a similar function for PCL.

Part 2: *Specific printer definitions.* As in Part 1, each option is defined as a printer code, except that each printer configuration begins with a label enclosed in square brackets: for example, [apple postscript ps]. Search for apple in the ifhp.conf file to see this definition.

NOTE *Part 2 is where the* model=name *option becomes relevant. If you put* :ifhp=model=apple: *in an entry in your* /etc/printcap, ifhp *will search for* apple *in the labels and use the modifications that configuration defines.*

Looking in `ifhp.conf` is the only way to find all the options available for your printer—or at least the ones `ifhp` knows about. Here are some of the more useful options your printer may or may not support.

`Duplex`	Enables duplex (two-sided) printing.
`Simplex`	Enables simplex (one-sided) printing.
`envelope, legal, a4, ..`	Sets paper sizes.
`inupper, inlower`	Printer uses upper or lower paper trays.
`outupper, outlower`	Printer uses upper or lower output trays.

You can expand `ifhp.conf`'s set of printers and options as described in the section below, Customizing PostScript Printers.

Testing ifhp on the Command Line

When dabbling with various `ifhp` options and testing customizations (explained in the next subsection), you may find it a pain to put them into a `printcap` and restart just to try something out. If you simply want to test your `ifhp` options, you can do so from the command line:

```
$ /usr/local/lib/filters/ifhp -Tdev=device,others args < file
```

Here, `device` is the device to print to, `,others` are any additional `-T` options you'd like to use, `args` are any additional arguments, and `file` is the input file. The device can be a regular file—this is handy when you want to look at what you're sending to the printer without actually printing (note that `ifhp` appends to that file if it already exists). The `trace` option to `-T` is a good one for debugging, as is `debug=n` (`n` is some number; the higher it is, the more debugging information you'll get).

Customizing PostScript Printers

If you need to add `ifhp.conf` entries, don't modify the file that came with the distribution. Use a separate file and tell `ifhp` to look at it in addition to the distribution's file. For example, if the distribution `ifhp.conf` is `/etc/ifhp.conf` and your new one is `/usr/local/etc/ifhp-ext.conf`, use a parameter like the following in your `/etc/printcap` to tell `ifhp` to look at both files:

```
:ifhp=config=/etc/ifhp.conf;/usr/local/etc/ifhp-ext.conf:
```

NOTE *Now you're going to need to dig up your PPD (PostScript Printer Definition) files to match features with the printer codes; there are plenty of examples in the system* `ifhp.conf` *to help you out.*

Printing Text

It's a funny thing, but users tend to expect their text files to actually *print* on their printer. But unlike other kinds of operating systems that run programs on the text file before sending it to the printer, under Unix, if you send a text file straight to a PostScript printer, the printer may not have a clue as to what to do with it.

If every user knew how to print text with a program like enscript or a2ps, this wouldn't be a problem. But (perhaps unfortunately) PostScript filters have always included autosensing software that checks the file to see if it's PostScript, and if not, converts it to PostScript, then hands it down to the printer. So that's what you're dealing with when you install a printer in a larger workgroup environment.

Luckily, ifhp provides a short and quick solution. If your printer is HP-like and supports PCL, enabling PCL support causes the option default_language=pcl to come into effect, and your text will come out. If you have a2ps installed on the system, it will be the default, and you won't have to think about it as long as you have these lines in the systemwide ifhp.conf file:

```
text_converter=/usr/local/bin/a2ps -q -B -1 -M Letter --borders=no -o-
text_converter_output=ps
```

The problem is, this won't work if your printer doesn't have native Post-Script support and you're not using ifhp (for example, if you're using Ghostscript in your print filter as described in Section 5.4). The quick fix is to make sure you have version 4.2 (or later) of a2ps installed on your system in /usr/local/bin. Then, in your filter, send the print job through this before it reaches gs (or whatever you use to rasterize):

```
/usr/local/bin/a2ps -1 -q -B -o-
```

The details of the ifhp case lie in the text_converter= and file_output_match= settings in ifhp.conf; have a look at it if you want, but don't worry too much over plain text printing—it's just not worth it. If a user wants better-looking plain text output, tell them to read up on a2ps.

Relevant man pages: a2ps (1), enscript (1)

AppleTalk Printers

Many Apple LaserWriters won't let you talk directly on a port, or you may be on a Macintosh-dominated network that only lets you reach the printers via AppleTalk. No problem—take a look at Chapter 4 for how to install this package, put an appropriate entry in your /etc/printcap, carry out the two steps outlined below, and you should be ready to go.

PROBLEM 56

Symptom: Someone printed a binary file and the printer is spewing garbage.

Problem: The print spooler doesn't reject binary files.

Fix: First get rid of the offending job. As root, stop the printer with `lpc` *printername* down. Remove the active job with `lprm -P`*printername*. The printer will probably continue to spew garbage pages; switch it offline, reset it, wait a little bit, and see if any print jobs remain in the buffer. Then start the printer again with `lpc up` *printername*.

After sending an optional nasty message to the user who caused the problem, install a binary filter (such as the one that comes with a2ps) to kick binary files out of the queue.

Here's the `/etc/printcap` entry:

```
lw|laserwriter|Apple LaserWriter:\
        :mx#0:sf:sh:\
        :sd=/var/spool/lpd/lw:\
        :lp=/var/spool/lpd/lw/null:\
        :lf=/var/spool/lpd/lw/log:pw#80:\
        :of=/usr/local/atalk/etc/filters/ofpap:\
        :if=/usr/local/atalk/etc/filters/ifpap:\
```

The filters here are ofpap, ifpap, and tfpap, which come with the Netatalk distribution (actually, they are all basically the same program, psf). These are no-frills filters—be careful not to use a filter with a rev at the end of the name because the filter will attempt to reverse the pages (this doesn't work particularly well because PostScript code is hard to parse without a full-blown interpreter). The ofmpap and ofwmpap variants of the filter turn on a couple of workarounds for certain printers that don't behave correctly. See the psf manual page for a description of those.

Your job doesn't end with the filters, though. Notice that the device is null, but for file-locking reasons it can't be a link to /dev/null. On Linux, the following creates the device:

```
# mknod spooldir/null c 1 3
```

One last point—the program that eventually sends the file to the printer, pap, needs to know the printer name, which may be different from what you call it on your system. Create a file called .paprc containing the AppleTalk name of the printer.

```
# cat > spooldir/.paprc
printername
^D
```

If this doesn't work right away, you can test a few things. First cd to the spool directory (the one containing the .paprc) and use

```
# papstatus
```

to see if you can at least talk to the printer (the papstatus command is in the bin directory of wherever you installed Netatalk). If the .paprc file doesn't contain the right name, you'll get an error like this one:

```
printer:LaserWriter@*: NBP Lookup failed
```

Use the -p option to find the right printer. If you have no idea what it is, try the nbplkup command (in the same directory as the papstatus command; see Chapter 4 for more information on nbplkup):

```
# nbplkup :LaserWriter
```

You should get a listing of the printers offering LaserWriter service and their AppleTalk network numbers. To list a different zone, tack @*zone* onto the end of :LaserWriter (Netatalk's getzones command lists the available zones). Of course, you could also use the Chooser on a Mac—the LaserWriter 8 service is the one you want.

Once you get a printer status report, such as idle, try sending the printer a PostScript file with pap:

```
# pap file.ps
```

By the way, a rather interesting option, -c, tells the printer this print job has been waiting forever, and tries to get the job in first ahead of any other jobs in the print queue.

Relevant man pages: psf (8), pap (1), nbp (1), getzones (1)

SMB Printers

If your printer is on an SMB share on a Windows machine, you can use SAMBA's smbclient program to print to it. The printcap will look much like the one with AppleTalk:

```
smbprinter|Printer on SMB Share:\
        :mx#0:sf:sh:\
        :sd=/var/spool/lpd/smb:\
        :lp=/var/spool/lpd/smb/null:\
```

```
:lf=/var/spool/lpd/smb/log:pw#80:\
:if=/usr/local/lib/filters/smbprint:
```

Again, you'll need to create a new null device:

```
# mknod spooldir/null c 1 3
```

where *spooldir* is the one sd specifies in the printcap (as in /var/spool/lpd/
smb above).

Now you'll need to set up the filter properly. The filter is probably not
installed in /usr/local/lib/filters. In Red Hat 6.1, for example, you'll find it
in /usr/bin, and if you installed SAMBA from source, it won't be installed by
default anyway (it's in the source, in the subdirectory examples/printing).

The filter is just a shell script and needs a .config file in the spool directory of the printer; that would be /var/spool/lpd/smb in the example above.
The .config file looks like this:

```
server=SERVER
service=PRINTER
password="PASSWORD"
```

SERVER, *PRINTER*, and *PASSWORD* are the details of the SMB printer (you
probably won't need a password for printing, so you can omit that line). You
may need to change the last line of the file to reflect where you installed
SAMBA (the example in the source assumes you put it in
/usr/local/samba/bin).

NOTE *Red Hat's* smbprint *differs from the example in that it sets the SMB log file to*
/dev/null *instead of* /tmp/smb-print.log, *and it gives the proper Red Hat location
of* smbclient.

You can use the smbclient program to look up the shares available on a
machine, as in this example:

```
$ smbclient -L printserver
Password:
Domain=[FOO] OS=[Unix] Server=[Samba 1.9.18p10]

        Sharename      Type      Comment
        ---------      ----      -------
        printers       Printer   All Printers
        hp160b         Printer   HP LaserJet 5Si in room 160b
        ...            ...       ...
```

For this to work, the printer must support PostScript. If it doesn't, you'll
need to run the file through Ghostscript before sending it off.

5.4 Ghostscript for Non-PostScript Printers

Most inexpensive printers do not have built-in PostScript support. These include most inkjets and a few low-end or older laser printers. However, the computer can often interpret and rasterize the file, ultimately sending a finished bitmap to the printer. Ghostscript, developed by Aladdin Enterprises, is a popular free interpreter and rasterizer that comes with most Linux distributions and has most or all of the devices configured.

While Ghostscript supports many printers, the correct options and drivers are not always obvious and its documentation is messy, with information scattered over a number of files. Certain options—those for color inkjets in particular—significantly change output quality. For example, the defaults for an Epson Stylus Color 850 are not the best for transparencies, although the printer is capable of producing very good results (ideally you would want unidirectional printhead movement to reduce streaking and perhaps a different kind of dithering from usual).

You typically integrate Ghostscript into Linux's print spooling system as a filter. PostScript goes in and printer-ready data comes out and goes to the printer. The filter is usually a shell script, which parses some arguments and then calls Ghostscript with some options. Here is a very simple script:

```
#!/bin/sh
/usr/bin/gs -q -dNOPAUSE -dBATCH -sOutputDevice=- -r720x360 -sDEVICE=epson -
```

The heart of this is, of course, the call to Ghostscript (gs). When you customize your filter, you will probably invoke gs on the command line to avoid specifying the many parameters that a print filter requires.

To send the output of a run on foo.ps straight to the parallel port, run this:

```
# gs -q -dNOPAUSE -dBATCH -sOutputDevice=/dev/lp0 -r720x360
- sDEVICE=epson foo.ps
```

Using the uniprint Driver

You'll generally want to call the uniprint driver as follows:

```
# gs @name.upp -q -dNOPAUSE -dBATCH -sOutputDevice=device [files]
```

name.upp is actually a parameter file in the Ghostscript library directory. For example, stc800p.upp is a 720-by-720-dpi plain-paper mode for the Epson Stylus Color 800. The file itself is a huge listing of options that set uniprint as the driver and tweak the parameters for this particular printer.

PROBLEM 57

Symptom: You don't know which driver is appropriate.

Problem: You've got too many drivers to choose from.

Fix: You ran a `gs -help` and got a huge list of driver names, and you don't know which one your printer understands. Maybe you picked one that has your printer's model number in it, but didn't get quite the result you expected. Here's a quick rundown of the main drivers:

bj10e, cj200, bjc600, and so on Canon BubbleJet drivers.

cdj500, cdj550, and so on HP Color DeskJet modules (color drivers).

epson Various Epson printers; see also the uniprint driver.

ljet3, ljet4, and so on HP LaserJet models that don't support PostScript. (Under the old convention, if the printer name ended with M, it did support PostScript.)

stcolor Color driver for Epson Stylus inkjet printers. The uniprint driver tends to do a better job on these printers, though.

uniprint A unified print driver capable of producing Epson, Canon, and other output.

You can obtain the full listing of these files with an `ls *.upp` in the Ghostscript library directory. However, you might also want to know what they do. The documentation appears by default at the end of the Devices document. (As of Ghostscript 5.50, this is all in HTML; `Devices.htm` spells out the device names. Older versions had documentation in plain-text format.)

Configuring Fonts and Fixing Font Problems

Ghostscript's font configuration file, `Fontmap`, is usually in the `lib`/*version* directory where you installed Ghostscript (or `/usr/share/ghostscript/`*version* in some distributions). It will resemble this:

```
/Times-Roman          (ptmr.gsf)       ;
% /Times-Roman        (Times-Roman.pfb) ;
/Courier-Oblique       /Courier-Italic  ;
```

The first field of each line is the font name, with a forward slash (/) marking it as a symbol; the second is the font's location; each line ends with a semicolon. If the second field is in parentheses, it's a filename. Ghostscript searches for the font in its configured font directory or directories (use `gs -help` and look at the `Search path`). The fonts can be in .gsf (a Ghostscript-native format), .pfa (plain-text specification), or .pfb (a newer binary format). If Ghostscript can't find the font, it uses Courier by default (it doesn't fail as a printer would).

To manipulate the fonts, edit the `Fontmap` file and move the files into the proper place within the font directory.

Font Problems

Certain fonts are considered standard in PostScript but, unlike the language specification, they're not free—so they don't come with Ghostscript. You can run into two problems here. One is that documents set for the particular metrics of one font look odd when you substitute another font. The other is that the font may be a bitmap, which doesn't look very good scaled. (The default fonts in many distributions are from the URW Nimbus series; they're scalable and have the same metrics as standard ones. For the most part, they work fairly well.)

Still, the only way to get rid of persistent font mismatch problems is to get the correct fonts. This means you'll either have to buy them or hope you have some piece of software that includes them, along with a use license. Adobe's Type Basics takes you up to Level 2 and includes a license for one rasterizer. Pirating fonts is mean and nasty, not to mention illegal, so don't do it.

Ghostscript Options

These are some of Ghostscript's more useful options. A `gs -h` also provides a quick reminder of them.

-sDEVICE=*devname*

Use the output device driver *devname*; for example, `-sDEVICE=epson` selects Epson-compatible printers.

-sPAPERSIZE=*papersize*

Selects the paper size (`papersize` may be `letter`, `legal`, `a4`, and so forth).

-r*n*x*m* or -r*n*

Specifies the resolution at either n dpi horizontally and m vertically, or just n for both. Choosing a resolution a printer doesn't support can have unpredictable results.

-dQUIET and -q

Ghostscript outputs some diagnostics while it parses files. -dQUIET gets rid of the intermediate messages and -q gets rid of the start-up messages. You'll need -q in a filter as well as -dSAFER, -dNOPAUSE, and -dBATCH (below).

-dSAFER

Removes file write capability. This is essential for filters; you don't want people to remove and alter system files just by printing rogue files!

-dBATCH

Exit after processing the last file.

-dNOPAUSE

Don't pause at the end of each page.

-sOutputFile=*filename*

Write output to *filename*. You can use a few special options here for *filename*, such as %pipe%*cmd,* which sends the output to the *cmd* program, and %stdout, which sends to the standard output. Also, *filename* can have a %d in it, which means each page goes to a separate file with the page number substituted for %d.

SMB Version

If you have to send output to a printer connected to Windows, you'll need to add a Ghostscript command to your filter, setting up the filter as if it were a PostScript printer (see the previous section on Ghostscript).

For example, let's say you used the smbprint filter example that comes with SAMBA:

```
) | /usr/local/samba/bin/smbclient "\\\\$server\\$service" $password -U
$server -N -P >> $logfile
```

Change it to two lines:

```
) | ghostscript_command | \
/usr/local/samba/bin/smbclient "\\\\$server\\$service" $password -U
$server -N -P >> $logfile
```

Here, *ghostscript_command* invokes Ghostscript—for example:

```
) | /usr/bin/gs -q -dBATCH -dNOPAUSE -r600x300 -sOutputDevice=
- sDEVICE=deskjet - | \
```

```
/usr/local/samba/bin/smbclient "\\\\$server\\$service" $password -U
$server -N -P >> $logfile
```

The effect is that Ghostscript runs on the input lpd feeds to the print filter, and Ghostscript sends a bitmap to smbclient.

5.5 printcap Generation and Distribution

For larger networks with many printers, getting the correct /etc/printcap to
the right machines can take a lot of time. You should automate this task using
a master list of printers—from that you can generate files based on host name.
The traditional Unix tool for the printcap is a macro-processing language
called m4. Practically everyone has their own system, so we might as well
describe our own.

In the directory support/printing/printcap on the included CD-ROM,
you'll find a collection of m4 files and a Makefile.

If you run m4 generic-lprng.m4, the output will be a generic LPRng client
printcap containing a number of printers. printer-list.m4 defines these printers, but before you examine that file, let's examine the generic-lprng.m4 file:

```
define(this_host,generic-host)dnl
```

This line defines the host that gets the printcap. This particular definition
can be used by a number of hosts, none of which have a local printer
attached. We use the name generic-host, which doesn't match any host name
on the network (more on matching host names later).

```
include(common.m4)dnl
include(lprng-printcap.m4)dnl
```

These lines pull in m4 source code from other files. The first one,
common.m4, defines some macros common to all kinds of output, such as spool
directory prefixes. The second one, lprng-printcap.m4, creates customized
output for LPRng.

```
include(printer-list.m4)dnl
```

Finally, m4 reads the printer list and creates the output.

The printer-list.m4 file

The file printer-list.m4 is a list of printers and descriptions with entries like
this:

```
HP4SI(hp160b,HP LaserJet 5Si,hp160B|160b,room 160b Ryerson,
    printserver.cs.uchicago.edu,
    HP_LaserJet_4Si_300_dpi,hp160b.cs.uchicago.edu)dnl
```

The first argument is the printer's primary name, the second a description, the third a list of aliases, and the fourth its physical location. This information makes up the first field of a printcap entry.

Because you can attach printers locally to different machines, printcaps vary across the network. For example, if the host mikado had an inkjet attached to its parallel port, its /etc/printcap would contain the spool directory and filter information required to send files to that printer. Any machine on the network other than mikado would need a printcap with an entry saying this printer is on mikado. That's what the fourth argument in the printer-list.m4 file is about—it's the machine that this printer is attached to. If the fourth argument matches the definition of this_host, you get output tailored for a local printer; otherwise it is a remote printer entry.

To add a new printcap variation, as in the local printer on the host mikado above, you'd make a new file called mikado.m4:

```
define(this_host,mikado)dnl
include(common.m4)dnl
include(lprng-printcap.m4)dnl
include(printer-list.m4)dnl
```

After that, the command

```
$ m4 mikado.m4 > mikado
```

would create a new printcap just for mikado. However, the Makefile offers a way to make everything at once; take a look at the description below.

Macro Definitions

The printer list is a set of macro invocations. For an LPRng printcap, the macro definitions are in lprng-printcap.m4 and they look like generalized printcap definitions. Each kind of printer (or printer configuration) has a different macro definition, and most are very similar (compare HPPSD with HP4SI). Adding a new kind of printer is typically only a matter of copying a similar definition, then modifying it to suit your needs.

Note, however, that when you add new types of printers, you may also need to do some work in other files. This system of printcap generation is flexible enough to accommodate other kinds of files that require information about your printers. These include printcaps for the original lpd (not LPRng) (done here in lpd-printcap.m4), Netatalk (netatalk-source.m4) and SAMBA (samba-source.m4) configuration files for allowing AppleTalk and SMB access, a script that creates appropriate spool directories (mkdirs.m4), and anything else you can write a macro list for.

If you add a new printer type and use these additional files (samba-source.m4, for example) to generate other files, you'll need to add that type of printer to them. Fortunately, you probably have the hard work behind you already, as some of the these files are quite trivial (look at netatalk-source.m4 for an example).

Finally, the Makefile wraps it up. A make in the printcap directory will generate all the files.

Example: Generating a New printcap for mikado

Say we want to add the new printcap for the machine mikado we talked about earlier. One definition in Makefile reads:

```
PRINTCAPS = printserver generic-lprng generic-lpd papd.conf \
        samba-printcap make-spool-script
```

To add mikado to the list, change it to

```
PRINTCAPS = printserver mikado generic-lprng generic-lpd papd.conf \
        samba-printcap make-spool-script
```

and then add

```
mikado: $(STD_DEPS)
```

after the line beginning with printserver. Otherwise, everything else stays the same. Now, a make will also generate a new file called mikado.

NOTE *This system is by no means set in stone. It's written in m4 to provide flexibility. If, for example, you need to group printers and only make certain printers visible on certain hosts, you can do that by splitting up* printer-list.m4 *and including the parts you need as you go.*

5.6 Utilities

There are a number of useful printing tools every systems administrator should know about.

a2ps

Short for ASCII to PostScript, this is the current state of the art in converting ASCII text files to PostScript. It doesn't come with some major distributions.

enscript

Similar to a2ps, it can't do as much. It comes standard with major distributions. Here's an example of its usage:

```
$ enscript -2Gr textfile
```

wordlist

```
Aarhus              abductors
Aaron               abducts
Ababa               Abe
aback               abed
abaft               Abel
abandon             Abelian
abandoned           Abelson
abandoning          Aberdeen
abandonment         Abernathy
abandons            aberrant
abase               aberration
abased              aberrations
abasement           abet
abasements          abets
abases              abetted
abash               abetting
abashed             abeyance
abashes             abhor
abashing            abhorred
abasing             abhorrent
abate               abhorrer
abated              abhorring
abatement           abhors
abatements          abide
abater              abided
abates              abides
abating             abiding
Abba                Abidjan
abbe                Abigail
abbey               Abilene
abbeys              abilities
abbot               ability
abbots              abject
Abbott              abjection
abbreviate          abjections
abbreviated         abjectly
abbreviates         abjectness
abbreviating        abjure
abbreviation        abjured
abbreviations       abjures
Abby                abjuring
abdomen             ablate
abdomens            ablated
abdominal           ablates
abduct              ablating
abducted            ablation
abduction           ablative
abductions          ablaze
abductor            able
                    abler
```

Figure 5-1: Saving paper with enscript

This takes *textfile* and prints what would normally be two pages onto one, as in Figure 5-1.

gv

A GUI front end for previewing files with Ghostscript.

psnup

A tool for printing multiple pages on one page. From time to time, psnup encounters a file that's difficult to parse. Using Ghostscript to filter the file (later in this section) can help. While we mention it here as a separate utility, you probably don't need to install psnup because a2ps has a psnup mode, too:

```
$ a2ps -4 -o out.ps in.ps
```

This example takes the file *in.ps* and outputs it on four sides per page in *out.ps*.

Additional Ghostscript Utilities

Ghostscript also offers filters useful for calming down rogue PostScript files. In particular, you can turn a PostScript file into an Encapsulated PostScript (EPS) file with the following:

```
$ gs -q -dBATCH -dNOPAUSE -sDEVICE=epswrite -sOutputFile=name.eps name.ps
```

The input and output files are *name.ps* and *name.eps*. You will come across this mostly when users are attempting to include a file in their documents. Ghostscript also has PDF and non-EPS drivers—pdfwrite and pswrite.

Converting PostScript to a Bitmapped Format

Ghostscript can convert PostScript to bitmaps in the same way it allows use of non-PostScript printers. This feature is particularly useful for Web site graphics, occasional presentations, and some other miscellaneous applications.

Depending on how you installed Ghostscript, it may offer a number of graphics format drivers along with its printer drivers, so a command such as

```
$ gs -q -dBATCH -dNOPAUSE -sDEVICE=jpeg -sOutputFile=name.jpg name.ps
```

will create the jpeg file *name.jpg* from *name.ps*. (Most distributions outfit Ghostscript with quite a few graphics format drivers, including ppm, tiff, jpeg, and png.)

Improving Your Conversions

The results of this conversion may not look anywhere close to optimal, since they get rasterized at whatever resolution you pick with the -r option, and therefore exhibit jaggies and font problems. You can improve on this by antialiasing; here is one way to do so with a jpeg file:

```
$ gs -r300 -q -dBATCH -dNOPAUSE -sDEVICE=ppmraw -sOutputFile=- name.ps | \
  pnmscale -xscale .2 -yscale .2 | cjpeg -quality 70 > name.jpg
```

Here, we're first rasterizing the PostScript file at 300 dpi, creating ppm output, then sending that to a program called pnmscale, which reduces the size here to a fifth of the original, antialiasing in the process. Finally, the file goes to cjpeg, which creates a jpeg file with the quality set to 75 percent. The pnmscale comes from the pbmplus toolkit (included in Red Hat 6.*x*). To create other formats, replace the cjpeg portion of the command with something like this:

```
$ pnmtopng > name.png
```

or

```
$ pnmtotiff > name.tiff
```

You'll usually have to tinker a little with options to get the best results.

Finally, while the pbmplus toolkit is quite good at batch processing, you may still find a program like gimp very helpful for manual manipulation.

Relevant man pages: gs (1), cjpeg (1), pnmtopnm (1), ppm (1)

5.7 Troubleshooting

When debugging print problems, it helps to know where to look for diagnostic output. If you run into a spooling problem, look first in your system log files in /var/log.

To test a printer on a parallel port, enter a command similar to this:

```
# cat testfile > /dev/lp0
```

If the problem printer lies on the network, you should be able to telnet to a port on the printer to see if it's working.

PROBLEM 58

Symptom: `lpq` or `lpc` reports that it can't open the device.

Problem: Bad permissions on the device or an incorrect device name.

Fix: Device names and files change frequently. If you upgraded your kernel, make sure you specified the right drivers, and check the bootup messages in `/var/log` or with `dmesg` to make sure a device did not change its name—for example, `lp1` becoming `lp0`. Also make sure the print daemon can write to the device.

PROBLEM 59

Symptom: Large files don't print.

Problem: The default maximum file size is too small.

Fix: Set `:mx#0:` in the `printcap` entry. The default for mx is 1MB, completely unrealistic for modern printers.

PROBLEM 60

Symptom: `lpq` or `lpc` reports an I/O error.

Problem: The device is not configured.

Fix: Either the print daemon is trying to write to the wrong device (see the above problem) or the kernel doesn't have the device driver configured. This happens most frequently with parallel ports, in the case of a recent kernel upgrade, or when the computer just didn't have a printer previously. If you haven't already done so, read Chapter 7 to upgrade your kernel. Then configure the kernel with parallel port support (under General setup), choose PC-style hardware, and make sure you've selected parallel printer support in Character devices. Then recompile the kernel and test the new version.

PROBLEM 61

Symptom: Output exhibits jaggies when printed through Ghostscript.

Problem: Incorrect resolution for a printer.

Fix: Adjust the print with the -r flag, as in -rnxm, where n is horizontal DPI and m is vertical DPI. Beware—your printer (or the driver) may not support the resolution you're asking for, resulting in anything from curiously wide, cut-off pages to complete garbage spewing from the printer.

PROBLEM 62

Symptom: Output is somewhat off-center, cuts off the bottom of the page, and so forth.

Problem: You selected an incorrect paper size.

Fix (case 1): Using Ghostscript, set the paper size with the -sPAPERSIZE=size option on the command line, with size as letter, a4, legal, and so on. To change Ghostscript's default, look in the file gs_init.ps in the library directory for lines that resemble this:

```
% Optionally choose a default paper size other than U.S. letter.
% (a4)
```

Remove the percent sign (%) in front of (a4) and change a4 to whatever paper size you want as the default. (Note that if you use gs as a screen viewer, this change takes effect there, too.) If for some reason you need to define a custom paper size, look in gs_statd.ps in the library directory.

Fix (case 2): For text files printed with a2ps, use the --medium=type option to choose the media (where type is the medium type, like Letter). If you want to make it a default, use the following in the a2ps configuration file (a2ps.cfg, found in an etc directory):

```
Options: --medium=type
```

PROBLEM 63

Symptom: Printer's default NVRAM values keep getting screwed up.

Problem: Some idiot keeps messing with your printer's front panel.

Fix: For example, if you want duplex mode as a default for your printers, and someone keeps changing it back to simplex on the front panel, you can either try to lock the panel or force a default. If you want to force it (we recommend this unless you have really meddling users, because after all you don't want to have to remember printer passwords), when you're running LPRng, put **:ifhp=duplex:** in your printcap file, making the default duplex. A user can override it for one job with lpr -Zsimplex. (Remember that users probably won't know how to do this, and if it's important they'll come to you for help—unless they've read this book.)

PROBLEM 64

Symptom: A user has a PostScript file that won't print on a particular printer or won't preview or print with Ghostscript.

Problem: Nonstandard PostScript commands.

Fix: This situation has no standard fix. Some PostScript files are simply corrupt and unprintable. Still, you might be able to get it working with one of two methods.

One is to get a version of Adobe's Acrobat Distiller and run it on the file to produce a PDF file. Then use Acrobat to print the PDF file to a PostScript Level 1 file.

Here's another option: If Ghostscript can preview the file, you can use the pswrite filter in gs to smooth it out as mentioned in Section 5.6 in "Additional Ghostscript Utilities." Here's a quick example—creating new-file.ps from file.ps:

```
$ gs -q -dBATCH -dNOPAUSE -sDEVICE=pswrite -sOutputFile=new-file.ps file.ps
```

6

INSTALLING SOFTWARE
FROM SOURCE CODE

6.1 Binary and Source Distributions

Developers traditionally distributed packages for Unix as source code. There
are various reasons for this: Binaries don't work over different architectures
and operating systems, it makes local modifications to programs possible,
users can install bug fixes, and so on.

Because source code is the most common way to distribute Unix packages,
knowing how to install stuff from source is helpful even if you're not a
programmer. You may want to use a version that doesn't have a binary release,
configure it with different default options, or put it in a different place.

Some site administrators install as many packages as possible from
source—anything the systems administrator doesn't feel is a core part of a
Unix system goes elsewhere on the system, usually in the /usr/local hierarchy. The main advantage to putting files in /usr/local is that everything there
survives major operating system upgrades.

Thankfully, building software is not nearly the hassle that it used to be.
Most software is written in ANSI C, and widespread use of GNU autoconf has
taken much of the pain out of configuration. (Of course, some packages just
have to be different—deal with those as best you can.)

6.2 Required Tools

The basic set of tools necessary for installing packages from source code consists of a C compiler, some associated tools, and a version of make. Most distributions call this the "development" set of packages. The tools are available with all Linux distributions (they are usually marked as optional). The following packages are the most important ones.

egcs or gcc C Compiler

A C/C++ compiler is a must. gcc is the traditional standard here, but you may come across a version of egcs in your distribution. If you're given a choice between egcs and gcc, and your gcc version isn't at least version 2.95.1, choose egcs. In any case, the commands gcc and g++ should exist on your system.

Full Set of Header Files

Header files (also called *include files*) contain operating system definitions the C compiler needs to compile almost any program (they usually have an extension of .h). In addition to the standard set (traditionally included in libc, also in glibc-devel packages in Red Hat distributions), you'll need the kernel include files that come with the kernel source code. Some distributions don't install any kernel source, and some may install only the header files that come with the source. Make sure you have a /usr/src/linux/include directory.

binutils

This includes the assembler (as), linker (ln), and library archiver (ar), among other things. These programs process and glue together the C compiler's output to make the final programs in machine code.

make

make oversees the compilation process. You should have GNU make installed; some Makefiles depend on its nonstandard extensions. You may also want the BSD make (usually called pmake) if you're looking at an item from one of the BSD projects.

perl

Larry Wall's "Swiss Army Chainsaw" of scripting languages—install it if you know what's good for you. Many configuration scripts, code generators, parsers, and associated utilities depend on perl.

X Window System Header Files

A distribution often defaults to not installing the include files and static libraries. You'll really want the include files, and you may perhaps want to link statically (that is, without shared libraries—see the Shared Libraries section below).

How Does It All Fit Together?

The source distribution contains a number of source files on which the compiler runs to create output specific to machines and operating systems. These output files are called *object files*. After building the object files, the compiler runs through them all and eventually invokes ln, the linker. ln gathers all the code it needs from the object files (as well as code and references from system libraries), then creates an executable.

Luckily, make automates the compilation and linking process. The make program reads a file called Makefile (sometimes makefile) to run the compiler and linker, and you usually use make install to put the programs in their proper place on the system. Sometimes you can run tests with make test.

Because systems can vary so much, one Makefile simply won't do for all Unix platforms. When installing a package in the bad old days, you always needed to edit the Makefile and change several settings in order to compile the program. It was time-consuming and could present a major headache, so various autoconfiguration programs were introduced to create the Makefile and some header files (the canonical example is Larry Wall's Configure script, which came with rn and perl).

Finally, the GNU autoconf system rose out of the mess, giving developers easy access to autoconfiguration. Since many packages now use GNU autoconf, we'll address it in detail in Section 6.4.

Shared Libraries

In the context of software development, a *library* is a collection of object files intended for inclusion by many programs; the linker copies the necessary code from a library into the executable program. The libraries are usually located in a lib directory like /usr/lib, and they end with .a; the standard static C library is /usr/lib/libc.a.

Because the code in libraries can get quite large, and many programs use the same libraries, using a library can waste a lot of disk space and memory—hence the introduction of *shared libraries*. When you link a program against a shared library, the linker doesn't copy code from the libraries; instead, it puts a reference to the libraries into the program. When the program runs, a part of the system called the *run-time linker* (or *dynamic loader*) is invoked, which looks for the library, and then pulls code into memory as needed, with only one copy of the library code in memory for all running programs. Shared libraries under Linux end with .so.*number*. Run **ls /lib/libc.so*** to have a look at your shared C library.

To find out which shared libraries a particular package uses, run ldd on the executable:

```
$ ldd /usr/X11R6/bin/xbiff
        libXaw.so.6 => /usr/X11R6/lib/libXaw.so.6 (0x40017000)
        libXmu.so.6 => /usr/X11R6/lib/libXmu.so.6 (0x40051000)
        libXt.so.6 => /usr/X11R6/lib/libXt.so.6 (0x40064000)
        libSM.so.6 => /usr/X11R6/lib/libSM.so.6 (0x400b0000)
        libICE.so.6 => /usr/X11R6/lib/libICE.so.6 (0x400ba000)
        libXext.so.6 => /usr/X11R6/lib/libXext.so.6 (0x400d2000)
        libX11.so.6 => /usr/X11R6/lib/libX11.so.6 (0x400de000)
        libm.so.6 => /lib/libm.so.6 (0x40187000)
        libc.so.6 => /lib/libc.so.6 (0x401a3000)
        /lib/ld-linux.so.2 => /lib/ld-linux.so.2 (0x40000000)
```

Problems arise when libraries are missing from the system, when the run-time linker uses the wrong library version, and when there's an incompatibility between the shared library and some part of the operating system (such as the kernel).

PROBLEM 65

Symptom: Programs fail to run, yielding an error message like

progname: can't load library '*libname*'

Problem: Missing or incorrect shared library.

Fix: At the very minimum, the run-time linker looks in /lib and /usr/lib by default. If you are compiling and linking a program against a shared library in a place other than the default, you need to pass special options to the linker (at compile time) to tell the run-time linker the library locations. These options are -L*dir* and -Wl,-rpath=*dir*. Section 6.4 also explains them.

The file /etc/ld.so.conf lists directories for the run-time linker to search in addition to /usr/lib and /lib. If you modify this file, you need to run ldconfig -v to put the changes into effect.

> **NOTE** *Use extreme care if modifying* /etc/ld.so.conf, *and do not add unnecessary entries (that is, don't add anything unless you really know what you're doing). Excess directories can slow system performance.*

6.3 A Typical Source Distribution

Source code is usually distributed as a compressed tar archive with a file suffix such as .tar.gz, .tar.bz2, or .tgz. Files created with gzip have suffixes of .gz (and sometimes, very rarely, .z). The .bz2 suffix comes from bzip2, a newer compression program. Finally, anything with a .Z suffix comes from the old Unix compress program; gzip can handle that.

PROBLEM 66

Symptom: Programs fail to run as in Problem 65, and no source code is available.

Problem: Missing or incorrect shared library.

Fix: Another way to modify the behavior of the run-time linker, one you should turn to only as a last resort, is the environment variable LD_LIBRARY_PATH. You can set this to a colon-separated list of directories, which the run-time linker searches to find shared libraries. Using this variable slows program start-up time and can lead to serious shared-library mismatches, but sometimes it's the only option.

> **WARNING** *Never set the* LD_LIBRARY_PATH *in any default user environment, and never, ever under any circumstances compile any package with* LD_LIBRARY_PATH *set. Your users will complain about programs not finding libraries and weird error messages referring to outdated versions of libraries.*

If you really need to use LD_LIBRARY_PATH to run a program for which you lack the source code—for example, a program called *prog*—rename *prog* to *prog*.bin and make *prog* a wrapper script like this (where *libdir* is the directory location of the shared library):

```
#!/bin/sh
LD_LIBRARY_PATH=libdir:$LD_LIBRARY_PATH
/usr/local/bin/prog.bin $@
```

Relevant man pages: ldd (1), ldconfig (8), ld.so (8)

What to Do with Those Tarballs

To unpack a compressed tar file (also called a *tarball*), do not first decompress the file and then run tar to extract it in two separate command lines; instead, do it all in one pipeline. GNU tar (which you almost certainly have on your system) makes the process simple for tar on gzip files with its -z option, which tells GNU tar to decompress the file with gzip first.

At the moment, there is no standard way to handle .bz2 files, so you'll need to do that in a pipe. Some examples follow.

To examine the contents of foo.tar.gz, use:

```
$ tar -ztvf foo.tar.gz
```

To extract the contents of bar.tar.bz2, use:

```
$ bunzip2 -dc foo.tar.bz2 | tar -xvf -
```

tar's -t option examines the archive's table of contents; -v tells tar to be verbose (give more detailed output), and -f says that what immediately follows is the file name. A dash (-) for the file name signifies that input comes from the standard input ("stdin"). In the second example, tar's standard input is the output of the bunzip2 command. You might also need the -p option, which preserves the file permissions in the tar file.

These options to tar may be the only ones you ever use, but if you need more information you'll find the current documentation for GNU tar in an info file (try **info tar** or access the page within emacs). Beware: The current documentation can be spotty.

Examine the Table of Contents

Before unpacking any source, have a quick look at the table of contents to see if it all unpacks into one directory. If the -tv (view table of contents) options show something like

```
package-1.23/Makefile
package-1.23/main.c
package-1.23/bar.c
..
```

you're in good shape. Extraction will create a new directory *package*-1.23 containing all the source files. However, if you get something like

```
Makefile
main.c
bar.c
..
```

and you extract just like that, the files Makefile, main.c, bar.c, and the rest of the distribution land in your current directory. (This can be really annoying, and most developers are aware of it.) The fix is simple—create a new directory, cd to it, and then extract the distribution.

Corrupt Files

Watch out for files that begin with a forward slash (/). If the contents include such items as

```
/etc/passwd
/etc/inetd.conf
```

you've downloaded a corrupt tar file. Remove it from your system.

Relevant man pages: gzip (1), bzip2 (1)

Taking a Look at the Extracted Source Files

Now that you've extracted the source and found your way into its directory, take a look around. There you'll find files with names like INSTALL, README, Makefile.in, and configure.

README and Other Installation Guide Files

If there's a README file, look at it first. Usually it describes the software package, but sometimes it contains a small manual, instructions, or other notes. You might also find some other README files such as README.linux or README.first, containing additional remarks about use under Linux, special cautions, and so on.

The installation manual (with a name like INSTALL) is probably the next item to inspect—that is, if there is one. Many packages that use GNU autoconf have generic installation instructions (for an in-depth look at autoconf, see below).

It's especially important to check the compile-time options, which set various devices. An incorrect or awkward configuration, whether it's for a default paper size or a standard device, can cause constant annoyance.

GNU autoconf and Makefile

If the package uses GNU autoconf, it most likely won't have a Makefile in the clean, untouched distribution. If it doesn't use autoconf, it might have an Imakefile (which uses a program called imake), or a special little script (called build, compile, or some similar name) from the author.

The Source Code

The source code files can appear pretty much anywhere—all in the main directory (which is fine if there aren't too many of them), or systematically parceled out into different libraries and packages. C source files have a .c extension, C++ files have suffixes like .cc, .C, and .cxx, and header files for either end with .h.

Object Files

There shouldn't be any object files (ending in .o) in normal, clean, out-of-the-box distributions. If object files are present, proceed with caution. It may be that the software author cannot release certain source code, and in that case you may need to follow special instructions to link the object files into the final program. But if the author simply forgot to delete the files, not only should you delete them (they may not even be for the ix86 or Linux), but look out for other mistakes that pop up in a sloppy distribution—hard-coded include file paths, incorrect compiler options, and so on.

6.4 If a Package Uses GNU autoconf

Building software has become much simpler since GNU autoconf's rise in popularity. GNU autoconf generates a script called configure that looks over your system configuration and options to create a proper Makefile and local configuration header files. You typically need only run the configure script to build the package and make to compile it.

First, though, make sure your program actually uses the autoconf system. If the main distribution directory includes files called configure, Makefile.in, and config.h.in, then the package uses autoconf.

Running configure

Let's run configure on a sample package, fdutils-5.3.tar.gz, a floppy disk utility package that you'll find in support/installsoft on the included CD-ROM. Unpack it and run **./configure** in the fdutils-5.3 directory. You'll get output that resembles the following:

```
creating cache ./config.cache
checking whether make sets ${MAKE}... yes
checking for gcc... gcc
checking whether the C compiler (gcc  ) works... yes
..

..
creating doc/Makefile
creating config.h
```

The last two lines indicate that you've created a Makefile and config.h.

Now type **make**. The compiler then runs on a number of files, with resulting output like this:

```
make -C src all
make[1]: Entering directory `/tmp/fdutils-5.3/src'
gcc -Wall -g -O2 -I. -I.  -DHAVE_CONFIG_H -DSYSCONFDIR=\"/usr/local/etc\" -c
 floppycontrol.c -o floppycontrol.o
floppycontrol.c:259: warning: return type of `main' is not `int'
..
```

After make finishes, you'll find a number of new files in the fdutils-5.3/src directory, such as floppycontrol.o, superformat.o, and superformat. superformat is an executable; floppycontrol.o and superformat.o are intermediate object files.

Now test a program you just compiled. Try to run the getfdprm program with

```
# ./getfdprm /dev/fd0u1440
```

(This program attempts to fetch your floppy drive parameters; if you're not root, it probably won't work.)

Now type **make -n install** (with the -n, this command won't actually install the program, but rather just print what a real make install would do). You'll see output like this:

```
make -C src all
make[1]: Entering directory `/tmp/fdutils-5.3/src'
make[1]: Nothing to be done for `all'.
make[1]: Leaving directory `/tmp/fdutils-5.3/src'
make -C src install-bin install-conf
make[1]: Entering directory `/tmp/fdutils-5.3/src'
/usr/local/bin/install -c -c -m 755 -o root -g floppy ./MAKEFLOPPIES
 /usr/local/bin
/usr/local/bin/install -c -c -s -m 755 -o root -g floppy diskd
 /usr/local/bin
```

If you really want fdutils installed on your system, run a make install.

If you choose to install fdutils, it goes in the /usr/local hierarchy with the programs MAKEFLOPPIES, floppy, and others going into /usr/local/bin. make install also places a few manual pages in /usr/local/man.

PROBLEM 68

Symptom: make install fails; error message in response to an install or cp command looks like the following:

pathname: No such file or directory

Problem: Makefile rule for install expects directories that don't exist.

Fix: These error messages can be persistently annoying if you run into a lot of them. The only way to get around it is to create the directories. The fastest way is with

```
$ mkdir -p pathname
```

This creates all parts of the *pathname* that don't exist already.

Important configure Options

The configure script takes options in typical GNU fashion (that is, in a --*item*{=*value*} format). These options are mainly for configuring a program with different defaults, but configure sometimes doesn't get everything right; if this is the case, you can override certain defaults and checks on the command line. Here are some of the most important configure options:

--prefix=*directory*

Changes the default installation prefix of /usr/local to *directory*. If you run ./configure --prefix=/tmp/fdutils on the fdutils package, the binaries would go in /tmp/fdutils/bin and the manual pages would go under /tmp/fdutils/man. Most packages stick strictly to their prefixes. Section 6.6 discusses further use of this option.

--bindir=*directory*, --sbindir=*directory*, and so on

With these options, you can influence where individual types of programs go instead of defaults like *prefix*/bin and *prefix*/sbin.

--disable-shared

This option keeps the package from creating shared libraries, if it has any. There are many reasons why you would not want to create a shared library. See the note in Section 6.6 under Organization for one reason, and have a look at Shared Libraries in Section 6.2 if you haven't already.

NOTE configure *options vary from package to package. Look at the output of* ./configure --help *for a (possibly incomplete) list of options.*

Environment Variables

Another way to influence configure is through the use of environment variables. Here's an example (assuming you're running bash):

$ **CFLAGS='-O2 -I/usr/local/*package*/include' ./configure**

Normally, configure uses both the -g (generate debugging information) and -O2 (optimize 2 levels) options as the initial CFLAGS. Although you end up with optimized code, it includes a large amount of extra stuff, taking up much more disk space than necessary (although the code never occupies excess memory unless you're actually using the debugger). If you're not writing the program, you don't need this extra stuff, so you only want to include the -O2 optimization option.

The -I/usr/local/*package*/include make `configure` and the compiler look in /usr/local/*package*/include for include files. Sometimes certain include files aren't in a standard place, and the CFLAGS environment variable is a handy way to convey the location to `configure`.

Here's another example to keep in mind—it solves problems with shared libraries:

```
$ LDFLAGS='-L../lib -L/opt/stuff/lib -Wl,-rpath=/opt/stuff/lib'
```

This tells `configure` and the linker to search in ../lib and /opt/*stuff*/lib for libraries, and causes the run-time linker to look in /opt/*stuff*/lib for shared libraries when you build and run the program. See Shared Libraries in Section 6.2 for further discussion of shared libraries.

PROBLEM 69

Symptom: `configure` fails with an error message such as

```
configure: error: installation or configuration problem:
C compiler cannot create executables.
```

Problem: Bad compiler or linker options; missing tools.

Fix: Check the end of the `config.log` file, where you should find at least some evidence of the error. The following example with a bogus compiler flag

```
$ CFLAGS=BAR ./configure
```

yields an error in the log file:

```
configure:673: checking whether the C compiler (gcc BAR ) works
configure:689: gcc -o conftest BAR   conftest.c  1>&5
gcc: BAR: No such file or directory
configure: failed program was:
..
```

The first line above indicates the compiler used. The second line is the command that `configure` tried, the third is an error message from the compiler, and the rest is the source code of the program the compiler failed on. (`configure` generates these programs, which are otherwise unrelated to the package's source code.)

6.5 When the Package Doesn't Use GNU autoconf

Some more heavily used programs, such as Ghostscript and perl, don't use the autoconf system. Categorization is difficult, but there are roughly three styles of such programs:

Edit Makefile and/or config.h

This is the traditional Unix style. If a program expects you to edit some files just to make it build, the edits probably won't be very complicated and may be unnecessary.

Imakefiles

Widely used for X applications, imake is at the heart of building the base X distribution itself. This system works on prespecified templates.

Other Schemes

These include anything from custom configuration scripts to Makefiles with special targets for different platforms. The latter scheme rarely works well; you may find these types of packages annoying at the very least.

Even though packages tend to fall into one of these three slots, there is no single formula for building and installation when a package does not use autoconf. Its instructions, if available, usually tell you the specifics. If they don't, or if it has no instructions whatsoever and you get really stuck, you have two choices: Either give up or find someone more experienced and ask for help. As always, if you choose the latter option, be considerate of their time.

Editing Makefile, config.h, and Variants

If the source directory has a Makefile, perhaps config.h, and instructions that tell you to type make—or more likely (and with a much better sense of reality), to look over the Makefile and then run a make—you've come across a fairly standard build. Some of the more thoughtful packages tell you to copy some item like Makefile.dist to Makefile and edit Makefile (if you're building Ghostscript, for example, you'd cp unix-gcc.mak Makefile and edit Makefile).

The Makefile

The Makefile typically consists of two sections: a number of definitions in *VARIABLE=value* format, and a target section that defines what you must do to compile the package. When you edit a Makefile to configure a program, you'll only change the section with the definitions.

Let's go through an example. Unpack the package hello_w-0.00.tar.gz on the included CD-ROM and cd hello_w-00.0. This is a sample program with a simplified Makefile. Copy Makefile.dist to Makefile and config.h.dist to config.h, then examine the Makefile. The first part looks like this:

```
# CC=gcc
# use -O to turn on the optimizer
MYCFLAGS=-g
# MYCFLAGS=-O
DESTDIR=/usr/local
BINDIR=$(DESTDIR)/bin
MANDIR=$(DESTDIR)/man/man1
# For X support, define -DHAVE_X and the include/lib directories
# XTRA=-DHAVE_X
# XINC=-I/usr/X11R6/include
# XLIB=-L/usr/X11R6/lib -lX11 –lXt
# -- Don't edit below this line
...
```

As in many Unix files, lines that begin with a hash mark (#) are comments. In a Makefile, hash marks often offer a quick means of specifying options. To activate the CC=gcc line, remove the hash mark and make sure it doesn't get redefined a line or two later.

CC specifies which C compiler to use. By default it's cc, and since Linux's cc is just a link to gcc, don't bother with these lines.

CFLAGS is set to the debug flag -g without any optimization, hinting that you might want to use the -O option instead.

The DESTDIR, BINDIR, and MANDIR definitions pertain to where to install the program when you call make install. DESTDIR is set to a root directory, and the executables and manual pages install in BINDIR and MANDIR, respectively. Notice the definition relative to DESTDIR; if you decide to install the program somewhere else instead of the default location, this saves tedious alterations to the Makefile, but keeps open the option of installing one part in a completely different place from the rest of the package. Sadly, not every Makefile allows this.

The XTRA, XINC, and XLIB definitions, commented out here, suggest that the program supports X; if you have the X libraries and include files, you can build that support. The values here assume an X root at /usr/X11R6, the default on most current Linux systems. This name will probably change in the future as new versions of X appear.

The most essential X definitions here are XINC and XLIB. XINC is the location of the X include files (preceded by -I), and XLIB shows where the libraries are and specifies which ones to use. Packages rely on a mix of variables for this. Ghostscript's Makefile, for example, uses three variables instead of two: XINCLUDE, XLIBDIRS, and XLIBS. For some reason or other, they always seem to have a bizarre default, so look them over carefully.

Editing the Makefile

Now go ahead and edit the Makefile. Set the CFLAGS to optimize (with -O) and the DESTDIR to /tmp. Don't bother with the X stuff yet; just type **make**. After the program builds, run it with **./hello** (since this is just an example program, it isn't terribly exciting). The lines pertaining to X don't do much; if you uncomment them, make clean, and make again, the only real difference is that if you run **ldd hello**, you'll see hello linked against a whole bunch of X libraries. You can do a make install if you like. Since you set the DESTDIR to /tmp, it's harmless, and you can remove it at your leisure.

config.h

The config.h file is another matter. This is a C header file with a bunch of definitions. When changing one of these, it's particularly important to make sure you're sticking to the C language. Try changing awfully to completely in config.h (in the example hello_w package), run a make to rebuild, and then see what ./hello does.

BSD or SVR4?

This example program doesn't include any real dependencies on the operating system, but others may. Since most Unix flavors are based on BSD or SVR4 (System V release 4), one option that comes up often is a choice between those two. Linux tends to lean more toward the SVR4 side in terms of its include files and libraries, but nonetheless includes many BSD-isms such as the printing system. Choose SVR4, but keep in mind that you might need some BSD options as well.

Common Path Names

You may have to fill in path names in a Makefile or header file before you build a package. Here is a short list of files and where most Linux systems keep them. Check out the file /usr/include/paths.h for a larger list, as well as the Linux File System Structure Standard (FSSNTD) at ftp://tsx-11.mit.edu/pub/linux/docs/linux-standards/fsstnd.

```
vi                /usr/bin/vi
maildirectory     /var/spool/mail
utmp file         /var/run/utmp
wtmp file         /var/log/wtmp
lastlog file      /var/log/lastlog
```

Imakefiles

The problem of interplatform differences prompted the authors of the X Window System to come up with their own configuration scheme. The result was the Imakefile. The imake program works with templates that run through the C preprocessor (cpp) to create a Makefile with the definitions for the particular system on which you're building. The advantage of imake is that it uses a standard tool that already exists on Unix systems. The disadvantage is that it's not terribly flexible. It doesn't look around the system as an autoconf-generated configure script would; it simply trusts few configuration files. It also doesn't usually present too many options for where to install a package.

You'll rarely call imake by itself. You'll use xmkmf, a shell script that calls imake with the (presumably) correct options for the system you're on. When you have a number of subdirectories with Imakefiles in them, some larger packages want an xmkmf -a to take care of all of the subdirectories and Imakefiles. Occasionally, there are configuration options in the Imakefile; as always, you should look over any installation instructions in advance.

After imake creates the Makefile, the next step is to do a make. Once you've completed that, you'll end up with the usual bunch of object files and programs. However, if the program is true to form with respect to the X Window System, you may not be able to run it successfully out of the build directory. To do so, you'll first need X resources (run-time configuration parameters), usually from an app-defaults file. We'll get back to this point.

Installing

The easiest way to test software is to install it. Unfortunately, if a program uses an Imakefile, it rarely presents the option to install it in any way but with a prefix of your current X root tree (usually /usr/X11R6). If you run a make install, the programs go into the *prefix*/bin directory, X resources go into the *prefix*/lib/X11/app-defaults directory, and perhaps some other files are thrown into the mix. A make install does not include the installation of manual pages, so run a make install.man to put them in place.

If you follow this convention, you probably won't have to do anything else, and you'll have the program in place with the shared libraries and other files it needs to run properly. However, even a minor upgrade of your X installation might delete the program, forcing you to reinstall it. But because the number of programs that use imake is diminishing, you may want to keep track of what you install with imake and hold on to the source code, since digging it up again could take some time.

If you don't want to use the prefix of your X root directory, the process gets a little more difficult. A make -n install tells you what files the final installed package includes, but the X resources present another problem: If they aren't in your X root's lib/X11/app-defaults directory, the package won't find them. There is a way to get around this.

X Resources

First, identify the application's X resources file; it's usually the name of the program with the first letter or two capitalized, ending with .ad. Once installed, the file loses that extension. Run a make -n install to see what will happen when you install the file. Sometimes it goes through a filter before installation. Put the file in a directory named *prefix*/app-defaults (you determine the *prefix*), and create the following wrapper script called *prog* in /usr/local/bin or your desired binary directory (where *prog* is the name of the program you're installing):

```
#!/bin/sh
XUSERFILESEARCHPATH=prefix/app-defaults/%N%S:$XUSERFILESEARCHPATH
export XUSERFILESEARCHPATH
exec progpath/prog $@
```

Now place the actual program in *progpath*. It's usually a path like *prefix*/bin; obviously, this can't be the same place where you put the wrapper script!

The Imakefile is a far from perfect way of configuring programs. The X Window System can run on different versions of an operating system, but some parameters that don't pertain to windowing may change, with the result that imake's templates end up wrong in one or all system versions. Don't expect imake to produce consistently clean compiles.

Relevant man page: xmkmf (1)

Other Build Procedures

Some packages have build procedures that don't fit into any of the schemes we've mentioned so far. Consisting of Makefiles with special targets for different operating systems or just plain bizarre build scripts, they can work perfectly, bomb out entirely, or anything in between. It's hard to give a formula for what to do about them, but a few hints can help. You can actually get most of these hints by looking at the output of configure on a relatively large package (like gtk+). For example, if configure says

```
checking for sys/time.h.. yes
```

then you know there's a /usr/include/sys/time.h include file on your system. If the build scheme of the package has an option such as HAVE_SYS_TIME_H, you know to define it.

Special targets in a `Makefile` usually pop up if you type **make** and get a message saying "Use make target, where target is one of..." with a list of operating systems. If Linux is an option and it works, fine. If not, the author of the program has made too many assumptions about their particular distribution, or has done the build on a version of Linux much older than the one you're using.

6.6 Recommended Practices

Certain ways of compiling and installing software can save time and frustration. A consistent method makes it easier to find things. However, if you strive to make all of your installed packages conform to the same scheme, you might have difficulty with a few oddballs that just don't want to play along. There's a tradeoff between how much time you spend installing a package and how much time you spend maintaining it.

Where and When to Compile Software

The place to put all software that doesn't come with the operating system is usually /usr/local, meaning that binaries go in /usr/local/bin, manual pages in /usr/local/man/man*, and so on. The default prefix of the GNU autoconf system is /usr/local, and most other packages default to this as well.

There are good reasons to put software in /usr/local: It will survive an upgrade without much fuss, it's easier to back up there, and if you install an enhanced version of a package that's already in the operating system, you don't clobber the old version.

But why would you want to install a package your Linux distribution can install for you? Linux distributions try to pile in as much free software as possible, so whether you install programs yourself ultimately boils down to how much of your time you want to spend making users happy. Follow the following guidelines to make a determination.

Advantages of compiling programs yourself:

- Distributing changes over the network becomes easier because there's a common installation prefix.

- The directory stays the same when you upgrade your operating system, and it's easier to back up.

- The newest version of a package always gets installed.

- You can customize defaults if the package allows.

- Optimizations are sometimes possible.

- You usually get a better overview of how to use the package.

Disadvantages:

- It can take some time.

- If no one actually uses the package, you're wasting your time.

Organization

Especially on larger sites, keeping track of what software has been installed can present quite a challenge. If every package simply goes into /usr/local, you may find odd files and programs there and wonder where in the world they came from. Knowing the origins of files is important: Lingering files from an old version of a program may cause a newer version to malfunction.

NOTE *On traditional Unix networks, normal users never install packages in system directories. As for programs that users install in their home directories, administrators typically don't care.*

Many Unix software organization schemes have evolved over the years. We'll go over just one: Encap. This scheme specifies where to put installed software and how to link it to the system so it's available to all users. You can find extensive information for Encap at http://encap.cso.uiuc.edu/. The Encap system has the following advantages:

- It keeps old versions of software packages intact.

- You can identify everything in /usr/local by package.

- It simplifies removal of old versions and of entire packages.

- Encap usually requires very little extra configuration and works fine with autoconf.

An Encap Example

Let's go over an example configuration using the Encap scheme with our sample package, fdutils-5.3. Assume /opt has plenty of disk space; that's where we will actually store our collection of locally installed programs, but we'll use /usr/local as a launching point for them.

After unpacking, configure the program:

```
$ configure --prefix=/opt/fdutils/fdutils-5.3
```

After running a make and a make install, **cd** to /opt/fdutils and run **ln -sf fdutils-5.3 default.** Then **cd** to /opt/fdutils/default/bin and do this:

```
# for file in *; do
> ln -s /opt/fdutils/default/bin/$file /usr/local/bin/$file
> done
```

Similarly, in /opt/fdutils/default/man/man1:

```
# for file in *; do
> ln -s /opt/fdutils/default/man/man1/$file /usr/local/man/man1/$file
> done
```

Now the package is ready to run right out of /usr/local/bin. Other packages may have some other files, such as manual pages, for which you'll need to create additional links.

PROBLEM 71

Symptom: After upgrading a library, programs using that library experience a segfault, can't find the library, or give wrong results.

Problem: Shared libraries are inconsistent over upgrades.

We have one caution about shared libraries. Their names change from one version to another, and this can create a horrible mess. Don't, for example, make a /usr/local/lib/libfoo.so.1 link to /opt/foo/default/lib/libfoo.so.1. If you're going to be linking against a library later on, choose one of the following methods.

Fix (case 1): If it's a relatively small library like libpnm, just make it a static library (that is, the library's installed name will be libpnm.a). If you want to make the library available to users for general development, put (for the pnm example) a /usr/local/lib/libpnm.a link to /opt/netpbm/default/lib/libpnm.a, as well as appropriate links for the include files in /opt/netpbm/default/include. The standard configure option to make static libraries with the GNU autoconf system is --disable-shared.

Fix (case 2): If it's a big library, such as libgtk, you can make a shared library. However, as mentioned above, don't make any links in /usr/local because this will cause upgrade problems. When compiling (libgtk, for example) use -I/opt/gtk/gtk-*version*/include and for linking, use the -L/opt/gtk/gtk-*version*/lib and -Wl,-rpath=/opt/gtk/gtk-*version*/lib options. You *must* use the version numbers instead of the default link, because a major upgrade of the library tends to wreak havoc on anything linked against it.

Be especially careful about removing old versions of any packages containing shared libraries. Not only may the system contain programs linked against the old libraries, but your users may have also done so.

Note that when, say, fdutils-5.4 comes out, all you need to do is `configure --prefix=/opt/fdutils/fdutils-5.4`, and then, after running a `make` and a `make install`, change the `/opt/fdutils/default` link. Because we contained everything for the previous version in one place (`/opt/fdutils/fdutils-5.3`), and there are no longer any specific links to that directory (we used `/opt/fdutils/default` instead), you don't need to worry about problems installing the new version. Sometimes new versions of programs do change file names around—keep an eye out for that.

So if you need to know what any item in `/usr/local` is, just use `ls -l`, and the link will tell you exactly what package it belongs to—for example:

```
$ ls -l /usr/local/bin/superformat
lrwxrwxrwx   1 root     root     36        /usr/local/bin/superformat ->
/opt/fdutils/default/bin/superformat
```

6.7 Troubleshooting Failed Compiles

So you ran a make, and things didn't happen quite the way you planned. Perhaps it didn't get past the compilation stage, or maybe the installed package doesn't work properly. The reasons can range from trivial—for example, an incorrect library path—to very serious—a poorly programmed package or even a hardware problem. Unfortunately, you can't tell exactly what the problem is unless you look at the source code. This does nonprogrammers little good. However, with a few guidelines you can guess at some common errors and develop appropriate fixes.

Reading Error Output

First, though, you must know how to read error output. Say a compile fails, make terminates immediately, and the last message you get before the prompt looks like this:

```
make: *** [target] Error 1
```

Some step of the process required to satisfy the requirements for *target* has failed. Usually it's a file name (probably an object file), and the compiler has failed to create it. (We'll discuss strategies on how to fix that problem shortly, in Compiler Errors.)

If you get an error message like this:

```
make: *** [target] Error 1 (ignored)
```

you can usually ignore it (an ignored error does not cause make to terminate). This error probably means make tried to create a directory or some other item that already existed, the command failed, and no one cares.

Compiler errors look like this:

```
t.c:1: junk.h: No such file or directory
t.c:5: `stuff' undeclared (first use this function)
```

Compiler *warnings* (as distinguished from errors) are clearly marked as such:

```
aacurses.c:128: warning: initialization from incompatible pointer type
t.c:2: warning: unused variable `t'
```

For the most part, you can ignore warnings. They don't cause the compiler or make to stop. An excessive number of warnings like the first one above might signal possible run-time errors (in this case, make sure you're using the right include files). If you're not the programmer, just ignore the warnings like the second above.

A Makefile sometimes turns on all compiler warnings (the -Wall option to gcc/egcs), because the programmer wants to know about them when developing the package. This often has the happy result that you get no warnings at all, but sometimes it goes the other way and you get a plethora. Because warnings appear inline with error messages, the actual errors can disappear amid a sea of warnings.

Linker (ld) errors resemble compiler errors, except that they refer to an object file instead of a source file:

```
foo.o: In function `baz':
foo.o(.text+0x62e): undefined reference to `__ctype_b'
```

That wraps up how to identify basic errors and warnings. The next sections cover specific errors and their solutions.

General Errors

PROBLEM 72

Symptom: You see the following Error message: make: Command not found.

Problem: You don't have the make program installed on your system.

Fix: Install make. If you're missing make, you're most likely also missing the rest of the development packages (see below).

PROBLEM 73

Symptom: You see the following Error message: make: *prog*: Command not found.

Problem: make can't find the program called *prog* anywhere in its path.

Fix (case 1): If *prog* is cc, gcc, cpp, as, or ld, you need to install the developer set of packages that came with your Linux distribution. The development packages have gcc (or egcs), the static libraries, include files, and binutils.

If *prog* is a full path name such as /usr/local/bin/prog, the program may exist elsewhere on your system. Look for it and change the Makefile accordingly.

Fix (case 2): make may have just built a program and is now trying to run it. If you don't have a dot (.) in your path (you should not), either put this at the end of your path temporarily or change the Makefile to include ./ before *prog*.

PROBLEM 74

Symptom: You just installed *foo* in /usr/local/bin, but even though /usr/local/bin is in your path, when you (or some user) try to run *foo*, it says

foo: Command not found.

Problem: Your shell is probably tcsh or csh, caching command names.

Fix: Try the rehash command. This only works if the problem is that you're using tcsh or csh. If you're running a windowing system, you may need to restart the login session. Otherwise, use another shell.

PROBLEM 75

Symptom: make ran a command like this:

```
cc   -o t t.o -lX11.
```

Then you got this error message:

```
ld: cannot open -lX11: No such file or directory.
```

Problem: The linker can't find a library.

Fix: Look for a file called either `libX11.a` (static library) or `libX11.so.`*n* (a shared library), where *n* is some version number. You need to place the directory containing it in the linker arguments, usually LDFLAGS. Let's say you found it in `/usr/X11R6/lib`. If you're using an autoconfed package, configure it properly with

```
$ LDFLAGS="-L/usr/X11R6/lib" ./configure.
```

If you find a shared library, don't forget to give the message to the run-time linker as well:

```
$ LDFLAGS="-L/usr/X11R6/lib -Wl,rpath=/usr/X11R6/lib" ./configure.
```

PROBLEM 76

Symptom: You get the following error message:

```
t.o: In function `main':
t.o(.text+0xd): undefined reference to `stuff'
```

Problem: The linker couldn't find a library call in a library or object file it received as input. You're probably missing a library.

Fix: Find the library containing the call (this can be difficult—use `strings` and `ar` if necessary). Let's say you found it in `libfoo.a`. Put `-lfoo` in your LDFLAGS as described in the previous problem, keeping in mind that you may also need to add `libfoo.a`'s directory with `-L`, also described above.

Skipping Lines in .c and .h Files

If you have to fool around with a source file, it's probably because the compiler needs to get a line or two from it. Let's say we have an excerpt from a file like this:

```
. . .
#include <stdio.h>
#ifdef JUNKOS
#include <junk/extracrud.h>
extern int junkerrno;
#endif
. . .
```

Notice the preprocessor directive, #ifdef JUNKOS, closing with an #endif, around two lines. This means if you define the macro (text substitution) JUNKOS, the preprocessor and compiler will read the next two lines. If you're not running anything like JunkOS, then the compiler under Linux usually skips these lines.

You define macros with either the -DMACRONAME[=value] flag to the C compiler (as in -DJUNKOS or -DSKY=blue) or in a source file with the #define directive (for example, #define SKY blue).

To get rid of an offending line guarded by #ifdef directives, first attempt to make the outcome of the #idfdef test false. If you just can't find the macro definition, there's an #undef directive for undefining macros, but first try to find and verify the original definition. Other mismatches, especially those related directly to the operating system, can cause the same error to appear many times, and a program that manages to compile despite an incorrect configuration may not run properly.

If #ifdef does not enclose an offending line, you may not have any choice but to exclude a line or two with #if 0/endif, as in this example:

```
#if 0
#ifdef JUNKOS
#include <junk/extracrud.h>
extern int junkerrno;
#endif
#endif
```

Even though it's not a true comment, #if 0/#endif is safer than using /* and */ because you don't run any risk of nested comments (which cause syntax errors).

Never delete a line. Only comment out as a last resort, and be careful when you do it. For example, if we switched the second and third lines in the first example above, catastrophic-looking errors would result.

Compiler Errors

Because of the nature of software development tools like the compiler and linker, we can't give a one-size-fits-all fix for any error they produce (although programmers would love it). There are, however, a number of common cases.

PROBLEM 77

Symptom: You get an error message like this:

```
t.c:10: foo.h: No such file or directory.
```

The compiler ran the C preprocessor (cpp) on t.c, which used the #include directive (on line 10) to read in another file, foo.h, but couldn't find that file.

Problem: Bad include path, or include file isn't installed.

Fix (case 1): If you have the include file installed on your system, then all you need to do is change the *CFLAGS* in the Makefile/Imakefile, or get configure to do it for you (see below). If you're missing the file outright, there's a chance it may not be critical and you can simply comment out the #include line in the source file, but that's a very slim chance. If it's a system file, chances are it has a different file name.

If the include file isn't rooted at /usr/include (or /usr/local/include), you need to tell the compiler's preprocessor where to find it by giving cc or gcc the -I*directory* option, where *directory* is the root location of the include file.

For example, if you get an error message stating that myjunk/junk.h couldn't be found, and the file is actually in /usr/convoluted/include/myjunk, you need to pass the option -I/usr/convoluted/include to the compiler.

If a package uses the GNU autoconf system, you can do so (while maintaining optimization) with the following:

```
$ CFLAGS="-O2 -I/usr/convoluted/include" ./configure
```

Fix (case 2): You could be missing a library on your system (and may be coupled with a missing -I compiler option in Fix (case 1) above). Libraries come with .h files. Look at the package's installation instructions to see if it mentions required libraries. Then see if you have the necessary libraries installed on your system. Find and install any missing libraries if possible.

One X library you may come across is Motif. The include files for it are in Xm and Mrm subdirectories, usually in /usr/X11R6/include. It's a commercial library, and most distributions include a work-alike free clone called lesstif. You can get it from http://www.lesstif.org/.

This library *does not* come with Red Hat.

Fix (case 3): You may have an incomplete or incorrect compiler installation. You not only need a full set of include files in /usr/include, but also a set of Linux kernel include files in /usr/src/linux/include/ linux. Verify that these directories exist and contain files (you may need to install the Linux kernel's source code), and also that /usr/include/ linux is a symbolic link to /usr/src/linux/include/linux.

Fix (case 4): It's possible that you're attempting to compile for an operating system other than Linux. Look over the Makefile and installation instructions to see if they make special mention of Linux. Look at the failed file around the place where the offending #include directive is located, and eliminate it as described in the Skipping Lines subsection.

PROBLEM 78

Symptom: You get an error message similar to

```
t.c:22: conflicting types for `errtype'
/usr/include/example.h:47: previous declaration of `errtype'
```

Problem: The programmer screwed up and put in a prototype that shouldn't be there.

Fix: This example shows an erroneous redeclaration of errtype on line 22 of t.c. /usr/include/example.h already made the correct declaration. Look at and around the offending line, and comment it out (see the Skipping Lines subsection).

PROBLEM 79

Symptom: You get an error message like this one:

```
t.c:3: `time_t' undeclared (first use this function)
...
t.c:3: parse error before `foo'
```

Problem: You're missing an #include directive.

Fix: Here, the problem is that the type time_t isn't defined. Find the line with time_t *foo* (they mean that *foo* is a variable). Examine what follows that declaration to see where *foo* is used—let's assume we find *foo* = time();. Now we can see if time is some sort of library call—try man -a time. In section 2, we find this:

```
SYNOPSIS
        #include <time.h>
```

The #include directives in the synopsis are the key. Placing them in the appropriate places within the source file will probably fix the problem. If you can't find the definition using that method, look in /usr/include and other include directories with a program like grep, then use an appropriate #include directive.

7

KERNEL UPGRADES

7.1 Introduction

The Linux kernel is the core of the operating system. It manages processes and resources, provides most of the hardware drivers, and handles the filesystem interface. The kernel is under constant development, so new drivers and bug fixes appear all the time.

If you plan to recompile your kernel, you're probably doing so to get better system performance, add a new device driver, or fix some bug. The fastest way to break a machine is to screw up the kernel. The good news, though, is that once you're familiar with the kernel, you'll find it relatively easy to recover from a broken kernel; it's not as though you've filled your hard drive with null bytes.

Sections 7.2, 7.3, and 7.4 outline the three steps involved in compiling a new kernel. Section 7.4 also contains detailed information on installing and booting the kernel—including how to use LILO (the Linux loader, also capable of dual-booting) and how to boot the kernel off a device other than a hard drive (for emergencies or bootstrapping).

7.5 explains kernel modules and a few aspects of the automatic kernel module loader. Kernel modules are dynamically loadable parts of the kernel that can simplify the configuration process and eliminate wasted system resources. For example, if you rarely use FAT-based filesystems, you can compile them as modules and leave them out of the kernel most of the time. Many device drivers, filesystems, and other options are available as modules. The automatic module loader attempts to make module insertion transparent by loading modules on demand from the kernel. Finally, if you dig yourself into a hole, 7.6 will try to lift you out of there.

Kernel Source Code and Versions

NOTE *You'll find all of the source code distributions for Linux kernels in ftp://ftp.kernel.org/ pub/Linux/kernel, but for faster downloading use a server specific to your country code. For example, ftp.us.kernel.org offers a fast link for the United States.*

Version releases—2.0, 2.1, 2.2, and so on—classify the kernel. There are two different kinds of release series, and it's important to recognize the differences between them.

If you want to know which kernel you're using, try the command *uname -a*. To see what version of the source code you have, look for the source code in /usr/src/linux. The top of /usr/src/linux/Makefile has the version number. Linux kernel versions have three numbers and have *major.minor.patchlevel*-type names. The first number is called the *major level*, the second is the *minor level*, and the third is the *patchlevel* (in 2.3.34, the major level is 2, the minor level is 3, and the patchlevel is 34). A *kernel release series* is a set of kernel releases that share the same major and minor levels. Series identified by even numbers (1.**0**.*x*, 1.**2**.*x*, 2.**0**.*x*, 2.**2**.*x*, and so on) are *production* releases. Intended for stability, they contain code that has withstood considerable testing. Within a production series, the driver set is the same, and developers release new versions only for bug fixes.

On the other hand, if the minor level is an odd number (1.**1**.*x*, 1.**3**.*x*, 2.**1**.*x*, 2.**3**.*x*, and so on), the kernel is a *development* kernel. These are released with an expectation of instability—basically, as a type of beta release. Early releases in a development series are particularly unstable, with driver interfaces gratuitously altered, new drivers added, and code removed without extensive cross-checking (that's left to the people who develop the kernel). This instability can cause some or most of the kernel to break in sometimes dangerous ways, so unless you know exactly what you're doing, stay away from development releases.

NOTE *Many distributions omit complete kernel source code by default (for example, the* kernel-source-version.rpm *in Red Hat 6.x distributions). Instead, they may include just the header files for* /usr/include/linux *and* /usr/include/asm *(sometimes not even those). If you don't see a* Makefile *in* /usr/src/linux, *or you see less than several megabytes of stuff in there, you don't have the complete source; you'll need to get it if you want to build a kernel.*

What You Need to Build the Kernel

To build a Linux kernel, you'll need:

- A C compiler (gcc) and make (found in the development packages of most distributions).

- Two assembler and linker programs called as86 and ld86 (from bin86-0.4-7.rpm in Red Hat 6.0, dev86-*version*.rpm in later releases).

See /usr/src/linux/README *for the version of* gcc *you need (found under 'COMPILING the kernel' heading as recently as 2.2). (Use* gcc -v *to find your version number.) If your Linux distribution is at all recent, you won't have a hopelessly outdated version of* gcc.

- Space—the source code is large. At version 2.2.12, a compiled kernel with a lot of modules took up 75MB. Unfortunately it's hard to say how much space future versions will take.

- A relatively fast computer with a decent amount of memory, if you plan to finish in any reasonable amount of time. It took me over an hour to compile a 2.2 kernel on a 486 with 20MB of memory, but my newer machines were much faster. (If you want the kernel on a slow machine but don't want the wait, you can compile it on a faster machine and then copy it to the slower one.)

Setting Up Kernel Source Code

Before you can set up the kernel, you need to unpack the source. Unpacking the source is as easy as with the packages described in Chapter 6. You use either

```
# cd /usr/src
# umask 022
# bz2cat linux-version.tar.bz2 | tar xvf -
```

or

```
# cd /usr/src
# umask 022
# zcat linux-version.tar.gz | tar xvf -
```

Your choice of unpacking command depends on the type of compression in your source file (see the underlined text above; an extension of .bz2 means you need the bz2cat program, whereas .gz means you should use zcat).

Put Your Unpacked Source Here

Unpacking the file in /usr/src creates /usr/src/linux, so before you extract the contents of the tar file, you want to move whatever is already there out of the way:

```
# mv /usr/src/linux /usr/src/linux.DIST
```

You can decide what to do with the linux.old directory later.

In fact, /usr/src/linux is an inconvenient name because it doesn't reflect the version number. Many administrators prefer this:

```
# cd /usr/src
# mv linux linux-version
# ln -s linux-version linux
```

Then the unpacking of a new kernel looks like this:

```
# cd /usr/src
# rm linux
# bz2cat linux-version.tar.bz2 | tar xvf -
# umask 022
# ln -s linux-version linux
```

The old version is still available in /usr/src/linux-version. Be careful, though; the source code is quite large, especially with object files in there, and if you leave too many old versions lying around, they take up a big chunk of space on your disk.

Checking Links

Once you get the source code set up, check a few links. Try these commands:

```
# ls -ld /usr/include/asm /usr/include/linux
```

If the output has this in it:

```
/usr/include/asm -> /usr/src/linux/include/asm
/usr/include/linux -> /usr/src/linux/include/linux
```

the C compiler will not have trouble with mismatched or missing kernel-specific include (header) files. If, however, asm and linux don't exist or are real directories (instead of symbolic links), do this:

```
# cd /usr/include
# mv linux linux.DIST
# mv asm asm.DIST
# mv scsi scsi.DIST
# ln -s /usr/src/linux/include/asm asm
```

```
# ln -s /usr/src/linux/include/linux linux
# ln -s /usr/src/linux/include/scsi scsi
```

This moves the old directories out of the way and sets up links so the C compiler can find the right header files. Kernel configuration is the next step.

Distribution Kernels

The kernels that come with Linux distributions are called *generic kernels* because they haven't been tuned for any particular hardware or applications. They tend to work on most machines, and the implementation of the automatic kernel module loader has eliminated many problems with these kernels, such as excessive size or driver conflicts.

Many distributions, including Red Hat, modify the standard kernel before shipping it. Thus, if you plan to install a new kernel apart from what your distribution offers, you should understand how the distribution's kernel is managed so you don't step on anything important.

7.2 Configuring the Kernel

When you configure the kernel, you decide which device drivers to include and which to build as modules, and you might also set some parameters. Although configuring the kernel is different from configuring any other software package, it's a fairly easy process once you have the source code installed. To begin, issue these commands:

```
# cd /usr/src/linux
# make menuconfig
```

The make menuconfig runs off and compiles a configuration program, then executes it. The configuration program is a full-screen text interface that uses the curses library, which comes standard with all distributions. It's not the most glamorous tool around, but it gets the job done. You'll see the opening main menu screen in Figure 7-1.

The big box in the middle contains the kernel options. Navigate in this box with the up and down arrow keys; you'll see the current selection highlighted or in a different color. The little strip at the bottom contains Select, Exit, and Help; you can move around here with the left and right arrows. An arrow (-->) next to an item indicates a submenu; pressing ENTER brings up that submenu.

Let's skip the first item in the list for now; move down to Processor type and features and press ENTER. The box will contain these options:

```
(PPro/6x86MX) Processor family
(1GB) Maximum Physical Memory
[ ] Math emulation
```

```
[ ] MTRR (Memory Type Range Register) support
[*] Symmetric multi-processing support
```

This is where you have to make your first real choices. `Processor family` allows you to make a kernel that suits your processor; press **ENTER** to bring up a little dialog box with 386, 486, and other options. Move to your choice with the arrow keys and press **ENTER** when you are happy. (We'll explain what the processor choice does in a moment.)

NOTE *The kernel configuration process has a help system with very comprehensive documentation for these options. To see the help for any option, type a question mark (**?**) after selecting the option. To leave the help and return to the configuration menu, type **x**.*

Submenus organize the configuration options. The rest of section 7.2 covers specific configuration options, which are current as of kernel 2.2; new releases will almost certainly bring changes.

NOTE *The default configuration file is* `/usr/src/linux/.config`, *and* `/usr/src/linux/.config.old` *contains a backup. You can look at these files to get a quick summary of the configuration.*

```
Linux Kernel v2.2.12 Configuration)
─────────────────────────────────────
+──────────────── Main Menu ────────────────+
| Arrow keys navigate the menu. <Enter> selects submenus ─->. |
| Highlighted letters are hotkeys. Pressing <Y> includes, <N> excludes, |
| <M> modularizes features. Press <Esc><Esc> to exit, <?> for Help. |
| Legend: [*] built-in [ ] excluded <M> module < > module capable |
| +────────────────────────────────+ |
| | Code maturity level options ─-> | |
| | Processor type and features ─-> | |
| | Loadable module support ─-> | |
| | General setup ─-> | |
| | Plug and Play support ─-> | |
| | Block devices ─-> | |
| | Networking options ─-> | |
| | SCSI support ─-> | |
| | Network device support ─-> | |
| | Amateur Radio support ─-> | |
| +──────-v(+)──────────────────+ |
+──────────────────────────────────────+
| <Select> < Exit > < Help > |
+──────────────────────────────────────+
```

Figure 7-1: make menuconfig—crude-looking, but effective

Once you're finished with the configuration, exit the first menu. The kernel will ask if you want to save the new configuration; select yes to write out the file and go to Section 7.3 (or no if you were just fooling around).

The main menu has two handy options at the bottom of the box: load from and save to alternate files. If you want to save your kernel configuration for later use on this or another machine, use the Save Configuration to an Alternate File option to save it to a file.

NOTE *There's a documentation directory* /usr/src/linux/Documentation. *This motley collection of documents contains everything from kernel-hacking instructions to driver notes. The configuration help often refers to files here.*

The Processor

Here are the various options under Processor type and features with a description of each.

Processor Family

This selection enables optimizations for specific processors. The architectures are organized roughly by age. The kernel probably won't run on a processor older than your selection (a 486 kernel will not work on a 386), though a 386 kernel works on everything (which is why many distributions install it as the default).

Math Emulation

Linux needs a floating-point coprocessor to operate, but if you don't have one, the kernel can emulate it. (This is only an issue for 386 and 486SX systems with no additional coprocessor.)

Loadable Module Support

See Section 7.5 for a more detailed explanation of kernel modules.

Enable Loadable Module Support

Only say no to this if you really know what you're doing; otherwise accept the default.

Kernel Module Loader

The kernel can attempt to load modules as needed. This offers the convenience of having a great number of kernel features available without loading them all by hand or compiling them directly into the kernel. For certain features this works particularly well; we'll talk about them in Section 7.5.

General Setup

This is a collection of fairly important stuff that doesn't fit anywhere else in the hierarchy.

Networking Support

Say yes to this.

System V IPC

Say yes to this as well.

Kernel Support for . . . Binaries

You'll definitely need to support ELF binaries (the default executable format in Linux distributions—your system won't start a single program without it), and it never hurts to build the others as modules in case you run into older or nonstandard programs. If you have an older system, you'll probably want make a.out binary support compiled into the kernel.

Parallel Port Support

To get your PC's parallel port to work, you need to select not only this option, but also the PC-style hardware option that appears next. That's not all, though—you must say what you want to do with the parallel port elsewhere in the configuration menu system. Parallel printer support is under the Character devices submenu in the main menu, Zip drives are in the SCSI submenu (under low-level drivers), and you'll find still other devices under Block devices.

Block Devices

Most of the choices here are pretty straightforward and deal with well-known devices and their drivers.

Include IDE/ATAPI Floppy Support

The two most common devices that require this driver are internal non-SCSI Zip drives and LS-120 floppy drives. Include this option if you have either device.

Loopback Device Support

This driver emulates a block device through a regular file on a filesystem. The long and short of it is that if you include this option, you can emulate and test floppy-disk and CD image files without actually writing the file out to a floppy or CD.

RAM Disk Support/Initial RAM Disk (initrd) Support

The idea of using part of random-access memory as a disk is nothing new; under Linux, it's primarily for installation and recovery boot purposes. But the initrd stuff that appears after you compile RAM disk support directly into the kernel (not as a module) has a new twist. Some distributions such as Red Hat use this on SCSI-only systems to avoid compiling SCSI drivers into the kernel. They first boot with an initial RAM disk, then load a kernel module on that RAM disk (one containing the driver for the SCSI controller), then mount the true / partition. You can wiggle out of this mess by compiling the SCSI driver you need directly into the kernel, and changing /etc/lilo.conf before you run lilo (the part of LILO that installs the boot sector); Section 7.4 offers more on the subject.

Networking Options

You can accept the default values here for most systems. Network firewalls and the options that appear after you choose it may be important if you're planning to do IP filtering or masquerading; turn to Section 2.4 for more details on that.

SCSI Support

You usually know when you need SCSI support (you've got a SCSI host adapter), but the Linux kernel also considers external parallel port Zip drives to be SCSI devices.

SCSI Disk Support

This turns on support for all sorts of hard disks, including removable-media disks.

SCSI Generic Support

A number of miscellaneous devices use this driver, most commonly SCSI scanners and CD burners.

SCSI Low-Level Drivers

Under this submenu, used to select drivers for individual SCSI controllers (host adapters), you may notice a few similar-looking entries if a device has more than one driver available (Symbios SCSI cards, for example), or if there is more than one version of the device (such as the two different versions of the parallel port Zip drive).

Network Device Support

You'll find the network interface drivers, Ethernet, PPP, SLIP, token ring, and others here.

Old CD-ROM Drivers

If you've got an older system with a proprietary CD-ROM drive, you might find support for it here. Most of these drives came with sound cards in some of the first multimedia kits, like the ones from Creative Labs or even MediaVision.

Character Devices

You're best off leaving many of these options set, including `Virtual terminal` and `Support for console on virtual terminal` (not setting these will cause a system to break).

Standard/Generic (Dumb) Serial Support

These are the standard PC serial ports that come with almost every computer. Modems, serial mice, UPS devices, and other gadgets hook up to serial ports (or emulate a serial interface).

Parallel Printer Support

Enables I/O to printers on a parallel port. This only shows up if you select `Parallel port support` (and most likely will only be useful if you select `PC-style hardware` as well) under `General setup`.

> **PROBLEM 80**
>
> **Symptom:** Upon installation of a new kernel, the printer doesn't work anymore.
>
> **Problem:** Renamed the printer device.
>
> **Fix:** Starting with production release 2.2, printers begin at `/dev/lp0` instead of `/dev/lp1`, so your former `/dev/lp1` device file is now `/dev/lp0`. Usually the only place you have to change this is `/etc/printcap`.

Mouse Support (not serial mice)

Selecting this enables a `Mice` submenu. Most modern mice use the so-called PS/2 port, for which the device is `/dev/psaux`. This submenu is *not* for mice that hook up to a serial port.

Filesystems

It's fairly safe to compile most filesystems as modules, *except* for the second extended and `/proc` filesystems (see below); you will almost certainly need to compile these directly into the kernel (in fact, you're not even allowed to build `/proc` as a module).

DOS FAT fs Support

Selecting this enables a few filesystems that use FAT, including the MS-DOS file system, UMSDOS (an extended MS-DOS filesystem), and the newer VFAT.

ISO 9660 CD-ROM Filesystem Support

Most CD-ROMs use this filesystem. The filesystems on CDs meant for Unix systems typically use the Rock Ridge extension, also included in the driver.

Minix fs Support

Best built as a module, the Minix filesystem is small and best suits slow devices such as floppy disks. If you need to compile it directly into the kernel, you're probably using a Minix RAM disk image.

/proc Filesystem Support

Modern Linux tools use the /proc filesystem for system status, kernel parameters, and other miscellaneous configuration. Compile it directly into your kernel.

Network File Systems

You'll find NFS, Coda, and SMB stuff here; all are client-side components and don't include server code. There's a way to look at SMB shares without kernel support using SAMBA (see Section 4.2 for information).

7.3 Building the Kernel

Now that you've got your kernel configured, it's time to compile it.

Verify Source Files

First run the following commands:

```
# make clean
# make dep
```

These commands attempt to verify that you have all of the required source files in place on your system. They take a little while to run; output should appear as in the following fragment.

```
make[1]: Entering directory `/usr/src/linux-2.2.12/arch/i386/boot'
make[1]: Nothing to be done for `dep'.
make[1]: Leaving directory `/usr/src/linux-2.2.12/arch/i386/boot'
scripts/mkdep init/*.c > .depend
scripts/mkdep `find /usr/src/linux-2.2.12/include/asm /usr/src/linux
2.2.12/include/linux /usr/src/linux-2.2.12/include/scsi /usr/src/linux
2.2.12/include/net -follow -name \*.h ! -name modversions.h -print` >
hdepend
...
```

PROBLEM 81

Symptom: You get the error message `make: *** No targets. Stop.`

Problem: You don't have the kernel source installed.

Fix: Either you're not in `/usr/src/linux` or the `/usr/src/linux` that came with your distribution is incomplete. Install the kernel source (see the previous section).

PROBLEM 82

Symptom: You get the error message `gcc: command not found`.

Problem: You don't have the C compiler installed.

Fix: Install the development series of packages (the one that contains `gcc`) for your distribution. Make sure it doesn't walk over your kernel source or symbolic links to include file directories.

Make the Kernel Image

Once you've successfully run these commands, you're ready to make the kernel image itself. While there are a number of ways to do so, start with

```
# make bzImage
```

and you should see the actual object code built with output resembling this:

```
scripts/split-include include/linux/autoconf.h include/config
gcc -D__KERNEL__ -I/usr/src/linux-2.2.12/include -Wall -Wstrict-
 prototypes -O2 -fomit-frame-pointer -fno-strict-aliasing -pipe
-fno-strength-reduce -m486 -malign-loops=2 -malign-jumps=2
 -malign-functions=2 -DCPU=586  -c -o init/main.o init/main.c
 ...
```

NOTE *This process takes a few minutes even on the fastest machines. If you've got a major problem with your build environment (such as a missing compiler), the* make *should abort early on in the process; you probably won't even get past the* make dep.

Test Your Image

Once this process completes, it leaves you with a `bzImage` file in `/usr/src/linux/arch/i386`. This is a compressed kernel image; you'll move it to a system directory later and tell the boot loader about it. But first you need a suitable test image—one that won't screw up your current kernel before you have a working replacement.

The safest way to make a test image is to write one to a floppy disk. It's very important to use a floppy if this is the first time you've ever built a kernel. Put a formatted disk in your first floppy drive and enter:

```
# make bzdisk
```

This command compiles a new kernel and writes it to the floppy disk, attempting to use your current root partition parameters on that floppy disk. The end result is a boot disk. If you ran the `make bzImage` above, `make` won't have to go through the process of making all the object files again, but because floppy disks are slow, you'll still have to wait for the image to copy.

PROBLEM 83

Symptom: A write to floppy fails. A boot from floppy fails.

Problem: You've got trouble with your floppy disks.

Fix: Your floppy might be bad, or it might need better formatting. Red Hat comes with a tool called `fdformat`—but `superformat`, which comes with the fdutils package, attempts to adjust to your floppy drive's particular alignment. It's one of the example packages in `support/installsoft` on the included CD-ROM, and you can also get it at http://www.tux.org/pub/knaff/fdutils/.

Another way to test your boot image, and perhaps one to try once you're familiar with LILO (see Chapter 8), is to add these three lines to `/etc/lilo.conf`:

```
image=/usr/src/linux/arch/i386/boot/bzImage
      label=test
      read-only
```

Then run `lilo`, and on reboot enter `test` at the `LILO` prompt. This test avoids the mess with the floppy disks, but if your `/etc/lilo.conf` wasn't correct in the first place, you won't be able to load your original kernel again. So it's worth repeating this warning: If you've never recompiled a kernel before and you've never changed your boot image with LILO, make sure you have a working boot floppy before you try this.

Build the Modules

Now it's time to build the modules. Run the following:

```
# make modules
```

The modules will appear in /usr/src/linux/modules. We'll install them in a different place later on, but we'll leave them here while we test the new kernel in the next step. (You may load the modules by hand if you wish, but the automatic kernel loader and any boot scripts that depend on modules won't work until they are installed in the proper place.)

7.4 Testing and Installing the Kernel

To test a kernel on a floppy disk, make sure you have your floppy drive set in your system's BIOS boot configuration to boot before the hard disk. Then put the disk in the drive and reboot the system.

PROBLEM 84

Symptom: You get the error message `can't mount root fs`.

Problem: You recompiled the kernel, but it doesn't boot all the way.

Fix: See Problem 92 in Section 7.6.

When your system is up, all essential system services should work as normal, but give yourself some testing time to make sure. Go through all the drivers you compiled directly into the kernel to see that they work; check them by using the appropriate devices and file systems.

Use the dmesg command and files created by syslogd to look through the kernel messages that flew by just after the kernel booted. Some distributions put kernel information in two places in /var/log—the dmesg file and the messages file (where all sorts of other stuff appears). To pick out the kernel stuff, run this:

```
# grep kernel /var/log/messages | less +G
```

Look through this log for errors. (You'll probably see some information about System.map and the kernel symbols; don't worry about this just yet as it's related to modules.)

When performing major kernel upgrades, you may find that some system tools cause the kernel to warn you that it considered what you just did obsolete. Sometimes minor tools don't work because of a really major change.

After you've tested all your hardware and system services and are sure you have a working kernel, it's time to replace your old default kernel image with the new one.

LILO

Unless you use a floppy disk or LOADLIN to boot all the time, you need to know about the standard Linux boot loader system, LILO. The configuration file is /etc/lilo.conf. This is a sample lilo.conf file, based on one set up on a Red Hat system:

```
boot=/dev/hda
map=/boot/map
install=/boot/boot.b
delay=50
image=/boot/vmlinuz-2.2.5-15
        label=linux
        root=/dev/hda1
        read-only
```

The following are the essential parameters.

boot=bootdev

This is where the boot sector is written. In this example, it's /dev/hda, which means it gets written to the master boot record of the first hard disk on the primary interface. If you're using another boot loader there already, you'll want to put this on your Linux root partition (that is, if your /dev/hda2 is mounted on /, /dev/hda2 is the device you want to use).

map=map_file

In order to load the kernel, LILO needs to know where on the disk the kernel is located. When you run lilo, *map_file* stores the information.

install=file

Here, *file* is the actual boot loader program placed on the boot sector.

delay=*num*

Wait *num* tenths of a second for other input before booting the default image.

image=*image_file*

This is the kernel image to load. You may specify multiple images, as long as you have a label for each one (see below).

label=*label*

Use label as the name of this image. To load this image at boot time, you may type this name at the LILO boot: prompt.

root=*rootdev*

After the kernel image loads, *rootdev* is passed to the kernel as the initial root device.

read-only

Mount the initial root device in read-only mode.

Running LILO

To make your new kernel accessible with LILO, first verify that the parameters are correct, then back up your old kernel image. Next, copy the new image file in /usr/src/linux/arch/i386/bzImage to /boot/vmlinuz-*version* (where *version* is the version of your new kernel).

Then, in lilo.conf, change the label of the existing default to backup, and insert these lines before the first image:

```
image=/boot/vmlinuz-version
      label=linux
      root=your_root_dev
      read-only
```

where *your_root_dev* is the root device, as specified in /etc/fstab.

Next, run this:

```
# lilo -t -v
```

You should get a message like this:

```
Reading boot sector from /dev/hda
Merging with /boot/boot.b
Boot image: /boot/vmlinuz-version
Added Linux *
Boot image: /boot/vmlinuz-2.2.5-15
Added backup
The boot sector and the map file have *NOT* been altered.
```

With the -t argument, lilo tests the lilo.conf file without actually changing anything on the system. The asterisk (*) indicates the default boot image. If the output looks acceptable, and you have a backup boot disk, go ahead and run

```
# lilo
```

to install the new boot sector and map file. Then reboot to activate your new kernel.

PROBLEM 85

Symptom: Editing the lilo.conf file has no effect.

Problem: LILO doesn't load the new kernel.

Fix: First, keep in mind that simply editing the lilo.conf file doesn't do anything by itself. To make a change to the boot sector, you must run the lilo command (usually found in /sbin).

If that doesn't solve the problem, it could be that lilo isn't writing the boot sector to the correct place. For the master boot record on a primary disk, the device is /dev/hda. However, you can put it on any partition and disk you like, including those the BIOS doesn't even look at. Either change the boot parameter to whatever the BIOS is looking at, or add your Linux partition to the OS loader you're using on the master boot record.

PROBLEM 86

Symptom: At boot time, only LILO appears, and then after a while, it just loads Linux.

Problem: You can't bring up the LILO boot: prompt.

Fix: When you see LILO, press the **SHIFT** key. Then boot: appears. There are actually two ways to do this. The illustrations we've used so far use the delay parameter. This requires the user to press the **SHIFT** key at LILO to get the rest of the prompt. The other way is to insert

```
prompt
timeout=num
```

in lilo.conf instead (where *num* is a timeout in tenths of a second). This causes the LILO boot: prompt to come up immediately; the default image boots in *num*/10 seconds.

PROBLEM 86 (CONTINUED)

Dual-booting with LILO is relatively easy. Let's say you have a disk with three partitions, /dev/hda1, /dev/hda2, and /dev/hda3; some other operating system is on /dev/hda1, Linux is on /dev/hda2, and /dev/hda3 is Linux swap space. Let's say there is already a loader for that other operating system on /dev/hda1. Your /etc/lilo.conf will end like this:

```
image=/boot/vmlinuz-version
        label=linux
        root=your_root_dev
        read-only

other=/dev/hda1
        label=junk
```

After you run lilo and reboot, you can type junk at the LILO boot: prompt, and LILO will start the other operating system's loader.

7.5 Kernel Modules

We've talked about how to configure and compile the modules that come with the kernel in Sections 7.2 and 7.3. To install them, you run another make command:

```
# cd /usr/src/linux
# make modules_install
```

Before doing this, though, look in /lib/modules for a directory with the same name as the kernel release you're installing. For example, if you're installing version 2.2.12, look for /lib/modules/2.1.12. If such a directory exists, move it to a different location before running make modules_install.

PROBLEM 87

Symptom: Boot-up scripts complain about an incorrect System.map.

Problem: System.map is not in place.

Fix: Copy the System.map file into either / or /boot (the location of the original file—make sure to back up the original), and reboot.

Kernel Module Commands

Here's a short kernel module command reference:

insmod *modname* [*parameters*]

Load *modname* into the kernel. The modname must either have a corresponding *modname*.o file somewhere in /lib/modules/*version*, or it must be a file in the current directory (or an absolute path name). Sometimes you'll need to give the module a parameter or two when you load it, in the form *param=value*; you may specify as many as you like.

rmmod *modname*

Remove *modname* from the kernel. You don't need to put the .o at the end of *modname*.

lsmod

This shows all currently loaded modules.

depmod [-a]

This builds a dependency list of all modules. One module may need a bunch of other modules to load first—for example, the msdos.o module (for the MS-DOS filesystem) needs fat.o. The dependency file is /lib/modules/*version*/modules.dep.

modprobe [*modname* | *option*]

This command works with the dependency list depmod generates. If you give a *modname* as an argument, it will first attempt to load any other modules *modname* depends on, and then load *modname*. modprobe -r *modname* will try to load *modname* and any other modules it depends on.

NOTE *The kernel module loader uses* modprobe *to load modules. Most current distributions are configured with the module loader, so it's important to keep the dependency list up to date. You do this at boot time with a call to* depmod -a *from one of the* init.d *scripts (described in Chapter 1). It's in* /etc/rc.d/sysinit *in Red Hat 6 systems.*

Filesystem Modules

As mentioned earlier, filesystems are among the best suited for modules, but you'll experience one minor difference in operation with modules versus direct compilation. Let's say you have a DOS filesystem on /dev/hda1. If you've compiled fat.o and msdos.o as modules, and they aren't loaded at the time, you can't simply mount the filesystem with this:

```
# mount /dev/hda1 /dos
```

The kernel can't identify the filesystem type, because the driver is not loaded. However, this slightly more verbose version of the command works fine:

```
# mount -t msdos /dev/hda1 /dos
```

Ideally, you'll have everything you need in /etc/fstab (or the Automounter map), so you won't have to do any of this as root.

Other Drivers

Other drivers you might want to modularize and use with the kernel module loader are the loopback device, parallel port driver, ISDN drivers, SCSI generic and tape support, and other instances in which one piece of hardware or service has only one associated driver. On the other hand, it's usually better to compile Ethernet and SCSI controller drivers straight into the kernel. These all use the same interface name (eth or scsi); the kernel usually has little idea what it's looking for there.

If you use the kernel module loader, put a line like the following in your system crontab file (/etc/crontab):

```
00 * * * * root rmmod -a > /dev/null 2>&1
```

This tells cron to remove all unneeded modules every hour (on the hour), reclaiming a little memory. (If you don't have a system crontab file, put it in root's crontab; it has a slightly different format. See Chapter 1 for details on cron.)

SCSI Modules

Be especially careful when handling SCSI modules. If you use a SCSI drive as your root device, you should compile the driver for it directly into the kernel. You would have a hard time loading a module that's located on a disk your kernel doesn't know how to find yet. Red Hat follows this procedure anyway, though—it uses an initial RAM disk (initrd), putting the SCSI driver modules on the RAM disk image, then loading the modules right after the RAM disk mounts. You may use this system if you like, but it's a roundabout method and takes much longer to set up for an upgrade. (As you might have surmised, you shouldn't set up SCSI disk support as a module if your root partition is on a SCSI disk.)

PCMCIA Cards

All PCMCIA drivers are modules, distributed not with the kernel but rather with another package, called pcmcia-cs. You can get it from http://pcmcia. sourceforce.org/.

Because PCMCIA cards are hot-swappable modules, this system works quite well. When you have a card plugged in, the card manager daemon detects what kind of card it is, runs modprobe on the driver, and then optionally runs a script to set it up. This is especially handy for Ethernet cards—upon insertion of the card, the script can run the proper `ifconfig` and `route` commands to get it working right away.

PROBLEM 88

Symptom: You get the error message `.. symbols don't match version`.

Problem: You have a kernel module mismatch.

Fix: You need to recompile this module with the current kernel's include files. Make sure beforehand that `/usr/include/linux` and `/usr/include/asm` point to places in the current source tree.

PROBLEM 89

Symptom: You get the error message `module.o: unresolved symbol symname`.

Problem: You didn't have dependency loaded when you attempted to use `insmod`.

Fix: Find the module with `symname`. If it's available, look at `/lib/modules/version/modules.dep` to see if it lists `module.o`; this will show a dependency if `depmod -a` found one. If all of that is correct, you can use `modprobe` to load the dependencies and the module.

7.6 Troubleshooting

One of the best ways to do a general checkup on a currently running kernel is with the `/proc` filesystem. Many of the files in here contain parameters and listings related to the configuration, but some don't do what you might think.

/proc/filesystems

If you run `cat /proc/filesystems`, you'll get a list of the filesystems known to the kernel. This list excludes filesystems in modules you haven't loaded yet.

/proc/ide/

You can verify a number of settings in this directory. For example, checking up on a driver for a CD-ROM drive at `/dev/hdc` goes like this:

```
# cat /proc/ide/ide1/hdc/driver
ide-cdrom version 4.53
```

/proc/scsi/

This is somewhat like /proc/ide, but not as well-organized.

/proc/pci

This is obsolete. If you run a cat on this, then a dmesg, you'll see a message to that effect. Use the pciutils package, which includes lspci and other programs.

/proc/ioports

A cat /proc/ioports lists the drivers that use I/O ports on the machine. This is handy for finding conflicts or bad configurations.

/proc/interrupts

This is like the ioports above, but deals with interrupts. There is one major difference: Devices not currently in use do not show up in this list.

/proc/devices

This indicates devices configured for files in /dev, along with their major device numbers.

/proc/partitions

This provides information about current partition tables on all disks.

/proc/ksyms

This provides the locations of kernel symbols.

PROBLEM 90

Symptom: You get the error message System is too big. Try using bzImage or modules.

Problem: During compilation, the kernel got too big.

Fix: You probably ran a make zImage or make zdisk instead of a bzImage or bzdisk. Linux has expanded, leaving bzImage (or bzdisk) as the only option for many configurations. After leaving the menuconfig menu, a message appears to the effect that you should run a make zImage (at least, that was true up to kernel version 2.2). Don't listen to that message. Also, use as many modules as possible.

PROBLEM 91

Symptoms: The kernel is using too much memory, you're running into driver conflicts, and so forth.

Problem: Your system has a bloated kernel.

Fix: If you don't need a driver right now, don't compile it into the kernel, thinking you may get that kind of hardware someday. Chances are you'll put a new kernel in before you install that device anyway. Build modules whenever you can.

PROBLEM 92

Symptom: You get the error message `Can't mount root fs ...`

Problem: You recompiled the kernel, but it doesn't boot all the way.

Fix: First verify that you configured the correct root device into your boot system. If you're using LILO, then `/etc/lilo.conf` must have a `root=device` line, where *device* is your root filesystem. If you don't know what it is, check the output of the `mount` command on your working system. At the `LILO boot:` prompt, you can bypass this by giving `root=device` as a parameter to your image name (`Linux root=/dev/hda1`, for example). You can also do this with the CD-ROM accompanying this book at its boot prompt (that is, `Linux root=/dev/hda1`).

If you have a root on a SCSI disk, there's a good chance you forgot to configure the proper SCSI device driver. You need to configure the drivers for both the SCSI controller and the SCSI disks directly into the kernel, or the new kernel can't see the disk.

Finally, make sure you compiled the ext2 filesystem directly into the kernel.

PROBLEM 93

Symptoms: When compiling, gcc sometimes gets a signal 11. You experience a random oops (crash) upon boot.

Problem: You're getting a hardware error.

Fix: You can fix some of these through the BIOS settings. One problem in particular has to do with DMA (direct memory access); if you disable UDMA support on a troublesome hard drive, you may get better results. However, PC hardware problems have a huge scope and can be quite frustrating to debug. Check your motherboard settings—are they correct? If you are overclocking the processors, you're probably destabilizing your system. Is your memory all it's cracked up to be?

General random kernel oops messages usually point to CPU, memory, or motherboard problems. These also tend to pop up when you compile the kernel for the first time, because in most cases it's the most CPU-memory intensive task the machine has ever undertaken.

PROBLEM 94

Symptom: You experience a horrific-looking crash at boot time.

Problem: You have a very broken kernel.

Fix: You might need to run a make clean before recompiling the kernel.

8

BACKUPS AND CRASH RECOVERY

8.1 Backups: Introduction

Tape drives are pretty much your only backup option; effective alternatives are hard to come by. And because tapes and tape drives are expensive, your backup strategy (how often you back up and what kind of backup you choose) depends primarily on how much money you're willing to spend on media and hardware.

There are two basic kinds of backups. One is a *full* (*level 0*) backup; this is simply a complete record of everything in a specific directory or filesystem. The other type is an *incremental* backup, which records only the changes since the last full backup. In other words, an incremental backup pays attention only to those files with a modification or creation time later than the last time you ran a full backup.

The longer you wait between full backups, the larger incremental backups get (especially with home directories), and of course, large backups take longer and use more resources. You may also find it more time-consuming and difficult to track down files if you don't do full backups often enough.

You might also consider keeping some of your backups off-site. No amount of regular on-site backups will help if a fire destroys your building.

What You Should Back Up

Home directories are obviously your first priority. Administrators of large networks should run incremental backups on home directories once a night, with full backups every one to four weeks. Home directories change more than system directories, so regular full backups of these keep the size of the incremental backups down.

System configuration and data are the next most important files to back up. Items located in etc directories, as well as select stuff in /var, change frequently, and you'll want to keep track of this. Incremental backups of /etc stay at a fairly constant size, so you won't need to perform full backups as often as for home directories.

Locally installed software sets are next on the priority list. If you lose a package, it's often not worth the trouble to look for a backup, especially since it may take less time to install a new version of a package than to find the old one.

System software is the least of your worries when it comes to backups, for several reasons. If you have several machines and you use rdist or an alternative to maintain identical software on them, several complete copies of the system exist on hard drives throughout the network. Also, system software isn't unique; if you back up your configuration files regularly, you'll be in good shape—you probably spent more time working on those files than you did installing the software.

8.2 A Survey of Devices

Before going over the details of specific backup software, we first need to review the backup device types available. While we've already expressed a preference for tape drives, you have a few other options for backups you don't need to do so regularly.

SCSI Tape Drives

SCSI drives are far and away the most reliable and convenient way to back up a lot of data. They are also the most expensive means. Travan and DAT drives currently make up the low end of the SCSI drive spectrum, with DLT at the high end. If you're halfway serious about backups, you'll want a SCSI drive.

Which one you choose depends on how fast you need it, how much capacity you require, and whether you have a huge amount of money to invest.

IDE Tape Drives

The Linux kernel supports IDE tape drives, but you probably only want to consider this option if you already have such a device. You can get a low-end SCSI counterpart at only a slightly higher price than an IDE drive, and the price of a cheap, narrow SCSI controller won't kill you. IDE tape drives have two main weaknesses: poorer, non-uniform driver support, and limited features—all high-end tape drives are SCSI.

Removable Disks

These work adequately only for small-time, ad hoc backups. If you have a small home directory, you can probably get away with tossing it and your system configuration files onto a Zip, Jaz, or similar disk every now and then with tar. Don't get any ideas about backing up your entire system on one, though.

CD Writers

These devices are pretty versatile; you may have one already. If you plan to use one for backups, you'll probably need free disk space equal to the size of a disc. CD writers are fine for backing up home directories and system configuration files every now and then, but for more regular backups you'll probably want a tape drive.

Duplicate Hard Drives

This is probably the cheapest option, but it's not the easiest to set up. Also, it isn't a true backup—it can't conveniently store older archives since filesystem changes get too large over time for disks to handle. Furthermore, if you do buy a new hard drive, chances are you'll end up using it as your primary hard drive anyway because it's bigger than any that you currently own.

8.3 Working with Tapes

While tape drives have changed in size and shape over the years, the principle behind them is still the same, and so is the Unix interface.

Setting Up Your Tape Drive

To get tape drives to work, you'll need a driver in your kernel. In the kernel series 2.2 configuration menu (see Chapter 7), you'll find SCSI and IDE tape drivers in the SCSI and block devices sections, and the QIC-80/Travan (non-IDE) type stuff under Ftape in the character devices section. When the kernel successfully recognizes a tape drive, you get a message like this:

```
(scsi0:0:3:0) Synchronous at 5.0 Mbyte/sec, offset 15.
Vendor: HP       Model: C1537A          Rev: L708
  Type: Sequential-Access              ANSI SCSI revision: 02
Detected scsi tape st0 at scsi0, channel 0, id 3, lun 0
```

SCSI tape devices in /dev have st in their names (as the message above suggests).

When a SCSI tape doesn't show up, three things could be amiss. First, the SCSI tape driver may not be configured into the kernel. The same may be true of the driver for your SCSI host adapter. In both cases, see Chapter 7 for an explanation of how to compile the drivers into the kernel or compile and load them as modules. Another possible explanation is that you don't have the hardware properly installed. Make sure the SCSI bus terminates properly, the cables are secure, and the SCSI host adapter's BIOS recognizes the drive on boot-up.

PROBLEM 95

Symptom: No matter what you do with the tape, its position resets after every access.

Problem: You're using the rewind tape device. Each time a command accessing a rewind device completes, the driver instructs the tape to rewind.

Fix: Use the no-rewind tape device. The so-called rewind tape devices have names without any prefix, like /dev/st0; the no-rewind device corresponding to /dev/st0, for example, is /dev/nst0. Remember that the devices don't depend on the names—these are only a convention.

Tape Layout

Tape format is simply a long string of files with file markers between them. You can envision the tape as follows:

Figure 8-1: Schematic rendering of tape format

When placed at the end of a file marker, the tape head points to the first block of the file after the marker. Writing a file to the tape inserts a new file marker after the file, and—assuming you're using the no-rewind device—the tape head goes to the end of the marker after a write, ready to write a new file.

When moving the tape around, you can position the tape so the head is at the beginning or end of a file marker. Usually you'll want it at the end of the marker so you can read or write the next file.

Since tapes are sequential, it doesn't make sense to write an item to the middle of a tape that contains valuable data later on. Tape files can be arbitrarily long, and there's no way of discerning their structure on the tape.

Most tape utilities use the TAPE environment variable for storing the device filename (as in /dev/nst0). If you've only got one tape drive, you should set this variable in root's start-up scripts.

mt

The mt utility moves the tape head position, puts markers in place, and so on. Assuming that you have the TAPE variable set to a valid device, you can put a blank tape in your drive and, after the access light goes off (this could take a while), input the following code:

```
# mt status
```

You'll get a response like this:

```
drive type = Generic SCSI-2 tape
drive status = 1024
sense key error = 0
residue count = 0
file number = 0
block number = 0
Tape block size 1024 bytes. Density code 0x0 (default).
Soft error count since last status=0
General status bits on (41010000):
BOT ONLINE IM_REP_EN
```

Probably the most important part of this message is the file number. In the above example, this is 0 since you're at the beginning of the tape. A block number of 0 means you haven't done any reads or writes to this file yet. Figure 8-2 shows how a blank tape looks in our simplified view.

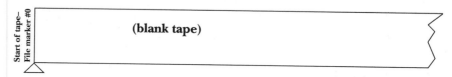

Figure 8-2: A blank tape in a tape drive—the triangle at the bottom left represents the tape head

Putting a File on Tape

Let's jump right to putting a file on the tape:

```
# cd /
# tar cvvp bin
```

(See the tar section below for an explanation of the different tar commands.) This places the contents of /bin after the first file marker on the tape.

When you run another mt status, you'll see that the tape position has advanced to 1. Go ahead and put another archive on the tape (we'll use it in later examples):

```
# tar cvvp lib
```

Reading from the Tape

Now practice reading back from the tape (for a list of mt commands, see the mt man pages). Run the following:

```
# mt rewind
# tar tvv
```

If the tape drive is working properly, you'll get a list of files in the /bin archive. tar's t option doesn't actually extract anything, but rather goes over the entire archive and makes sure that there are no errors on the tape.

Note, however, that an mt status yields a response like this for the file number and block number:

```
file number = 0
block number = 72870
```

After a read access, the tape does *not* advance to the end of the next file marker, but rather places you at the beginning, as shown in Figure 8-3.

To get to the next file, tell the tape head to advance to the end of the file marker (Figure 8-4 shows the result of this command):

```
# mt fsf
```

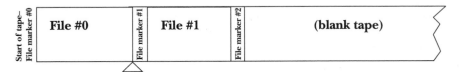

Figure 8-3: Note the position of the tape head

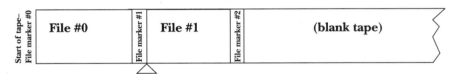

Figure 8-4: The tape head at the end of the file marker

Extracting a File from the Tape

Let's extract from the archive at our present position. We'll extract the files into /tmp:

```
# cd /tmp
# tar xvv
```

The output looks the same as before (with the t option), but this time the contents of the /lib archive (remember, that's the second one we put on the tape) go into /tmp/lib.

To move around on the tape, rewind it to the beginning and use mt to move the tape forward again, as in this example:

```
# mt rewind
# mt fsf
```

mt fsf moves the tape forward one file marker (in this case, to the /lib archive).

PROBLEM 96

Symptom: Using mt bsf (back a file marker) doesn't take you to the right file.

Problem: mt bsf doesn't do what you think it should when you place the head at the end of a file marker.

Fix: Let's say you're using a tape, and you're right at file position 2—that is, mt status shows this information:

```
file number = 2
block number = 0
```

If you run **mt bsf** and then **mt status**, you'll get this:

```
file number = 1
block number = -1
```

The head has hardly moved at all; it's only moved to the beginning of the file marker (that is, at the end of file 1, hence the -1 as a block number). Another **mt bsf** takes you to the end of file 0. To get to file 1, you need to use mt fsf.

If this sounds confusing, you may want to consider using mt rewind, then mt fsf n to get to the nth file.

When you're finished with a tape, you can use mt offline to rewind the tape, take it offline, and eject it (if possible).

Relevant man pages: mt (1)

tar

We've already demonstrated the three basic main modes of tar: for creating, extracting, and testing archives. To make tar work, you must put it into a mode. You may specify the modes and modifying options together; in the examples above, we've used the v option twice (vv) to get an extra-verbose listing of the files involved. The three mode options mentioned so far are c for create, t for test, and x for extract. Important modifying options include these:

f The file name of the device or archive follows. When you use this option, the next argument must be the file name. Use a hyphen (-) to indicate standard output, as in this example:

```
$ zcat foo.tar.gz | tar tvf -
```

v Be verbose; show more information about the files in the archive. If you give this option twice, you'll get a listing similar to that of ls -l.

p Preserve permissions when extracting, overriding any permissions mask (set with umask).

z Use GNU zip compression. New archives (when tar is used with the c option) run through gzip -c first; extractions and tests (tar's x and t options) use gzip -dc.

NOTE *There is nothing special about a* tar *archive. You can put any file on the tape; for example, if you wanted to put* /etc/services *at the current place on the tape, you'd run:*

```
# dd if=/etc/services of=$TAPE
```

Relevant man page: tar (1)

dd

One of the hidden treasures of Unix is a program called dd. It stands for convert and copy. dd differs from cat in that dd knows a bunch of obscure data coding formats as well as tricks on buffering and regulation of I/O flow. If you need to use your tape drive, disk, or other block device for some task that's a little out of the ordinary, dd is the first command you should look at, because it knows how to deal with the fixed-length chunks of data that block devices want. dd also works on plain files, but the block size specification is irrelevant in this case (other than for a few special tricks).

To see what dd can do on a device, try this:

```
$ dd if=/dev/zero bs=1k count=6 > /tmp/foo
```

While not terribly useful in itself, this command does demonstrate dd's option structure. This example is as straightforward as it looks: It takes 1-kilobyte blocks of input from /dev/zero (with standard output, the default) into /tmp/foo six times.

dd's size options are normally specified in bytes, but you can modify this with k (1024 bytes), b (512 bytes), w (2 bytes), and a few other choices described in the info and manual pages. The most important options are:

bs=*n*, ibs=*n*, obs=*n*

Set block sizes to *n*. Since there are two block sizes (one for input and one for output), there are three options: bs sets both, ibs sets the input block size, and obs sets the output block size. The default is 512 bytes.

count=*n*

Read a maximum of *n* blocks.

if=*name*, of=*name*

Set the input and output files (the defaults are standard input and output).

conv=*method*

This option is mostly for conversion of non-Unix formats. For example, it can convert EBCDIC to ASCII and back (with the ascii and ebcdic methods). See the info page for more details.

Like a number of GNU versions utilities that come with Linux, dd has expanded beyond the versions that come with other Unix variants; the manual page doesn't list all of the options because GNU wants you to use info documentation. However, dd --help does offer a quick summary.

cpio

From time to time, you may encounter a cpio archive. This format (or rather, collection of formats) is common on tapes coming from systems such as HPUX and Stardent Titans. The following section covers what you need to know to extract a cpio archive.

cpio has modes, much like tar: extract mode (initiated with -i), create mode (-o), and a pass-through mode (-p) for copying files. Testing an archive is part of the extract mode, and you would input the following:

```
$ cpio -i -t -I archive
```

where *archive* is the name of the cpio archive (it can be a tape drive). To extract the archive, run this:

```
$ cpio -i -d -I archive filename(s)
```

Here, *filename(s)* is optional; this instructs cpio to extract only items matching those names. The -d option creates directories as needed (tar does this automatically). Although GNU cpio tries to detect formats automatically, you may also need one of these options after the -i:

-b

The default format for cpio depends on the byte order of the machine's architecture. This option swaps the byte order.

-C *n*

Use *n* as the block size of the archive.

-H *name*

Use *name* for the type (format) of cpio archive. Options directly relevant to old cpio archives are bin, crc, hpbin, hpodc, newc, odc, tar, and ustar. Note that these are for the GNU version of cpio; other versions (such as the one that comes with BSD systems) don't support as many archive types, and they use different names.

-v

Verbose (somewhat like tar's verbose setting).
Relevant man page: cpio (1)

dump and restore

Alternatives to tar, the dump and restore programs come from older Unix utilities that backed up filesystems by looking at their internal structure on the disk (unlike tar and cpio, which use only information from the kernel's filesystem interface). These programs come with a number of Linux distributions, and though they don't work quite the same way as traditional dump and restore programs, they do share the same file format, so you can use them across platforms.

Interactive restore

You can use restore in automatic and interactive modes. The interactive mode is more popular:

```
# restore ivf filename
```

where *filename* is the name of the archive (either a device or a file). The command line above grabs the index information from the front of the archive and throws a new command prompt at you:

```
restore >
```

At this prompt, you can run cd, ls, and pwd commands (help offers a short summary). As you navigate the filesystem, use the add command to add a file or directory to the list of files and directories you would like to restore. When you add an item to an extract list, an asterisk (*) appears next to it, and if you choose a directory, restore instantly creates it (along with all of its subdirectories).

When you're finished selecting files, use the extract command to proceed with the actual restoration of the files. restore asks for a volume; just give it 1, since you probably have only a single-volume archive. It also asks if you wish to set the owner and mode for the . directory. If you say yes to this, the current directory will have the same permissions as the mount point of the original archive. If you're restoring into a different place from the original file location, you probably want to say no to this.

Automatic restore

To do an automatic restore, run this:

```
# restore rvf $TAPE file1 file2 ..
```

where *file1 file2* .. specify what to restore. If you omit them, you'll restore the entire archive.

dump

To back up (dump) a directory, use a command like this:

```
# dump -0 -f filename fs|directory
```

The 0 means it's a full level 0 dump, *filename* is the device or file in which to store the archive, and *fs* or *directory* is the filesystem or directory to back up. In addition to this information, you may need to provide the -d *n* and -s *n* options to specify the density and length of your tape.

We don't recommend using dump for backups. It's not flexible enough, especially when you're backing up multiple disks. GNU tar works fine and addresses the traditional arguments against using tar: GNU tar supports single filesystem backups, multiple volumes, and special/sparse files.

8.4 Automated Backups with Amanda

Manual backups can be a pain. You can automate the process somewhat by setting a cron job to back up some stuff every night, but it's difficult to come up with a satisfactory organization when you're juggling everything else a systems administrator has to do.

Amanda (http://www.amanda.org/) is a package for automating backups. Consisting of a client program that runs on the machines you're backing up and a server for use on the machine with the tape drive, Amanda works across Unix platforms—you just have to install the client side of the program on all the machines. You'll need a large disk with plenty of free space.

The format Amanda writes to the tapes is nothing special. The first file is an index and the rest consist of a bunch of archives, which can be of any type (tar, dump/restore, cpio, etc). When everything is in place, you can use amrecover for casual file restoration. If you get in a real bind, you can always look up the files and restore them with the usual utilities, such as tar.

Configuring Amanda

The hardest part about Amanda is starting out. Once you get the ball rolling with at least a partially correct configuration file and familiarize yourself with a few of its programs, fine-tuning your installation is simple; Amanda's online documentation is complete and descriptive enough to smooth out the rough edges. Therefore, this section will introduce Amanda to the point of getting it running—not necessarily perfectly, but so you can change the setup if it isn't appropriate for your needs.

You'll probably need to build the package, which you'll find on the included CD-ROM in support/backupcrash, from source as described in Chapter 6. When configuring, specify which users have write access to the filesystems on the machines you're backing up (with the --with-user=*user* option to configure—probably root if you're using GNU tar), as well as which group can run the programs that setuid to root (with the --with-group option, used for non–root operator access). You might also want to change the default configuration directory to *dir* using --with-configdir=*dir* because it's difficult to maintain a default over a larger network. We strongly recommend the option --with-amandahosts; this tells the clients to use a .amandahosts file instead of the .rhosts file for dump access (we'll mention this again a little later in this section).

After you've installed Amanda, you need to create at least one configuration directory. This is where Amanda keeps information about which machines and directories it should back up, a list of tapes to use, tape settings, and so on. If you give an installation prefix of /usr/local and make a directory named /usr/local/etc/amanda/servers, then servers is a valid configuration directory name.

You'll need three files in the configuration directory: amanda.conf, disklist, and tapelist. General backup parameters are in amanda.conf, and disklist contains a list of the directories to back up. Amanda creates the tapelist file for you after one run of amdump.

amanda.conf

The best way to create amanda.conf is to copy an example and modify it to suit your needs. When you configure Amanda, you'll get an example amanda.conf in the source code's example subdirectory. Make a copy of this file, edit the copy, skip the first section, and go down to the part that reads as follows:

```
runtapes 1          # number of tapes to be used in a single run of amdump
tpchanger "chg-manual"  # the tape-changer glue script
tapedev "/dev/null"     # the no-rewind tape device to be used
rawtapedev "/dev/null"  # the raw device to be used (ftape only)
changerfile "/usr/adm/amanda/DailySet1/changer"
changerfile "/usr/adm/amanda/DailySet1/changer-status"
changerfile "/usr/local/amanda/amanda..."
changerdev "/dev/null"
```

Here you'll need to make some changes. First change the /dev/null for tapedev to your tape device. This should be, as the comment suggests, the no-rewind tape device. The line that mentions ftape may not apply; newer versions of the ftape driver should provide full file-marker emulation. Comment all of the changer lines out—these are for tape changers; even if you have one, it's easier to start with a simple configuration.

The next line in the file is this:

```
tapetype HP-DAT          # what kind of tape it is (see tapetypes below)
```

Unless you're using an HP DAT drive, change this line. The list of tape types appears later in the file, with definitions like this:

```
define tapetype HP-DAT {
    comment "DAT tape drives"
    # data provided by Rob Browning
    length 1930 mbytes
    filemark 111 kbytes
    speed 468 kbytes
}
```

Make sure you change these specifications accordingly. If you can't find the specifications in your tape drive's manual, try the extensive tapetype reference available from the Amanda Web site.

Next, change the definition for the holding disk (a large disk partition for storing backup data before writing it to tape). The default looks like this:

```
holdingdisk hd1 {
    comment "main holding disk"
    directory "/dumps/amanda"
    use 290 Mb
    chunksize -1
    }
```

Change `/dumps/amanda` to some directory where you have enough disk space; you should call it `amanda` (or some other identifying name), because you'll be creating a number of things inside this directory. Don't bother with the `chunksize` parameter for the moment, since you'll start out with one holding disk.

Now change the index and log locations:

```
infofile "/usr/adm/amanda/DailySet1/curinfo"    # database DIRECTORY
logdir   "/usr/adm/amanda/DailySet1"            # log directory
indexdir "/usr/adm/amanda/DailySet1/index"      # index directory
```

Under Linux, `/usr/adm` isn't the standard place to put items of this nature, so use another place, such as `/var/log/amanda`. Make sure, however, that you have enough disk space. If you've got a significant number of machines and files to back up, the index files can grow to tens of megabytes. Prior to running any Amanda programs, make sure the directories you've set for the database, index, and log locations exist.

After the `tapetype` definitions, you'll come across a number of dump type definitions with this structure:

```
define dumptype global {
}
define dumptype root-tar {
    global
    program "GNUTAR"
    comment "root partitions dumped with tar"
    compress none
    index
    exclude list "/usr/local/lib/amanda/exclude.gtar"
    priority low
}

define dumptype user-tar {
    root-tar
    comment "user partitions dumped with tar"
    priority medium
}
```

Note how each define usually builds on a previous one. The global define, which you should include in all definitions, is blank by default. root-tar has a list of settings for a / partition (GNU tar format, indexing, no compression, and a file listing to exclude). user-tar has almost the same structure, so its definition simply includes root-tar. (We'll examine these definitions in greater detail in the "Advanced Configuration" section below.)

disklist

The disklist file has a format like this:

```
atlantic    /home        user-tar
mikado      /etc         root-tar
pacific     /usr/local   root-tar
```

The first field specifies the machine to back up (here we are backing up the machines called atlantic, mikado, and pacific), the second identifies the target directory, and the third names the type of dump (one of the dumptype definitions in amanda.conf; see the previous section). To start out, you should place just one line in this file—make it a small directory on some machine that isn't too busy. Start small, because it takes longer to debug Amanda on large lists of machines and directories.

Install the Client Software

After you have the amanda.conf and disklist files configured and on the server, put the Amanda client software in place on the machines you're backing up. This is a pretty standard inetd service, with lines like this in /etc/inetd.conf:

```
amanda dgram udp wait root /usr/local/libexec/amandad
amandaidx stream tcp nowait root /usr/sbin/tcpd
/usr/local/amanda/libexec/amindexd
amidxtape stream tcp nowait root /usr/sbin/tcpd
/usr/local/amanda/libexec/amidxtaped
```

The /etc/services file contains:

```
amanda          10080/udp          # amanda backup services
kamanda         10081/tcp          # amanda backup services (Kerberos)
kamanda         10081/udp          # amanda backup services (Kerberos)
amandaidx       10082/tcp          # amanda backup services
amidxtape       10083/tcp          # amanda backup services
```

Testing Your Configuration

Put a blank tape in the drive and look at the labelstr in amanda.conf. The one
in the example amanda.conf (in the example directory) is

```
labelstr "^DailySet1[0-9][0-9]*$"
```

This is a regular expression; here it matches any string that starts with
DailySet1 followed by at least one number. To get Amanda to accept a tape
for backups, you'll have to create a new label on the tape. Let's say you stuck
with the default. To write a tape label that matches labelstr, run this (assuming 01 is the first tape number in this series of tapes):

 # amlabel servers DailySet101

Now you can run an amcheck to see if the backup will go properly (still
assuming that our configuration directory is servers):

 # amcheck servers

The output will be as follows:

```
Amanda Tape Server Host Check

/var/spool/amanda: 1331470 KB disk space available, that's plenty.
NOTE: skipping tape-writable test.
Tape dailytape01 label ok.
Server check took 31.260 seconds.
```

```
Amanda Backup Client Hosts Check
Client check: 3 hosts checked in 1.029 seconds, 0 problems found.

(brought to you by Amanda 2.4.1p1)
```

The first part, the server host check, looks at the the tape loaded in the tape drive and the configuration to see if the backup will record properly. The client hosts check simply connects to the hosts you're backing up to see if they are ready. Errors involving nonexistent files and directories will probably crop up, so create them (with touch and mkdir) and run amcheck until they go away.

PROBLEM 98

Symptom: Client host denies access.

Problem: Host access.

Fix: By default, Amanda looks at the .rhosts file of the Amanda user's directory on the client machine to see if the client has access. You can use --with-amandahosts to configure Amanda to use an .amandahosts file if you don't want it to use the .rhosts file. Make sure that you specify only the tape server in your .amandahosts file and that your server is secure. If you want better authentication, a --with-krb4-security option allows Kerberos 4 authentication.

Backing Up with amdump

Once everything passes amcheck, you're ready to try a backup with amdump.

```
# amdump servers
```

instructs Amanda to dump the directories you specified in the disklist file to tape. If this is the first time you've done this, a full backup takes place, and the process might last a while if you have an extensive disklist file.

If the backup seems to have gone all right, look in the directory to which you set logdir in amanda.conf. You should see at least one log file in there named log.*yyyymmdd*.*n*, *yyyy* being the year, *mm* the month, and *dd* the day. *n* is most likely 0 (*n* differentiates log files created by different Amanda runs on the same day). Look at the log file to get familiar with the format and to see if there are any errors.

PROBLEM 99

Symptoms: Amanda backups fail, rejecting the name of the tape. Amanda writes to the wrong tape.

Problem: The label doesn't match the `labelstr`, or `labelstr` matches too many tape labels.

Fix: The example `amanda.conf` uses

```
labelstr "^DailySet1[0-9][0-9]*$"
```

as its label string for the tapes, although the default matches anything. If you use more than one configuration (for example, one configuration for incremental backups and another for full backups), you should use two different sets of tapes and two distinct names for each, and set `labelstr` accordingly. For example, your `amanda.conf` for incremental backups would contain

```
labelstr "^Incremental[0-9][0-9]*$"
```

and the `amanda.conf` for full backups would contain

```
labelstr "^Full[0-9][0-9]*$"
```

Automating Amanda

Now that you're sure Amanda is backing up properly, finishing the setup for automatic backup is relatively easy. All you have to do is put amcheck and amdump in your crontab files (see Chapter 1 for information on cron and crontab). Put an amcheck *config* in your crontab a little while before each amdump *config* so if you have the wrong tape loaded in the drive, Amanda alerts you in time to fix it.

If you want to force level 0 dumps every week, use a separate configuration, with dumpcycle set to 0. Then set up the crontab to run Amanda with this configuration only once a week.

Relevant man page: amanda (8)

Advanced Configuration: Important amanda.conf Settings

The manual page for amanda contains a section explaining each parameter you can put into `amanda.conf`. This subsection describes how a few groups of options fit together.

When you go back to put the final touches on your `amanda.conf` file, keep the amanda manual page handy so you can check the default value of every parameter. Example configuration files have all sorts of little quirks that may not apply to your situation.

Tape Cycle Options

Incremental backups, occurring in cycles, reuse old tapes. Every now and then, you should do a full backup so the size of the incremental backup doesn't become overwhelming. How long a cycle you choose depends more or less on how many tapes you want to buy. With a larger incremental backup cycle, you have more of a likelihood of recovering files or modifications between full backups, but the chance that you'll want files from an incremental backup drops drastically after a a few weeks. Many sites use four weeks as the basic cycle.

Here's a rundown of the basic tape cycle options:

runspercycle *n*

Sets the number of backups per cycle to *n*. This does not have to correspond to a scheme that includes a daily backup. You may set up your crontab to have amdump do incremental backups every other day or skip them on the weekend, for instance.

tapecycle *n*

Each run gets at least one tape. If you set tapecycle to more than runspercycle, you can perform multiple-volume backups. However, this may be useless for incremental backups unless you have a tape changer, since they normally run when no one is around to put a new tape in the drive.

dumpcycle *n*

This parameter controls how often a directory or filesystem gets a full backup; a full backup occurs at least once every *n* days, so *n* tells you how long the dump cycle is (in days).

Network Regulation Options

It's important to keep control of network usage for two reasons. First, if you try to push your machines harder than they can go, backups take longer. Repeated disk usage is system-intensive, especially if you're running low on memory. Also, if the network is active at the time of backups, users' work and external services slow down, sometimes to a crawl.

These options have the most impact on system resources:

inparallel *n*

This is a cap on the number of backups you can run at once. You should probably set this only if you have an overloaded tape server.

maxdumps *n*

Here *n* is the limit of simultaneous backup connections to run on one backup client. You can overload ("thrash") a machine by asking it to back up two disks at once, especially if one of the disks is a system disk or has active swap space (even if you don't thrash the machine, you'll slow it down). To allow finer control of which disks and machines to back up in parallel, you can also change maxdumps on a per-backup basis by including it in a dumptype declaration in the amanda.conf file (and then choosing the appropriate dump type in the disklist file). There is no precise formula for calculating maxdumps; in practice, it should turn out to be roughly the number of disks per machine you're backing up.

netusage *limit*

Specify *limit* in terms of network usage per second, as in 1000 Kbps. Remember to keep an eye on the default value, as it may be far too small for a modern system.

Restoring Files with amrecover

The preferred way to get lost files from tape is with amrecover, a program that works much like restore. To start it up, run

amrecover *config* **-t $TAPE**

where *config* is the name of the configuration you want to use (this also tests your modifications to /etc/inetd.conf). If everything's working, you'll get a response like this (here, atlantic is the tape server):

```
AMRECOVER Version 2.4.1p1. Contacting server on atlantic ...
220 atlantic AMANDA index server (2.4.1p1) ready.
200 Access OK
Setting restore date to today (1999-11-29)
200 Working date set to 1999-11-29.
200 Config set to daily.
200 Dump host set to atlantic.
Can't determine disk and mount point from $CWD
amrecover>
```

First determine if the dump host (that is, the machine that lost files) is correct; if it's not, type

sethost *host*

at the amrecover> prompt to get it to look at filesystems on *host*. Next you'll type

setdisk *disk*

to set the directory (on the *host* above) where the files once were. You also probably want to specify

setdate *yyyy-mm-dd*

to get a look at the file indexes on a certain date (rather than the most recent). Now you can use cd and ls to explore the contents of the directory in the backup. When you find a file or directory that you want to extract from the archive, use

add *name*

to add *name* to the list of files or directories to be extracted. Continue browsing the archive until you've used add on everything that you want to recover, and then type

list

to confirm what you've chosen. When you're ready, type

extract

to extract the files from the archive. You'll have to go through a few questions; here's an example transcript:

```
Extracting files using tape drive /dev/nst0 on host atlantic.
The following tapes are needed: dailytape01

Restoring files into directory /tmp
Continue? [Y/n]: y

Load tape dailytape01 now
Continue? [Y/n]: y
...
```

After you've gone through the questions, Amanda grabs the stuff off the tape for you (in this example, it restores files rooted at /tmp; if you don't like this, use lcd to change the local working directory). Remember that restores often take a while.

Access the online help for amrecover with the help command; it's fairly terse, but can give you a little hint when needed.

Relevant man pages: amrecover (8), amrestore (8)

Using Amanda Log Files for Recoveries if amrecover Is Unavailable

If the Amanda utilities amrecover and amrestore are unavailable, you can pull archives directly off tapes. To do so quickly, you need access to the log files (of course, you should be familiar with their diagnostics already).

Once you've found one (we'll call it *logfile*) with the appropriate file date, find a line near the beginning that reads like this:

```
START taper datestamp 19991110 label Daily05 tape 0
```

This line tells you which tape to use. Now you must figure out which file number on the tape is the one you're looking for, so find the parts of *logfile* that relate to the tape:

```
# grep 'SUCCESS taper' logfile > /tmp/stuff
```

Now you must find the line that corresponds to the machine and directory you want to recover. To do this fairly quickly in vi, use view /tmp/stuff (to invoke vi read-only), search for the directory with the /dir command, and when the cursor is on the proper line, press CTRL-G. The line number appears at the bottom of the editor.

Once you've found this, you've found the file number on the tape—since Amanda indexes the tape with the first file (which is 0), the file number should be the same as the line number.

8.5 Crash Recovery

It may sound a little hackneyed, but don't panic if you run into a serious problem with your system. Short of someone doing a little "fine-tuning" on your hard drive with a sledgehammer, getting your system back online is just a matter of putting files back in place.

Before you jump into action to fix a system problem, make sure you have a very clear idea what is wrong and how to fix it. For example, if you deleted your init program, you should plan on booting the machine so you can access the filesystem (and a copy of init) and put init back. But don't get carried away with planning: More often than not, a method you thought would work perfectly just won't.

The Rescue CD-ROM

In addition to containing tools that other sections of this book reference, the bundled CD-ROM can boot up your system with a bunch of crash recovery tools.

Creating a Boot Floppy

To boot off the CD-ROM drive, you need to have either an ATAPI drive with a motherboard BIOS that supports CD-ROM bootups (all modern motherboards do), or a SCSI controller with an on-board BIOS that supports a CD-ROM boot. If you don't have a supporting BIOS, you can make a boot floppy that works like the CD. To do so, find the boot.bin file in the boot directory on the CD. This is a 1.44MB floppy image. Under Linux, you can dd it to your first floppy drive with

```
# dd if=boot.bin of=/dev/fd0 bs=18k
```

As mentioned in section 7.3, floppy drives and disks tend to be slow and unreliable, but you can get them to work reasonably well with the superformat program in the fdutils package.

You can also use one of the RAWRITE programs supplied on the CD to write the image to the floppy in DOS. There are two versions (rawrite1 and rawrite2); see the README file in the tools/rawrite directory for more details.

Booting Up

The boot image supports all processors (but does not include math coprocessor emulation). It also includes standard disks, SCSI disks, tapes, and CD-ROM support, as well as a number of controller drivers, including the Adaptec AIC7*xxx* controllers (*x*9*x*0 series) and NCR/Symbios controllers. It does not support non-ATAPI or non-SCSI drives.

PROBLEM 100

Symptoms: The kernel can't find the disk or the CD-ROM drive.

Problem: The image on the CD doesn't support the device.

Fix: See the Different Boot Kernels subsection.

When you boot off the CD-ROM, a message comes up:

```
Linux Problem Solver
Bootable CD
boot:
```

boot: is a prompt from the SYSLINUX system; it's not LILO, but resembles it. The kernel image is named linux, and you can pass options to the kernel in the same way as with LILO.

If you just press ENTER at the boot prompt, the kernel loads and runs a system from a small *boot image* (the same image you get when you make a floppy disk). This system includes a small init with two virtual consoles. The first console runs a setup script, and the second (accessed with the usual ALT-F2) starts a shell.

The setup script asks if you want to mount the CD, and proceeds to mount it if possible. The boot image contains a number of small, stripped-down utilities (in case you need the CD-ROM drive for another purpose, or just can't use it), but the CD contains many full versions of programs.

You'll notice other differences between the CD and the boot image once you start using them. For example, the shell that comes on the boot image is a very small sh version that doesn't offer command-line editing and other stuff, but the CD includes a full-fledged bash. The same is true of text editors.

How you go about trying to fix your system is up to you. Sometimes you won't need to do much to get your system back in action. For example, if your CD-ROM is complicated to set up, you can just jump to the other virtual console with ALT-F2 after booting up and do a quick fix. However, some utilities aren't available from the boot image.

Using an Intermediate RAM Disk

If you need to use a utility on the CD-ROM along with a file on another CD, you can create a new, empty RAM disk and copy the utility from the boot CD-ROM to the RAM disk. Then you can unmount the boot CD-ROM, mount the other CD, and run the utility from the RAM disk.

There are preconfigured RAM disks of any size from 1MB to 16MB. To attach a 5MB RAM disk to /rd, type this:

```
# rdmount /rd 5
```

The rdmount program is simply a script in the bin directory of the CD-ROM.

ACKNOWLEDGMENT *We based the floppy boot image for the CD on the install/rescue image that comes with the Debian distribution. We appreciate the Debian team's efforts at creating a lucid, easy-to-modify image.*

Different Boot Kernels

If you have some peculiar hardware that the kernel on the CD doesn't support, you can make your own boot image. This image is a FAT filesystem; you just make a kernel that supports your device, then you replace the original on the disk image. First compile a suitable kernel as described in Chapter 7, including RAM disk and initrd support. Then mount the disk image like this:

```
# mount -t msdos boot.bin /mnt -oloop=/dev/loop0,blocksize=1024
```

To make this command work, you need the loop-back device and msdos filesystem support. If you don't have loop-back device support and you don't want to fool around with it, dd the image to a floppy and mount the floppy directly, or just work with it via an operating system like MS-DOS. The blocksize parameter specifies the loop-back device's block size.

Next replace the `linux` file in `/mnt` (or wherever you've mounted the image) with the kernel you just made. Your new image is now ready.

If you want to change the root RAM disk image (for example, adding a utility to it), the file containing the image is `root.bin`, a Minix filesystem compressed with gzip. You can use the same loop-back device and the line above (replacing `boot.bin` with `root.bin` and `msdos` with `minix`) to mount the root image (make sure it's decompressed).

8.6 Fixing Filesystems

The cornerstone of repairing a damaged filesystem is the `fsck` program. It goes over the entire filesystem structure, finds errors, and repairs them if you want it to. It normally runs at boot time; because filesystem errors can lead to very serious problems, Unix systems make extra sure of filesystem stability.

`fsck` itself is a wrapper program that calls the appropriate `fsck` for the filesystem. The `fsck` for a Minix filesystem, for example, will not work on a second extended filesystem. The real `fsck` programs are usually located in `/sbin` and named `fsck.`*fs* where *fs* is the target filesystem; two standard `fsck`s on most systems are `fsck.ext2` (usually just a hard link to `e2fsck`) and `fsck.minix`.

Operating fsck Manually

At times you'll have to run `fsck` manually—don't let this alarm you. Just run the following (for example, if the partition you need to check is `/dev/hda1`):

fsck /dev/hda1

`fsck` checks `/dev/hda1` for errors and if it finds any, asks if you'd like to fix them. It does this on an error-by-error basis, which can get very tedious if the disk has a lot of problems. Use `fsck -p` to force yes answers to the questions.

If you have an `/etc/fstab` available, you can make `fsck` look up a device. In this example, `fsck` looks up the `/home` device:

fsck /home

When no `/etc/fstab` is available, and you can't remember the device name of the desired filesystem, use `fdisk -l` to list the current partition table (along with the device names) of a disk.

NOTE   *Do not run* `fsck` *on a currently-mounted filesystem unless it's mounted read-only.*

PROBLEM 101

Symptom: fsck can't find a superblock or filesystem on a partition.

Problem: You have a bad superblock.

Fix: Superblocks contain data critical to the layout of a filesystem on the disk, and fsck needs to look at one of them to go over the partition. Creating a filesystem also creates a number of superblock backups. Normally fsck just looks at the normal superblock, but if it can't find that superblock, it uses fsck's -b option, like this:

```
# fsck -b 8193
```

This points fsck to another superblock. Normally, there are superblock backups at 8193 and 16385.

PROBLEM 102

Symptom: You're unable to remount / read-only.

Problem: mount wants to change files to remount a filesystem.

Fix: For /, use

```
# mount -n -o ro,remount /
```

The Clean Bit

Many filesystems have a *clean bit*, a parameter set to true when you mount the filesystem read-only or unmounted. The bit signals when the filesystem is in good condition and doesn't need a check. This is most relevant at boot time, because people don't want to wait hours for their computers to start up. However, it can sometimes get in the way if there's a problem the operating system doesn't know about (such as bad memory). If this is the case, use fsck's -f option.

Relevant man pages: fsck (8), e2fsck (8)

tune2fs and debugfs

A program called tune2fs can sometimes resolve filesystem performance problems. These often stem from the previously mentioned maximal mount count (modified with tune2fs -c), plus the reserved blocks percentage (tune2fs -m). The manual clearly describes the rest of the options. As with fsck, don't use this on a currently mounted filesystem unless it's mounted as read-only.

PROBLEM 103

Symptom: Even though the filesystem is clean, a `maximal mount count` `exceeded` error forces full `fsck` at every boot, causing long boot times.

Problem: You've exceeded the maximal mount count; a forced check doesn't reset the counter.

Fix: Go to single-user mode (for example, with `init s`), `umount -a`, `remount / read-only` (see above), and run `fsck` manually. This problem should not occur in modern installations.

PROBLEM 104

Symptom: Even though you shut down the machine properly, the filesystem is always dirty upon reboot and requires a check.

Problem: Unclean shutdown.

Fix: This problem can be a little time-consuming to track down, but you can usually do it without *too* many headaches. Try this:

1. Look at the single-user mode `init` runlevel (it will be in some `rc*.d` directory—check `/etc/inittab` as described in Chapter 1) and make sure there are no huge differences between it and the runlevel for reboot (if there are, it's likely that you don't have the reboot runlevel set correctly in `/etc/inittab`). The single-user mode version will start up a shell instead of a `reboot`.

2. Go to single-user mode with `init s` (or whatever the appropriate runlevel is). Single-user mode should kill all processes and try to umount all filesystems except for `/`.

3. Verify the last step by executing `umount -a`. If nothing else is running, you'll just get a message saying that `/` is busy. If you get more messages, your reboot `init` configuration is probably not killing processes and unmounting all filesystems properly. If you do get that message and everything seems fine, skip to Step 5.

4. Check that the file before the actual `reboot` command (which should be the very last file that starts with S in the `rc*.d` directory for reboot) has `umount -a` and `mount -n -o ro,remount /` commands, in that order. On Debian systems, for example, this appears in `/etc/rc6.d`; the first file (actually a link) is S40umountfs, and you do the reboot with S90reboot. The commands should be in the files (unless someone removed them by hand), but a test inside the files may prevent the commands from running; if this is the case, find out and fix whatever is causing the tests to fail.

   You might also have a problem with lingering processes. Run a full process listing with `ps auxww`. There shouldn't be all that many processes active. See if any on the list is running inappropriately in single-user mode (only some low-numbered kernel processes should use this mode). Kill off any process that looks wrong, then try the `umount -a` again.

   Once you've found the culprit, you have two ways to turn it off during system shutdown. The proper way (described in Chapter 1) is through the `rc*.d` convention for stopping services, scripts, or links to scripts starting with K; this convention makes `init` pass the `stop` argument to the script. The other way to turn off the problematic process is to do a generic kill-off by sending signals to all processes (for example, with `killall5 -15` followed by `killall5 -9`). Most distributions do this near the end of their shutdown configuration (for example, in Debian it's `/etc/rc6.d/S20sendsigs`). So if you see a problem here, the process is probably going into a bad zombie stage, which usually indicates driver problems, but also results from not giving it enough time to shut down.

5. If none of the above seems relevant, you may just need to allow more time for shutdown. Do so with a `sleep` inside one of the `init.d` scripts after you've killed all processes.

If you have really serious problems with a filesystem that `fsck` can't fix, the `debugfs` utility can help by performing low-level actions. Take special care when using `debugfs` commands that change the filesystem; `debgfs` allows you to clear blocks and wipe out inodes.

Like `tune2fs`, `debugfs` has a good manual page. When you use `debugfs`, either you want to look at the filesystem's internal structure or the kernel is complaining about some bad inode that `fsck` can't seem to find. In the latter case (probably a result of bad memory corrupting a cache), you'll want `debugfs`' `clri` command.

Of course, you should not even think about having the filesystem mounted when using debugfs.

If you modify a filesystem with tune2fs or debugfs, run fsck on the filesystem to get rid of any inconsistencies your change may have brought about.

Relevant man pages: tune2fs (8), debugfs (8)

Recognizing and Repairing System File Problems

Half of the battle in getting a broken system up and running again is making sure the various files (usually in /etc) are correct, and getting them back into the right format if they aren't.

PROBLEM 105

Symptoms: You don't know the root password. Commands say they don't know who you are and ignore /etc/passwd.

Problem: You're having passwd file difficulties (corrupted file, missing entries, incorrect data, and so on).

Fix: If you don't know the root password, and you've got the root filesystem mounted from a rescue CD or some similar medium, you can delete the second field of root's /etc/passwd entry (but don't leave it this way for long):

```
root::0:0:Super-User:/:/bin/bash
```

This change allows you to log in as root without a password (the second field in the passwd file is the encrypted password). Check out /etc/shadow as well if you're using shadow passwords; you may need to make similar changes there.

If you somehow deleted the passwd file, get one started again with at least this (you can restore the rest later):

```
root::0:0:Super-User:/:/bin/bash
daemon:*:1:1:daemon:/usr/sbin:/bin/sh
```

Finally, check /etc/nsswitch.conf. You're probably looking for trouble if you don't have

```
passwd:        compat
```

or

```
passwd:        files
```

in there.

PROBLEM 106

Symptoms: The boot fails after mounting the root filesystem. You get a partial boot.

Problem: init errors.

Fix: Aside from deleting /sbin/init completely, in which case you're stuck with the task of putting it back, the most likely cause of init not starting is that you're mounting the wrong filesystem. Try giving the root=/dev/*devname* argument to LILO (or whatever you use to boot your kernel). If this doesn't work, either the filesystem is corrupt and you need to fix it, or you need to compile the correct filesystem driver (ext2) into your kernel.

On the other hand, if the root filesystem mounts but the system boots up only part of the way, there's some problem in one of the rc*.d directories. Device drivers or network failures often cause rc*.d problems. First make sure all of the files are actually in place. Look carefully at the boot messages to see if you can tell which one is failing. If you can't zero in on it, try renaming the start-up script links (in such a way that they don't start upon boot), then rebooting the system.

9

USER ENVIRONMENTS

9.1 Introduction

Do not underestimate the importance of solid, stable user environments: Incorrect user startup files and environments can make good internal system configurations useless. Poorly thought-out defaults and examples can produce bad paths, bad aliases, inefficiency, and confusion.

Another complication is the domino effect of bad startup files. Sometimes users who like to tinker with their environments are coming from another system, and they bring all their startup files with them. If they know what they're doing, that's fine. Unfortunately, they sometimes feel the urge to share their files with everyone, and soon you have a whole bunch of users wondering what happened to their environment and why they can't read mail anymore.

This kind of stuff happens to a certain extent no matter what you do, but you can reduce its frequency (and your workload) by giving people less incentive to change the user environment. That means writing default files so users don't give them much thought. This chapter will take you through shell and window configuration files and demonstrate some effective, simple samples that will not break over time.

9.2 Shell Startup Files: Basics

Messing around with a `.cshrc` or `.login` file is a good way to shoot yourself in the foot. For example, people sometimes put this in their startup files:

```
blah
blah
blah
..
..
exit
```

This situation warrants a problem box right off the bat.

PROBLEM 107

Symptom: The `exit` in a `.profile` (or some other startup file) unexpectedly logs you out.

Problem: You think shell startup files run in subshells.

Fix: Understand that shells, unless you explicitly tell them to start in a subshell, read and execute commands in startup files as they would on the command line.

When writing a shell startup file, you need to keep in mind that *a shell runs programs you tell it to run.*

That's the long and short of it. To run the programs, the shell needs to know the locations of the programs (that is, their paths), some environment settings the programs require, and maybe some shortcuts you can type in as commands. Keep shell environments simple: There's no need to check whether you're on Jupiter and get a weather report every time you start up a shell.

Systems administrators often use system default startup files to set environment variables that certain packages need to start properly. Most shells read a special auxiliary file (if it exists) before a user's start-up file; tcsh reads `csh.cshrc` in `/etc` prior to any `$HOME/.cshrc`, for example.

Setting the Path

The path is the most important part of a shell's startup file. You'll probably want it to include these directories, in this order:

```
/usr/local/bin
/usr/bin
```

Symptoms: Users wonder where environment variables come from and complain about being forced to use the default system startup files.

Problem: Using a shell's 'system default' startup file.

Fix: Use customized system startup files instead. Make the default startup files include some code like this excerpt from a default .profile:

```
# Read in some system-wide defaults
/usr/local/etc/sys-profile
```

Make sure that you document /usr/local/etc/sys-profile well, and don't make this file large—if it becomes too large (say, more than 10 lines that aren't comments), you're probably doing something wrong.

```
/bin
/usr/X11R6/bin
$HOME/bin
```

It also wouldn't hurt to include

```
/usr/local/sbin
/usr/sbin
/sbin
```

because programs like traceroute are in these directories, and users like to tinker with such utilities. However, you'd most likely be making a mistake to include anything else.

All user programs should be executable from one of the four bin directories listed above. If they aren't, don't change environments around to reflect where the programs are, because that makes the environments much more difficult to maintain. Instead, create symbolic links from the programs to /usr/local/bin.

You may also want to get rid of the /usr/X11R6/bin in the path and make symbolic links from the X programs to /usr/local/bin. The X11R6 name, after all, depends on X11R6 (X version 11, release 6), which some other version may supplant in future.

Dot (.)

Then there is the matter of the dot (.) in the path. Putting the dot in the path allows you to run programs in the current working directory without additional syntax (such as using ./ in front of the program name). The troublesome part here is that you could accidentally run a Trojan horse instead of, say, sl (if you mistype ls). You already know, of course, that you should never have the dot in root's path and never put it at the *front* of anyone's path.

A further problem arises if the dot is the last directory in a path. If a user is working on a program in the current directory with the same name as a program in the path, the user ends up running the wrong program. My advice is to keep the dot out of the path and just field those "Hey, I compiled this from program but I can't run it" questions as they come. Make a Frequently Asked Questions file if you have to.

Manual Page Paths

man uses the MANPATH environment variable, similar to the PATH environment variable, to find manual pages. You should set it to something like this:

```
/usr/local/man:/usr/man:/usr/X11R6/man:$HOME/man
```

Prompts

In general, putting the kitchen sink into a prompt is a bad idea. We've seen a lot of elaborate prompts, from cryptic five-letter symbolic strings to multi-line monstrosities, and they have one feature in common: People only use prompts to figure out whether the command they just typed in has finished or not. So our advice is to keep prompts clear and simple: They can usually include the host name (unless you have really long host names), the login name, and perhaps a command number.

Avoid goofy punctuation—characters like

```
{ } = & ? <word>
```

will cause confusion.

Also avoid using the shell's default prompt (that is, what a shell yields when you *don't* set any prompt in a startup file). Users often want to change the prompt, and they'll go to great lengths to do so (even if they don't need to). Havoc ensues when they modify their startup files without any guidance. To avoid this, create a simple prompt in the default shell startup file(s). Make it really obvious, as in this bash example, which yields *username*$ as the prompt:

```
# Make a simple prompt
PS1=$USER'\$ '
```

You may also want to provide one commented-out example of a more complicated option, like this:

```
# To put your current working directory in your prompt, try this:
# PS1='\w\$ '
```

Keep in mind that it's not a great idea to include the working directory in the prompt. The directory takes up a lot of real estate on a command line and can be quite distracting.

Aliases

You can easily get carried away with putting aliases in default files. It's all too tempting to provide a huge number of aliases and expect these aliases to help your users with day-to-day tasks and even familiarize themselves with the system. This is not a very good approach. Your aliases will not only have sparse online documentation, but if you intend them as universal shortcuts, they will discourage users from exploring Unix systems. Whatever you do, don't use aliases to start up big, complicated packages with special options—the packages won't work consistently and reliably. Instead, use shell script wrappers to force environment variables and options before starting the package itself.

That said, you should perhaps provide a small set of aliases in start-up files to serve as examples. Most users want a few comfortable shortcuts, and they'll want to know how to create them. If you have inexperienced users, you may wish to alias cp and mv to include the -i argument, but don't push it beyond that. Also, don't put aliases in any system startup files (this confuses users because they don't understand where the aliases come from).

Default Programs: Shells, Editors, and So On

Which default programs should you include in new user accounts? This section provides a brief overview and recommendations on the essentials.

Shells

Originally, the only two real choices for shells were sh and csh. Since the barebones sh was a bit trying as an interactive shell, csh quickly gained popularity as a login shell (with some carryover to tcsh), and it has stuck.

It's time to get rid of this habit. You should use bash as the login shell for all new users. The only real reason anyone ever used csh was because of its extra interactive features (such as command history). bash supports this stuff, and there are some very compelling reasons to use bash and not inflict csh or tcsh on people.

- Some users have a tendency to write shell scripts in their login shells because that's what they are used to. As a systems administrator, you should be more than aware that csh is a really awful tool for writing scripts. If you need serious convincing, have a look at http://www.faqs.org/faqs/unix-faq/shell/csh-whynot/.

- tcsh can be frustratingly slow because it tries to second-guess you all the time. It can also get behind on system updates, as evidenced by the fact that it needs a built-in rehash.

- bash uses GNU readline. Though readline is really kind of a beast, many people already know how to use it, and that familiarity counts in its favor.

- tcsh is not as standard on Linux systems as bash. It's true that on other flavors of Unix, bash doesn't come with the operating system, but tcsh doesn't, either.

- tcsh syntax is weak. If you think the single-quote and double-quote conventions are a bit funny under bash, just wait until you see what tcsh makes you do.

Yes, there are other shells out there, like ksh, zsh, es, and my personal favorite, rc, but none is as suitable for a beginning login shell as bash.

Editors

Yes, it's vi versus emacs again. Guess what? It doesn't really matter which one you give users, because they'll learn how to use either option soon enough. You should give them either vi or emacs, though—mostly for the sake of the users, who may move to other systems where they'll likely find one of these two options. After all, you don't want to put a needless obstacle in the way of your users. Not only that, but they may come back and bother you about how to install an unfamiliar editor on a new system.

That said, you should not provide large editor setup files. A little set showmatch in a .exrc file never hurt anyone, but avoid set showmode, autoindent, wrap margins, and so on because they actually change the editor's appearance and behavior.

Pagers

Unlike editors and shells, pagers (set with the PAGER environment variable) are fairly passive programs. All most users ever do with a pager is press the spacebar or ENTER key until they've read enough. A fairly good choice is less, with the LESS environment variable set to mie so the options -m, -i, and -e are on all of the time.

Relevant man page: less (1)

Mail and News Readers

In addition to the Netscape, you should offer users some options for mail and news readers. Two popular full-terminal screen readers are mutt and pine. Of these, the older one, pine, has more users, but don't let that keep you from recommending mutt for mail. emacs has a number of mail readers. Avoid elm, as it's currently evolving into even more of a fossil than the old Berkeley mail program.

As for news readers, the old standby is trn, but there are some doubts on its user friendliness. Alternatives include slrn and tin (and, of course, emacs and pine). Don't forget to go out and start a flame war on Usenet about which one you choose.

A Default User

A well-thought-out environment is worthless unless you test it. Let's face it—as the systems administrator, you probably won't rely on the user defaults. You may use some configuration close to it, but with a few alterations. That's why you need to create a default test user and make sure everything works.

The default user should have the same privileges as any user, except that for security reasons you should lock the account when you're not testing it. The home directory's contents should be identical to what a new user gets. When you make changes to the default environment, unlock the test account, log in as the test user, and test the following:

- Try a bunch of file commands in /tmp.

- Make sure that both vi and emacs work.

- Send and receive mail.

- Run Netscape (with Java and JavaScript).

If all of these work properly, delete any new files you may have created (like a Mail or .netscape directory), lock the default user account again, and make sure the files that you just tested are the ones all new users get. Take a careful inventory of the files in the test user's home directory; tar them into an archive if you want.

Default Permissions

The only question here is whether you should make home directories default to mode 700 with a umask of 077 (which creates files that only the user can read), or mode 755 with a umask of 022 (world-readable). In an ideal world, all new users would learn about permissions and chmod the first day they receive a Unix account. But since this is unrealistic, you need to make a decision about what type of users you have. Certainly, email and Netscape caches should stay unreadable (these programs take care of that), but what about other files?

If, for example, you have an academic system with both professors and students, the professors probably want world read access turned off from day one. However, they may require group read access for collaborative efforts. On the other hand, users of a small company's network may not have to worry about students getting a sneak preview of next Friday's exam, and may find it counterproductive not to have complete access to all work files.

Commands in Shell Startup Files

People tend to do too much with commands in shell startup files (that is, check certain parameters on the machine or setup files). This cripples startup speed, which can lead to all kinds of frustration (see Section 9.4, on tcsh and csh). Large shell scripts also slow down shell interaction.

Each command in a shell startup file requires creating a new process, loading and executing the program, and transferring the exit status. If you don't specify an absolute path name, the shell also has to look for the program in the current command path. For single commands, this is usually no big deal, but multiple commands may pile up and noticeably slow the whole session down. To keep the process as simple, small, and fast as possible, avoid executing any programs inside shell startup files, opting for faster built-in shell features when they're available. If you must use external programs, use only small ones that run quickly; avoid long pipelines.

The test Command

You know the obvious command invocations in shell start-up files, such as this one:

```
FOO=`cat /var/run/blah.pid`
```

Then there is the matter of the test command—a command in /bin, also identified by the left square bracket ([)—which often appears in start-up files. Innocent-looking tests like

```
if [ "$FOO" = 4 ]; then
  stuff
  ..
fi
```

actually use the bracket form of the test command to figure out whether $FOO is equal to 4. Try it yourself on the command line (remember that $? is the exit status of the last command that ran):

```
$ [ 4 = 4 ]
$ echo $?
0
```

You can easily convert a test like ["$FOO" = 4] into a form that uses a shell built-in—avoiding execution of external commands:

```
case "$FOO" in
    4) stuff
      ..
    ;;
esac
```

If you're testing parameters and configuration data in a start-up script, use the case built-in to sh/bash (and the switch/case in csh/tcsh), a fairly powerful mechanism for comparing strings. It also supports the asterisk (*) as a wildcard and the pipe (|) for multiple matches:

```
case $blah in
  this|that*|the*other)
```

```
        stuff
          ..
      ;;
esac
```

Some of you may be wondering, "Isn't [a built-in to bash?" Yes, as a matter of fact—which means you shouldn't experience a performance penalty when you use it in .bashrc. We bring this up because you don't want to set a bad example for shell scripts (which may run on other systems' /bin/sh, with virtually the same syntax as .bashrc) or for other shells.

A Few Startup File Don'ts

To avoid headache and frustration with your start-up files, follow these rules:

- Don't put X commands in shell startup files.

- Don't set the DISPLAY environment variable in shell startup files.

- Don't set the terminal type in a default shell startup file.

- Don't give default shell startup files without good comments.

- Don't print anything in shell startup files.

- Don't put xeyes in default X Window System startup files.

9.3 bash and sh

One confusing thing about bash is that it reads any of a multitude of configuration files upon startup: .bash_profile, .profile, .bash_login, and .bashrc, among others. So which one do you use?

Unfortunately, bash uses different files depending on the *kind* of shell it thinks it is. When a user interacts with the Unix command-line interface, the user's shell is called an *interactive shell.* bash starts as an *interactive login shell* on a terminal when /bin/login invokes it (the traditional Unix login method). On the other hand, an example of an *interactive non-login shell* is one running inside xterm (unless you explicitly tell xterm to run a login shell).

For login shells, bash looks for a number of startup script files and *only* runs the first one it finds. The search order is first .bash_profile, then .bash_login, then .profile. bash also runs any commands in /etc/profile prior to the files in the user's home directory (we've already noted that having a file like /etc/profile on your system isn't a good idea).

For the other interactive shells, bash looks in .bashrc for commands. You'll encounter many arguments among systems adminstrators over how to run a shell, and consequently which startup files to choose. Since this book advocates simplicity, you might guess that our recommendation is to treat the login and non-login shells as one and the same.

We recommend this because the majority of users no longer log in through /bin/login. Most users have individual workstations that run xdm (or similar facility), bypassing /bin/login. Any shells starting up will use whatever files the non-login shell uses. If you use, say, .bash_profile, the settings there won't take effect for non-login shells, and you'll be wondering why the path is set wrong, why aliases don't work, and so on.

To avoid these problems, make your startup file .bashrc, and link it with ln -s to .bash_profile. There is no reason why a user's shell should behave one way when it's running in an xterm and another way as a remote login.

Here is an example of a bare-bones .bashrc including comments:

```
# Command and manual paths
PATH=/usr/local/bin:/usr/bin:/bin:/usr/X11R6/bin:$HOME/bin
MANPATH=/usr/local/man:/usr/man

# PS1 is the prompt. Substitutions include:
# \u username          \h hostname       \w directory
# \! history number    \s shell name
PS1='\h\$ '

# EDITOR and VISUAL control the editor that programs like less
# and Pnews invoke when editing a file.
EDITOR=emacs
VISUAL=emacs

# PAGER is the name of a paging program to view text files or streams
with.
# The man command uses this, for example.
PAGER=less
LESS=mei

# Shell variables are not environment variables until you export them.
export PATH MANPATH PS1 EDITOR VISUAL PAGER LESS

# umask 022 means most files will be created world-readable by default.
umask 022
```

If you need to run extra commands when the shell is interactive, run them as follows:

```
case "$-" in
   *i*)    command 1
           command 2
           ..
           ;;
esac
```

You should only really need to do this if you have the BASH_ENV variable set to the startup file, since noninteractive shells normally don't read any startup files.

Note that the above code exploits bash's built-in $- variable, which includes an i if the shell is interactive (other shells require you to take strange actions, such as checking to see whether the prompt exists). When you use a case statement with pattern matching, you incur no performance penalty for running external commands like test.

bash Aliases

You set aliases in bash with

```
alias newname=command
```

Remember that aliases are simply text substitutions. If you need to do something more complicated (such as pass parameters to an alias), you should probably use a shell script instead.

You'll find these aliases standard with many installations:

```
# A few aliases that change cp and mv to ask for confirmation when you're about
to clobber a
# file. If you don't like this, just remove them.
alias cp='cp -i'
alias mv='mv -i'
```

9.4 tcsh and csh

Still a staple among those used to older systems, tcsh is an enhanced version of the C shell. It owes its rise in popularity to its command-line editing and interactive features, which csh lacks.

Even though this book suggests dumping tcsh in favor of bash as the default shell for new users, you should probably write default environments for tcsh because so many people are used to it.

tcsh first looks for .tcshrc as a start-up file; if that doesn't exist, it tries .cshrc. The reason for .tcshrc is to let you enable tcsh extensions without worrying about csh breaking. There is no good reason to use .tcshrc, though—stick with .cshrc. There aren't many csh users out there anymore (and on most Linux distributions, csh is just a link to tcsh), and furthermore, you can test to see if you're running tcsh inside a .cshrc without causing speed or compatibility problems (we'll get to an example soon).

It's important to optimize .cshrc files because some programs execute a user's shell in order to start other processes. (The old Berkeley mail program offers an example—it had a habit of spawning shells if you asked it to use a pager other than the default.) Because csh and tcsh stupidly read the .cshrc file every time they start up, slow .cshrc files can make a simple task, like reading mail, painfully slow.

Optimize .cshrc files as you would a .bashrc file, by eliminating external command invocations and getting rid of unnecessary tests. In addition, keep the PATH environment variable especially short and simple.

A .cshrc file like the example .bashrc (see the example in Section 9.3) would read like this, including aliases:

```
# Command and manual paths
setenv PATH /usr/local/bin:/usr/bin:/bin:/usr/X11R6/bin:${HOME}/bin
setenv MANPATH /usr/local/man:/usr/man


# EDITOR and VISUAL control which editor programs like less and Pnews
# invoke when editing a file.
setenv EDITOR emacs
setenv VISUAL emacs


# PAGER is the name of a paging program to view text files or streams
with.
# The man command uses this, for example.
setenv PAGER less
setenv LESS mei


# Set the prompt. Substitutions in tcsh include:
# %n username       %m hostname       %~ directory
# %h history number


# First check to see if the shell is interactive.
switch ($?prompt)
    case 1:
    # If so, see if we're running tcsh or csh.
    switch ($?tcsh)
      case 0:
        # A simple prompt for csh.
        set prompt="% "
      breaksw
      case 1:
        # In tcsh, this expands to hostname%
        set prompt="%m%% "
      breaksw
    endsw
    # You may also want to run commands for interactive shells here
    # (aliases, terminal checks, and so on)
```

```
        breaksw
endsw

# umask 022 means most files will be created world-readable by default.
umask 022
```

For the most part, this example resembles the example.bashrc in the previous section. The prompt is somewhat complicated because we're checking to see whether we have an interactive shell, and if so, whether we're using tcsh or csh. The distinction between interactive and noninteractive is important with tcsh and csh, because alias definitions and terminal modifications in noninteractive shells can cause errors and incur performance penalties.

PROBLEM 111

Symptom: Interactive shell commands in .cshrc unexpectedly run upon startup of noninteractive shells.

Problem: .cshrc does not check to see if the shell is interactive or sets the prompt before the interactive check.

Fix: Make sure the prompt variable checks to see if the shell is interactive (compare with $?prompt in the .cshrc example above). If you do this and the interactive commands still run unexpectedly, see whether you accidentally set the prompt somewhere before this check (make sure it's not in any .login file).

As with the .profile stuff in bash, tcsh reads a .login file if it considers a shell a login. Try to avoid using .login files, since they confuse matters when it comes to windowing systems.

9.5 A Few X Window Start-up Files

In addition to the shell start-up files, certain files related to the X Window System tend to cause additional problems when a user logs in: .xinitrc, .xsession, and .Xdefaults. In this section, we'll go over these files, and we'll also talk about the X Display Manager (xdm), used for console logins. We will *not* talk about how to set up a window manager. If you want advice on that, here it is: Make it as plain and simple as possible, because people will wonder about your bad taste if you embellish. Seriously, though, adding a huge number of obscure options will just annoy users. Furthermore, you'll find it frustrating to maintain the configuration every time a new version of the window manager comes out, probably breaking all of your customized options.

X Startup: .xinitrc and .xsession

The difference between .xinitrc and .xsession is how you start the X Window System. If you run xinit or startx to start the server from a console, you'll need a .xinitrc file; xdm-based systems use .xsession files.

Starting X with startx or xinit is a pretty roundabout method: First you have to log in to a console, then you use another command to start the X server and clients (such as the window manager). Unfortunately, because of the many difficulties with PC graphics hardware, Linux installations often leave X server configuration until later, which means they boot into a console mode and expect the user to take it from there. As a consequence, the systems administrator never configures xdm, and gets used to starting the X server with xinit or startx.

On the other hand, xdm starts up the X server at boot time and presents the user with a login window. Because starting the X server is usually the most system-intensive part of beginning a session, xdm saves a lot of time (see the X Startup: xdm section below for how to configure xdm).

.xinitrc and .xsession Files

There really isn't much difference between .xinitrc and .xsession files—they both start a window manager and some clients. These differences only matter in terms of X terminals (issues such as where the console messages go). To get around this, you can check for an X terminal in a startup file, but they're becoming increasingly obsolete.

Here's a sample .xsession or .xinitrc file:

```
#!/bin/sh

# The background color and foreground colors (dark blue/white)
BG='#003'
FG=white

# Start up a terminal.
xterm -geometry 80x24+50+50 &

# Mail notification program.
xbiff -geometry -100+0 -foreground $FG -background $BG &

# Clock.
xclock -geometry -0+0 -foreground $FG -background $BG -hands $FG &

# Set the background color to a dark blue.
xsetroot -solid $BG

# Start the window manager.
twm
```

The BG and FG variables are a cheap way of making the desktop uniform. Nothing much starts here, just a clock and xbiff. Avoid starting especially slow applications, such as file browsers and Netscape.

The last item in the script generally controls a logout (here it's the window manager, twm). When that program exits, the X session ends. All other continuously running clients such as xclock and xbiff go into the background with an ampersand (&).

PROBLEM 112

Symptom: Users log in (with xdm login) and get kicked out again.

Problem: A bad .xsession won't let the user log in anymore.

Fix: First, press F1 instead of the ENTER key after entering the password. This drops the user into *failsafe mode*, which runs an xterm. Then find out what's wrong with the .xsession file; more often than not, it's an inadvertent ampersand at the end of the last command in the list.

The Window Manager

We can't recommend which window manager to use. We selected twm because it comes with X11R6. However, twm can feel pretty inadequate on modern systems. It doesn't really matter if you choose a window manager that has a Windows, mwm, or NEXTSTEP look and feel, or a totally different option, like Enlightenment. The crucial factors are stability and ease of maintenance.

PROBLEM 113

Symptom: You get kicked out of an X session without running the .xsession.

Problem: You have a nonexecutable .xsession file.

Fix: Run chmod u+x .xsession. Also note how to get into fail-safe mode (in the previous problem box).

X Startup: xdm

The X Display Manager (xdm) offers a way to log into X directly and avoid the lengthy startup of the X server. The xdm daemon starts the X server, places a login box on it, and upon login runs some startup programs (.xsession or a system default). When the user finishes the session, xdm does some cleanup and presents the login box again.

xdm Configuration Files

A number of configuration files control xdm; the default location off the X installation root is lib/X11/xdm, so on most Linux machines you'll find xdm's configuration files in /usr/X11R6/lib/X11/xdm.

If you're going to mess around with the xdm configuration (as you probably should, since its defaults aren't very good), make another xdm directory somewhere else and copy all files in the default xdm directory over to the new one.

The first item to change is the xdm-config file (in the new directory you just created, of course). Find these lines:

```
DisplayManager.errorLogFile:    /usr/X11R6/lib/X11/xdm/xdm-errors
DisplayManager.pidFile:         /usr/X11R6/lib/X11/xdm/xdm-pid
DisplayManager.keyFile:         /usr/X11R6/lib/X11/xdm/xdm-keys
```

Change them to the following:

```
DisplayManager.errorLogFile:    /var/log/xdm-errors
DisplayManager.pidFile:         /var/run/xdm.pid
DisplayManager.keyFile:         /var/run/xdm.keys
```

Then create the directory /var/run/xdmauth with mode 700, and add these two lines:

```
DisplayManager.authDir:         /var/run/xdmauth
DisplayManager.requestPort:     0
```

In the rest of the lines, such as

```
DisplayManager.servers:         /usr/X11R6/lib/X11/xdm/Xservers
```

change /usr/X11R6/lib/X11/xdm to the directory you created. For example, if you chose /usr/local/etc/xdm for the new location of xdm-config (the file you're editing now), change the above line to this:

```
DisplayManager.servers:         /usr/local/etc/xdm/Xservers
```

Now remove the Xaccess file and replace it with an empty file. This tells xdm not to let anyone but the local server have a login window. You may want to use ipchains (described in Chapter 2) to turn off all incoming traffic on the xdmcp port (known to have security exploit problems).

The Xresources file contains a bunch of definitions, including the setup for failsafe mode. The only features you may want to change here are the colors and fonts of the login box.

Xsetup_0 runs programs auxiliary to the login box for display :0. By default, it contains code resembling this:

```
xconsole -geometry 480x130-0-0 -daemon -notify -verbose -fn fixed
 -exitOnFail
```

You can make a few good additions:

```
xsetroot -solid '#003'
xset dpms 600 1200 6000
```

The xsetroot command sets the background to some better option than the awful stippled default, and the xset dpms command turns on the Display Power Management System (DPMS), to shut the monitor off when you haven't touched the machine for a while.

The Xsession file runs after a user logs in. This shell script runs the user's .xsession file to retrieve a custom startup, if one exists; if the file is not available, Xsession starts a default environment. Here you should make a few modifications. Find this final part:

```
if [ -f "$startup" ]; then
        exec "$startup"
else
        if [ -f "$resources" ]; then
                xrdb -load "$resources"
        fi
        exec xsm
fi
```

Change it to this:

```
if [ -x "$startup" ]; then
        $SHELL -c $startup
else
        if $SHELL -c /bin/true; then
            xterm -geometry 80x24+0+0 &
            twm
        fi
fi
```

The $SHELL -c parts perform two tasks: They check for a valid login shell (so users with no access to the machine can't log in), and they run shell startup files if the user's shell wants to (for example, tcsh reads its startup files at every invocation). We've gotten rid of xsm because it's a feeble attempt at creating a flexible, friendly user environment, and no one really uses it. Make sure to change twm to your default window manager (or replace the xterm and twm lines to an invocation of a systemwide default .xsession file).

To wrap it up, start xdm with your new configuration using the -config option. If your new xdm-config file is in /usr/local/etc/xdm-config, use

```
# xdm -config /usr/local/etc/xdm-config
```

Relevant man page: xdm (1)

X Resources

X resources are a type of preferences for X Window System applications, although not all X programs use them. You'll generally find them in two places: *application default* (*app-default*) files and users' .Xdefault files. They are plain text files, with entries on single lines. Here is a sample entry for changing the xterm text font:

```
XTerm.vt100.font:     -b&h-lucidatypewriter-medium-r-*-*-14-*-*-*-*-*-*-*
```

The resource specification on the left consists of a bunch of classes and names in a hierarchy. Sometimes it's well designed; sometimes it leaves a little to be desired. The so-called *application class name* (here, XTerm) is the first. A program's app-defaults filename is the application class name (that is, if the program has an app-defaults file). Each X program has a different application class name, chosen by the programmer. The rest of the resource specification (here, .vt100.font) is a series of various *widget class names* and subclass names, ending with a name of a property (a *widget* is a partition of an X application's appearance; it can be a grouping of other widgets, or a single element, such as a button).

PROBLEM 115

Symptoms: Applications look hideous. You encounter unexpected changes in applications other than the one you're trying to modify. X applications stop working.

Problem: You're using * to start a line in an X resource file.

Fix: This is one of the worst things you can put in an .Xdefaults file:

```
*foreground: blue
```

Because this matches all applications' class names (and the widget class names underneath), be ready for a lot of blue windows. Find the full name of the specific widget you want; tools like editres can help you.

Finding Widget Class Names with editres

Figuring out a widget class name is usually the hardest part of changing that class's setting. Manual pages usually help, but sometimes it's just not that easy; they may talk about a name only as the last portion of a class hierarchy. When you just can't track a name down and you're willing to tear the entire widget tree apart, bring out the big guns in the form of a program called editres. You can also use editres to figure out undocumented settings for commercial programs.

Although it comes with most modern X distributions, editres is not well known. It's a somewhat crufty GUI for navigating the resources in X widget trees. Start it up without any arguments. When you get the window, pull down the **Commands** menu and select **Get Tree** (see Figure 9-1). The mouse pointer then changes to a cross. Move it to a simple application that's running on your desktop (xclock, for example), then click. The editres window responds by showing a tree of names. If the tree is too large to fit in the entire window, use the map box in the upper left corner.

Click on one of the leaf names on the right (such as "clock" for the xclock tree) to invert it, then select **Show Resource Box** from the **Commands** menu. A window pops up showing all the resource names under that leaf—but that's not all (see Figure 9-2). Select one that looks promising (like the foreground setting in xclock.clock—let's say you're having trouble with xclock's foreground color). If you want to change the resource value of the current program (and you don't mind too much if the program crashes), type an option (such as red for xclock.clock.foreground) in the box at the bottom, to the right of Enter Resource Value. Click on **Apply** to see if this actually changes the program. To get rid of the Resource Box window, click the close button, conveniently labeled as the **Popdown Resource Box** button.

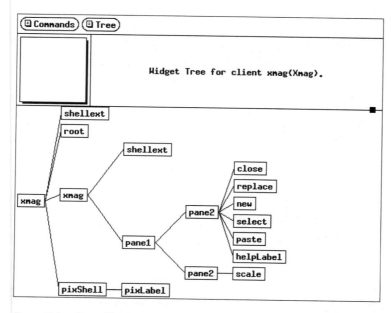

Figure 9-1: editres, like many Xaw programs, is not known for aesthetics

For a good time, try using `editres` on Netscape version 4—but only when you have nothing better to do.

Activating X Resources

One of the more confusing aspects of X resources is how to activate them. It's really not that hard. You just put entries in a .Xdefaults file and start the application. Unfortunately, startup scripts tend to use xrdb to force the server to store X resources for a session, overriding the .Xdefaults and app-defaults files.

xrdb works through a mechanism called the RESOURCE_MANAGER of the X server, which presumably makes it easier for remote X applications (sent to a display other than the local machine's) to adjust to the local quirks of the X server. However, overriding .Xdefaults and app-defaults files is a such a serious annoyance that you'll start to wonder whether letting the X server store its own resources was such a great idea in the first place.

To see if an X Window session has used xrdb, enter this:

```
$ xrdb -query
```

To get rid of all xrdb-supplied resources all at once:

```
$ xrdb -remove
```

If you don't see any effect, use the appres command to list the current resources for an application. For xterm, for example, you would use this:

```
$ appres XTerm
```

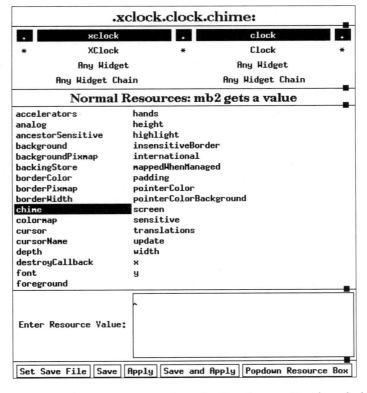

Figure 9-2: The Resource Box in editres: Popdown Resource Box closes the box

XUSERFILESEARCHPATH

The environment variable XUSERFILESEARCHPATH causes an X application to look in a place *in addition* to the usual app-defaults search path. If, for example, you want to put files containing application defaults (say, XTerm) into $HOME/lib/app-defaults, put this line in .bashrc or .cshrc:

```
XUSERFILESEARCHPATH=$HOME/lib/app-defaults/%N%C%S
export XUSERFILESEARCHPATH
```

A Touch of Color

Ever wonder why, in spite of the fact that all sorts of files in /usr/X11R6/lib/X11/app-defaults end with -color, your programs still appear in monochrome? Try this on the command line:

```
$ XUSERFILESEARCHPATH=/usr/X11R6/lib/X11/app-defaults/%N-color%S
$ export XUSERFILESEARCHPATH
```

Then run a program like `oclock` or `editres`. So why isn't the %C *customization resource* set to `-color` for color displays, you ask? Well, that's a good question—and we don't have an answer.

XFILESEARCHPATH

Steer clear of the environment variable `XFILESEARCHPATH`. This is a complete and absolute override of the normal app-defaults path. The only real reason to set this variable is when you're explicitly trying to *avoid* loading X resources from a certain place. Its specification is like that of `XUSERFILESEARCHPATH`.

If you really want to see a horrendous manual page on this stuff, have a look at XtResolvePathname (3).

Default .Xdefaults Files

What should be in a default `.Xdefaults` file? Probably only this, which adds some comfort to `xterm`:

```
XTerm.vt100.font:    -b&h-lucidatypewriter-medium-r-*-*-14-*-*-*-*-*-*-*
XTerm.vt100.scrollBar:    on
```

The more customization you add to users' default `.Xdefaults` files, the greater chance you'll make a mistake or enter some option that, once outdated, makes applications look terrible or otherwise go awry.

A Final Word on Simplicity

Throughout this book, we've advocated simplicity. Whether it's because log configuration files don't hold up well over package upgrades, or because more bells and whistles means more can break, the overall goal is saving your time. In this chapter, simplicity is especially important because the default startup files for new users greatly affect how they learn the system. If you give them a very complicated setup that malfunctions at the drop of a hat, they'll come to you for help more often than if you give them a setup they can understand quickly.

But don't remove all of your files in the ultimate pursuit of simplicity!

LEXICON

alias   A type of shell shortcut designed to reduce typing (different than a
mail alias or shell function).

Amanda   A free automated backup system.

antialiasing   A method of pixel interpolation used to smooth out "jaggies" in
graphics.

automatic kernel module loader   A kernel facility that loads kernel modules
as needed. Useful for keeping the size of the core kernel low.

bitbucket   A Unix slang term. Any piece of data thrown away goes to the bitbucket. The term can also refer to /dev/null, a character device that
throws away any input it receives.

block device   A type of device where the interface is in fixed-length blocks.

boot image   A bootable image (usually of a floppy disk) that contains a kernel.

Bourne shell   /bin/sh. The standard shell on Unix systems; a standard for
shell scripting. On Linux systems, /bin/sh is a link to /bin/bash.

CHAP (Cryptographic Handshake Authentication Protocol)   A type of
authentication for PPP.

character device   A type of device where the interface is character-wise.

clean bit   A flag that gets set when the filesystem is clean and does not need a
check before mounting.

cron   A system daemon that runs jobs at user-defined intervals.

crontab files   The configuration files for cron.

curses library   A library containing many display routines for terminals.

default route   In general network setup, the default route is where all network traffic goes when its destination does not match any destination the systems administrator has specified.

development kernel release   Kernel releases that emphasize new features. Not always stable, development kernel releases evolve into production series after extended development. The minor version numbers of these releases are odd numbers.

disk cache   In Web browsers, a directory structure that holds temporary copies of large, frequently used data, such as images.

dithering   A process that distributes pixels to emulate a large variety of colors when only a limited number are available. Most common in inkjet printers.

domain name resolver   A library routine that translates Internet names into Internet addresses.

dump   A backup (either the act of making a backup, or the archive itself). Also the name of a specific backup program.

dump host   A network host that manages backups in Amanda.

ELF (Executable and Linkable Format)   The binary format most Linux programs use.

environment variables   Variables present in every process in the environment. You set them in a shell such as bash by first running `VARNAME=value` and then export `VARNAME`.

even number series   See *production kernel release.*

executable (binary)   A compiled program, ready to run.

gateway   A router that serves as an entire network's link to any other network.

generic kernel   A type of kernel included in many distributions. Generic kernels typically support a very large number of drivers and make few assumptions about the processor.

getty   A program that runs on a terminal and waits for a user to type a username. It then runs `/bin/login`.

header (include) file   A source code file that contains mainly definitions rather than actual program code.

holding disk   A temporary storage location Amanda uses before writing backup data to a tape.

hostname   An identifying name given to a Unix machine, usually the first part of its fully qualified domain name (FQDN). For example, if the FQDN is *mikado.example.com,* the hostname is usually *mikado.* However, the hostname can also be the entire FQDN or something completely different.

HUP (hangup)   A signal that any process may receive. Many system daemons use this as a signal to reload their configuration files.

Imakefile   An input for templates that generate Makefiles. Used with some X Window System packages.

kernel image   The end result of a kernel compile. Usually named `bzImage` or something similar.

kernel module   A kernel driver or facility compiled into a separate object file and therefore not active immediately after boot. To activate it, run `insmod` on the module.

level 0 backup   A complete backup.

library   A precompiled set of routines linked into an executable program at the link stage.

LILO (Linux Loader)   Boots the kernel after you turn on a machine.

linker   A utility that joins many object code files and libraries into executable programs.

log host   A system set up to receive the system logging messages from multiple Unix machines on a network.

major device number   A group of devices using the same driver is usually assigned a single major device number (illustrated by `ls -l` in `/dev`).

Makefile   A control file for `make`, a program that oversees automatic building of software packages.

minor device number   Each device under the same major device number (see above) is assigned a different minor device number.

name mangling   In SAMBA, the process of compressing a long Unix filename into an MS-DOS–style name.

netatalk   Client and server software that gives Unix machines access to Apple-Talk networks.

NFS (Network Filesystem)   A Unix system for file sharing.

NIS (Network Information System)   One of many methods for distributing small information maps, such as password and group information, over a network.

object file   A piece of compiled source code at an intermediate stage. To use an object file, you must link it into an executable.

odd number series   See *development kernel release.*

PAP   A type of authentication for PPP.

PID (Process ID)   An identifying number that the kernel assigns to a process.

PostScript   A page description language. Widely adopted by Unix as a printing standard.

production kernel release   Kernel release that emphasizes bug fixes. Typically very stable. The minor version number of these kernels are even numbers.

pseudoterminal   An emulated terminal that the kernel provides for programs relying on a terminal interface.

rasterize   The process of turning vector-format graphics into bitmaps.

respawn   To restart a process after its termination.

restore   A backup retrieval. Also the name of a specific retrieval program.

runlevel (init)   System V init runlevels are numbered 0 to 6 and correspond to different states of the operating system: normal, single-user, halt, and reboot are some examples.

run-time linker   A program that links shared library code into a running executable program after it starts.

SAMBA   Client and server software that gives Unix machines access to SMB (CIFS) networks.

SCSI host adapter   Another name for a SCSI controller.

squid   A popular, free Web proxy server.

source code   The program author's code. To build an executable program, you must compile its source code.

system logger (syslogd)   A facility for collecting diagnostic messages from system daemons.

TCP wrapper   A small wrapper for filtering and logging TCP connections.

Trojan horse   A type of attack where the intruder replaces a system program with his or her own version of the program.

UID (User ID)   A unique identifying number for a user (set in /etc/passwd).

virtual console   An emulated terminal running on the Linux SVGA console.

wrapper script   A shell script that sets a few environment variables before running a binary.

PROBLEMS LIST

Basics

Network Installation

Network Installation (continued)

NFS, NIS, and rdist

MS-Windows and AppleTalk Networks; Web Proxy Server

Printing

Printing (continued)

Installing Software from Source Code

Installing Software from Source Code (continued)

Kernel Upgrades

Backups and Crash Recovery

Backups and Crash Recovery (continued)

User Environments

ABOUT THE CD-ROM

You'll find the packages mentioned in the book in the support directory. We have split them up into further subdirectories by chapter. Here is a short index with descriptions.

support/introduction (Chapter 1)

foo.1: An example manual page

The text uses this as an example of a manual page you can format manually. You can also use it as a template for writing your own manual pages.

support/nfsnisrdist (Chapter 3)

expn-netgroup: Utility to expand NIS netgroups

Because NIS netgroups tend to get too large for the underlying database library to support, they are often split up into several entries. This utility unifies these distributed netgroups.

rdist6: rdist, a remote file distribution program

This is a popular package for distributing complex directory structures to one or many hosts at once.

support/atalksamba (Chapter 4)

netatalk+asun: Netatalk, with the asun additions

The Netatalk package contains clients and servers that can interact with Macintosh AppleTalk networks.

Initappletalk: init.d script for starting or stopping netatalk

This is a small script intended to start Netatalk at boot time. It follows the System V init.d system.

support/printing (Chapter 5)

printcap/: m4 printcap creation

These m4 macros facilitate the automatic generation of different printer configuration files from a single printer list.

LPRng-*.tgz: LPRng, advanced print spooler

The traditional print spoolers for Unix lack many modern features. LPRng allows for much more than simply sending a file to a printer.

ifhp-*.tgz: ifhp, advanced print filter

This print filter is intended for use with LPRng. Due to its high number of configuration options, ifhp may be the only print filter you ever need.

support/installsoft (Chapter 6)

fdutils-5.3.tar.gz: Floppy disk utilities

In the text, we use this as a package that uses the GNU autoconf system to facilitate configuration and compilation. It is a set of useful floppy disk utilities.

hello_w-0.00.tar.gz: Example package

Some packages don't use the GNU autoconf system. This is a simple (somewhat contrived) sample that doesn't do anything useful.

support/backupcrash (Chapter 8)

amanda: Package for automated backups

If you have a number of machines to back up, keeping track of regular backups is difficult to do by hand. Amanda schedules and runs automatic archiving.

support/userenv (Chapter 9)

killx: Kills all active X applications

In response to the problem of lingering X Window System applications after logout from an X terminal, Bill Fenner wrote this program. It turns out to be highly effective for xdm logouts as well.

HOWTOs

The CD contains all the Linux HOWTOs, including the mini HOWTOs:

3Dfx-HOWTO

AI-Alife-HOWTO

AX25-HOWTO

Access-HOWTO

Adv-Routing-HOWTO

Alpha-HOWTO

Assembly-HOWTO

Bash-Prompt-HOWTO

Belgian-HOWTO

Benchmarking-HOWTO

Beowulf-HOWTO

BootPrompt-HOWTO

Bootdisk-HOWTO

Busmouse-HOWTO

C++Programming-HOWTO

C-C++Beautifier-HOWTO

CD-Writing-HOWTO

CDROM-HOWTO

COPYRIGHT

CVS-RCS-HOWTO

Chinese-HOWTO

Chroot-BIND-HOWTO

Commercial-HOWTO

Config-HOWTO

Consultants-HOWTO

Cyrillic-HOWTO

DNS-HOWTO

DOS-Win-to-Linux-HOWTO

DOSEMU-HOWTO

Danish-HOWTO

Diald-HOWTO

Diskless-HOWTO

Diskless-root-NFS-HOWTO

Distribution-HOWTO

Ecology-HOWTO

Emacs-Beginner-HOWTO

Emacspeak-HOWTO

Enterprise-Java-for-Linux-HOWTO

Esperanto-HOWTO

Ethernet-HOWTO

Filesystems-HOWTO

Finnish-HOWTO

Firewall-HOWTO

Font-HOWTO

Framebuffer-HOWTO

Francophones-HOWTO

From-PowerUp-To-Bash-Prompt-HOWTO

Ftape-HOWTO

GCC-HOWTO

German-HOWTO

Glibc2-HOWTO

HOWTO-HOWTO
HP-HOWTO
Hardware-HOWTO
Hebrew-HOWTO
Hellenic-HOWTO
INFO-SHEET
IP-Masquerade-HOWTO
IPCHAINS-HOWTO
IPX-HOWTO
IR-HOWTO
ISP-Hookup-HOWTO
IngresII-HOWTO
Installation-HOWTO
Intranet-Server-HOWTO
Italian-HOWTO
Java-CGI-HOWTO
JavaStation-HOWTO
Jaz-Drive-HOWTO
Kernel-HOWTO
Keyboard-and-Console-HOWTO
KickStart-HOWTO
Kiosk-HOWTO
Kodak-Digitalcam-HOWTO
LDAP-HOWTO
Laptop-HOWTO
Large-Disk-HOWTO
Linux-From-Scratch-HOWTO
LinuxDoc+Emacs+Ispell-HOWTO
Loopback-Encrypted-Filesystem-HOWTO
MGR-HOWTO
MILO-HOWTO

MIPS-HOWTO
MP3-HOWTO
Mail-Administrator-HOWTO
Mail-User-HOWTO
Majordomo-MajorCool-HOWTO
mini
Modem-HOWTO
Multi-Disk-HOWTO
MultiOS-HOWTO
Multicast-HOWTO
Mutt-GnuPG-PGP-HOWTO
NC-HOWTO
NCD-HOWTO
NET3-4-HOWTO
NFS-HOWTO
NIS-HOWTO
Net-HOWTO
Networking-Overview-HOWTO
Online-Troubleshooting-HOWTO
Optical-Disk-HOWTO
Oracle-7-HOWTO
Oracle-8-HOWTO
PCI-HOWTO
PCMCIA-HOWTO
PHP-HOWTO
PLIP-Install-HOWTO
PPP-HOWTO
PalmOS-HOWTO
Parallel-Processing-HOWTO
Plug-and-Play-HOWTO
Polish-HOWTO
Portuguese-HOWTO

PostgreSQL-HOWTO

phhttpd-HOWTO

Printing-HOWTO

Printing-Usage-HOWTO

Process-Monitor-HOWTO

Program-Library-HOWTO

Psion-HOWTO

Qmail-VMailMgr-Courier-imap-HOWTO

Quake-HOWTO

RPM-HOWTO

Reading-List-HOWTO

RedHat-CD-HOWTO

Root-RAID-HOWTO

SCSI-Programming-HOWTO

SMB-HOWTO

SMP-HOWTO

SRM-HOWTO

Secure-Programs-HOWTO

Securing-Domain-HOWTO

Security-HOWTO

Serbian-HOWTO

Serial-HOWTO

Serial-Programming-HOWTO

Shadow-Password-HOWTO

Slovenian-HOWTO

Software-Building-HOWTO

Software-RAID-0.4x-HOWTO

Software-RAID-HOWTO

Software-Release-Practice-HOWTO

Sound-HOWTO

Sound-Playing-HOWTO

Spanish-HOWTO

TclTk-HOWTO

TeTeX-HOWTO

Text-Terminal-HOWTO

Thai-HOWTO

Thinclient-HOWTO

Tips-HOWTO

Turkish-HOWTO

UMSDOS-HOWTO

UPS-HOWTO

UUCP-HOWTO

Unicode-HOWTO

Unix-and-Internet-Fundamentals-HOWTO

User-Group-HOWTO

VAR-HOWTO

VME-HOWTO

VMS-to-Linux-HOWTO

VPN-HOWTO

Vim-HOWTO

Virtual-Services-HOWTO

VPN-Masquerade-HOWTO

WWW-HOWTO

WWW-mSQL-HOWTO

Wacom-Tablet-HOWTO

Wearable-HOWTO

XFree86-HOWTO

XFree86-Touch-Screen-HOWTO

XFree86-Video-Timings-HOWTO

XWindow-User-HOWTO

mini HOWTOs

NFS-Root-Client

Netrom-Node

Netscape+Proxy

Netstation

News-Leafsite

Offline-Mailing

PLIP

Partition

Partition-Rescue-mini-HOWTO

Path

Pre-Installation-Checklist

Process-Accounting

Programming-Languages

Proxy-ARP-Subnet

Public-Web-Browser

Qmail+MH

Quota

README

RPM+Slackware

Remote-Boot

Remote-X-Apps

Saving-Space

SLIP-PPP-Emulator

Secure-POP+SSH

Sendmail+UUCP

Sendmail-Address-Rewrite

Small-Memory

Soundblaster-AWE

StarOffice

Swap-Space

TT-Debian

Term-Firewall

TkRat

Token-Ring

TransparentProxy

Ultra-DMA

Update

Upgrade

VAIO+Linux

VPN

Visual-Bell

WordPerfect

X-Big-Cursor

XFree86-XInside

Xterm-Title

ZIP-Drive

ZIP-Install

Emergency Boot Support

In addition to the packages mentioned in the book, you will also find a set of emergency and recovery utilities on the CD-ROM. It offers a boot image, as well as a number of basic system programs to help you out. The following is a brief breakdown of the emergency boot-related directories:

bin   The emergency boot CD-ROM binaries.

boot   Boot floppy images.

info; man   Manual and info pages.

lib; libexec   Auxiliary data and programs for the programs in /bin.

modules   A large set of kernel modules that can go with the kernel boot image.

Because CD-ROMs have a peculiar way of booting on PCs, there are two ways you can start up a session from the CD-ROM. One is to use the CD-ROM only for booting, which gives you a very basic system. The other is to boot this image, then mount the CD-ROM and access a larger set of utilities. The basic system asks if you'd like to do this after boot time. To stay with the basic system, type **n**. If you type **y**, the system will attempt to mount the CD-ROM for you. If the system succeeds in doing so, it asks if you'd like to use bash (you'll have access to a full version of bash, as well as many other programs such as vi and dc, after the system mounts the CD-ROM).

There are more details on the CD-ROM boot in section 8.5.1, including how to make a boot floppy and how to attach a temporary RAM disk.

The executable programs on the CD-ROM (not on the boot floppy) are statically linked; they do not depend on any shared libraries. They come from these packages:

bash-2.04 fileutils-4.0 gzip-1.2.4a rpm-2.5.1

bc-1.05 findutils-4.1 inetutils-1.3b sh-utils-2.0

cpio-2.4.2 gawk-3.0.4 less-340 tar-1.13

diffutils-2.7 grep-2.4.2 nvi-1.79 textutils-2.0

If you like the boot CD-ROM, please consider giving some money or equipment to the Debian people (http://www.debian.org/). The boot image on this CD-ROM is partly based on their installation image.

INDEX

chap-secrets, 28, 30

character devices, 11

    kernel support of, 172

characters, literal, 14

chat (program), 22

chat scripts, 24, 30

cjpeg, 131

class and subclass names, 235

clean bit, 212

clear-text passwords, 84

clients

    Macintosh, 42, 87

    NFS, 52–56

    NIS, 59–62

    Solaris NIS, 61, 66

    Windows, 42, 87

clients, configuration of Web

    browsers for, 102

cmdspecial (in Distfile), 70–71

Coda, 59, 173

collisions, troubleshooting

    excessive, 45

color displays with X Windows,

    238–239

commands

    illustrated in this book, 3

    in ipchains options, 34

    kernel module, 181

    network configuration, 18–19

    rdist, 69–71

    in shell startup files, 224–226

    substitutions, 16

compare dist option, 71

compiler errors, 155, 159–161

compiler warnings, 155

compiles, troubleshooting

    failed, 154

COM ports, 27

compress, 138

compressed tar files, unpacking,

    139–140

computers. *See also* clients;

    Macintosh machines; servers

    boot-up problems on, 53

    choosing, on which to run

        rdist, 75

    shutdown errors, 213–214

    that have lost files, 206

    using Windows and Linux,

        77–90

    Windows machines, 87–89

config.h, editing, 146, 148

config.log, 145

configure

    influencing, with

        environment

        variables,144–146

    options, 144

    troubleshooting, 145

connect *command* pppd option

conventions used in this book, 3

convert and copy. *See* dd

corrupt files, 140

cp, 143, 222

cpio, 195–196

crash recovery, 208–211

cron, 8–9

crontabs, 8–9

csh, 222, 228–230

.cshrc, 218, 228–230

ctrlatldel, 5

cu, 30

cua device names, 28

D

daemons
- NTP (network time protocol), 46
- print, 106–112
- SAMBA, 78–79
- troubleshooting, 93

data, sending via modem, 26

daytime, 39

dbm files, 62

dd, 194–195, 208

Debian distribution, 210

debugfs (utility), 214–215

debugging
- ifhp, 117
- inetd, 21
- NIS with ypcat, ypmatch, and ypwhich, 62
- pppd with nodetach, 26
- with route, 18
- SAMBA, 80
- with younger dist option, 72

debug pppd option, 27

default permissions, setting, 224

defaultroute pppd option, 25

default routes, 19, 25

default startup files, 219, 220

default user, creating a, 223–224

default .Xdefaults files, 239

denial-of-service attacks, 34

depmod, 181

/dev, 10

development kernel, 164

development set of packages, 136

device drivers, 170–171
- conflicts between, 185
- modules, 182
- for network devices, 18
- printer, 132
- for tape drives, 189

device pppd option, 25

devices
- block, 170–171
- changes in names of, 132
- examining and creating, 11–12
- faking, 114
- files and names (*See also* /dev), 10–11
- kernel configuration of, 170–172
- network, 17
- removable media, 55
- serial, 27
- troubleshooting, 209

df, 12

diagnostics, 14, 44–49

dial-ups
  connecting to, 28–29
  prompts from, 24
dig, 48
directories
  asking SAMBA server for
    home, 89
  empty, 56
  exporting to Windows
    clients, 87
  home, 224
  to include in startup files,
    218–219
  troubleshooting, 143, 159
discard, 39
disklist, 198, 201
disks, working with, 12–13
Display Power Management
  System (DPMS), 234
Distfile, 67
dist options, 68–69, 71–72
distribution kernels, 167
distributions, 4. *See also* Red Hat
  Linux; software; source code
distributions
  binary and source code, 136
  Debian, 210
  lacking complete kernel
    source code, 164
  large-scale, 75
  old versions of, dealing
    with, 166

starting complicated, 221
tools accompanying, 136
dmesg, 176
DNS and BIND, 3rd Edition (Paul
  Albitz and Cricket Liu), 49
DNS (domain name service), 20
  avoiding, 35
  domain, 59
  query program, 48
  using host command, 48
dollar sign ($) before strings, 15
domainname, 60
domain name resolution,
  disabling, 19–20
DOS FAT filesystems, kernel
  support of, 172
dot (.) in a path, 219–220
double quotation marks ("), 15
DPMS (Display Power
  Management System), 234
drivers. *See* device drivers
du, 12
dual-booting, 180
dump and restore programs, 196
dynamic loader, 137

E

e2fsck, 212
echo, 16, 39
editors, 223

eth0, 17

Ethernet configuration, 18

expn-netgroup, 66

extract, 197

F

facility names, 8

fdformat, 175

fdisk, 12

fdutils, 143, 175

Fenner, Bill, 235

file handles, stale, 56

filenames

    extensions for object files, 142

    extensions for source
        code, 141

    suffixes for compressed
        files, 138

    on Unix, 88

files

    accidental deletion of,
        preventing, 222

    AppleVolumes files, 95, 98

    beginning with a forward
        slash (/), 140

    binary, and printers, 119

    compressed, 138–140

    conversion of non-Unix
        format, 195

    copying from one machine to
        others, 67

    copying to and from remote
        files

    hosts, 42

    dbm, 62

    dependencies among,
        problems caused by, 53

    device, 10

    editor setup, 223

    gdbm, 59

    graphics, 130

    locking, 10

    long, 87

    m4, 126–128

    object, 137, 142

    postscript, 94

    PPD (PostScript Printer
        Definition), 117

    putting on a tape, 191–192

    recovering, with Amanda log
        files, 207–208

    repairing Linux system,
        215–216

    restoring, with amrecover,
        206–207

    source code, 141

    startup, 218, 219, 224–226

    troubleshooting problems
        involving, 69, 88, 143,
        159, 220

    updating NIS master
        server, 64

    X Windows startup, 230–235

K

Q

quotation marks
  double ("), 15
  single ('), 3, 14–16
  usage in this book, 3
  to get literal characters,
    14–16

R

RAM disk
  after a crash, 210
  kernel support of, 170–171
RAWRITE programs, 209
rc.atalk script, 92
rc*.d
  location, 6
  troubleshooting, 216
rdist, 51–52, 67–75
  choosing machine on which
    to run, 75
  distributing, when and with
    what, 75
  options, 68–69
  troubleshooting, 70, 71, 72, 74
  with ssh, 72–74
Red Hat Linux
  assembler and linker
    programs, 165
  handling of SCSI
    modules, 182

and PPP, 30–31
PPP/PAP configuration, 29
smbprint, 121
references to manual pages, 4
rehash, 156
remote distribution. *See* rdist
remote hosts, troubleshooting, 68
remote printers, 108
  name and host options, 110
remount errors,
  troubleshooting, 212
removable media, 55
  for backups, 189
  kernel support of, 171
rereading /etc/inittab, 6
rescue CD-ROM, 209
respawn, 5–6
restore
  equivalent program to, 206
  modes of, 196–197
rexecd, 39
.rhosts, 203
rlogin, 40
rlogind, 39
rm -i, 222
rmmod, 181
root (/) device, 78, 185
root password, 215
route command, 18, 19–20
routers, 31
routes, adding, 19
routing tables, 19

Y

Z

THE NO B.S. GUIDE TO
RED HAT LINUX 6.x

by BOB RANKIN

This book is a thorough yet concise guide to installing Red Hat Linux 6 and exploring its capabilities. Author Bob Rankin (*The No B.S. Guide to Linux*, No Starch Press) provides easy-to-follow instructions for installing and running Red Hat 6.x. Through examples and helpful illustrations, the author guides readers through these topics and more:

- Installation — in ten easy steps!

- How to use and configure GNOME — the new Linux GUI

- How to write Bash or Perl scripts and use the Bash shell

- How to connect to the Internet with SLIP/PPP and how to run the Apache Web server for Linux

- How to access DOS files and run Windows programs under Linux

The CD-ROM contains Red Hat Linux 6.*x* — one of the most popular Linux distributions available. It's easy to install and requires minimal configuration — you'll be up and running in a snap!

BOB RANKIN is a programmer and nationally recognized expert on the Internet. He is a columnist for *Boardwatch Magazine* and a contributor to several computer publications. His books include *Dr. Bob's Painless Guide to the Internet* (1996) and *The No B.S. Guide to Linux* (1997).

402 pp., paperback, $34.95 w/CD-ROM
ISBN 1-886411-30-1

LINUX MUSIC & SOUND

by DAVE PHILLIPS

Linux Music & Sound offers in-depth instruction on recording, storing, playing, and editing music and sound under Linux. The author, a programmer and performing musician, discusses the basics of sound and digital audio, and covers software and hardware issues specific to Linux, including:

- A clear introduction to the fundamental concepts of digital sound
- Linux-specific issues including available toolkits, GUI libraries, and driver support
- Reviews of available software with recommendations
- Recommended components for building a complete system including a digital audio player/recorder, soundfile editor, MIDI recorder/player/editor, and software mixer
- Coverage of hard disk recording, advanced MIDI support, network audio, and MP3
- A complete bibliography and an extensive list of Internet resources
- A CD-ROM with dozens of software packages

A performing musician for over 30 years, DAVE PHILLIPS became interested in computers as a means for playing, editing, and recording music. He is an expert in MIDI, Csound, and Linux. He currently maintains several educational Web sites on these topics.

300 pp., paperback, $39.95 w/CD-ROM
ISBN 1-886411-34-4

STEAL THIS COMPUTER BOOK: WHAT THEY WON'T TELL YOU ABOUT THE INTERNET

by WALLACE WANG

"A delightfully irresponsible primer." — *Chicago Tribune*

"If this book had a soundtrack, it'd be Lou Reed's 'Walk on the Wild Side.'" — *InfoWorld*

"An unabashed look at the dark side of the Net — the stuff many other books gloss over." — *Amazon.com*

Steal This Computer Book explores the dark corners of the Internet and reveals little-known techniques that hackers use to subvert authority. Unfortunately, some of these techniques, when used by malicious hackers, can destroy data and compromise the security of corporate and government networks. To keep your computer safe from viruses, and yourself from electronic con games and security crackers, Wallace Wang explains the secrets hackers and scammers use to prey on their victims. Discover:

- How hackers write and spread computer viruses
- How criminals get free service and harass legitimate customers on online services like America Online
- How online con artists trick people out of thousands of dollars
- Where hackers find the tools to crack into computers or steal software
- How to find and use government-quality encryption to protect your data
- How hackers steal passwords from other computers

WALLACE WANG is the author of several computer books, including *Microsoft Office 97 for Windows for Dummies* and *Visual Basic for Dummies*. A regular contributor to *Boardwatch* magazine (the "Internet Underground" columnist), he's also a successful stand-up comedian. He lives in San Diego, California.

340 pp., paperback, $19.95
ISBN 1-886411-21-2

Phone:
1 (800) 420-7240 OR
(415) 863-9900
MONDAY THROUGH FRIDAY,
9 A.M. TO 5 P.M. (PST)

Fax:
(415) 863-9950
24 HOURS A DAY,
7 DAYS A WEEK

E-mail:
SALES@NOSTARCH.COM

Web:
HTTP://WWW.NOSTARCH.COM

Mail:
NO STARCH PRESS
555 DE HARO STREET, SUITE 250
SAN FRANCISCO, CA 94107
USA

Distributed to the book trade by Publishers Group West

UPDATES

This book was carefully reviewed for technical accuracy, but it's inevitable that some things will change after the book goes to press. Visit the Web site for this book at **http://www.nostarch.com/lps_updates.htm** for updates, errata, and other information.

CD-ROM LICENSE AGREEMENT FOR *THE LINUX PROBLEM SOLVER*

Read this Agreement before opening this package. By opening this package, you agree to be bound by the terms and conditions of this Agreement.

This CD-ROM (the "CD") contains programs and associated documentation and other materials and is distributed with the book entitled *The Linux Problem Solver* to purchasers of the book for their own personal use only. Such programs, documentation and other materials and their compilation (collectively, the "Collection") are licensed to you subject to terms and conditions of this Agreement by No Starch Press, having a place of business at 555 De Haro Street, Suite 250, San Francisco, CA 94107 ("Licensor"). In addition to being governed by the terms and conditions of this Agreement, your rights to use the programs and other materials included on the CD may also be governed by separate agreements distributed with those programs and materials on the CD (the "Other Agreements"). In the event of any inconsistency between this Agreement and any of the Other Agreements, those Agreements shall govern insofar as those programs and materials are concerned. By using the Collection, in whole or in part, you agree to be bound by the terms and conditions of this Agreement. Licensor owns the copyright to the Collection, except insofar as it contains materials that are proprietary to third party suppliers. All rights in the Collection except those expressly granted to you in this Agreement are reserved to Licensor and such suppliers as their respective interests may appear.

1. Limited License. Licensor grants you a limited, nonexclusive, nontransferable license to use the Collection on a single dedicated computer (excluding network servers). This Agreement and your rights hereunder shall automatically terminate if you fail to comply with any provision of this Agreement or the Other Agreements. Upon such termination, you agree to destroy the CD and all copies of the CD, whether lawful or not, that are in your possession or under your control. Licensor and its suppliers retain all rights not expressly granted herein as their respective interests may appear.

2. Additional Restrictions. (A) You shall not (and shall not permit other persons or entities to) directly or indirectly, by electronic or other means, reproduce (except for archival purposes as permitted by law), publish, distribute, rent, lease, sell, sublicense, assign, or otherwise transfer the Collection or any part thereof or this Agreement. Any attempt to do so shall be void and of no effect. (B) You shall not (and shall not permit other persons or entities to) reverse-engineer, decompile, disassemble, merge, modify, create derivative works of, or translate the Collection or use the Collection or any part thereof for any commercial purpose. (C) You shall not (and shall not permit other persons or entities to) remove or obscure Licensor's or its suppliers' or licensor's copyright, trademark, or other proprietary notices or legends from any portion of the Collection or any related materials. (D) You agree and certify that the Collection will not be exported outside the United States except as authorized and as permitted by the laws and regulations of the United States. If the Collection has been rightfully obtained outside of the United States, you agree that you will not reexport the Collection, except as permitted by the laws and regulations of the United States and the laws and regulations of the jurisdiction in which you obtained the Collection.

3. Disclaimer of Warranty. (A) The Collection and the CD are provided "as is" without warranty of any kind, either express or implied, including, without limitation, any warranty of merchantability and fitness for a particular purpose. The entire risk as to the results and performance of the CD and the software and other materials that is part of the Collection is assumed by you, and Licensor and its suppliers and distributors shall have no responsibility for defects in the CD or the accuracy or application of or errors or omissions in the Collection and do not warrant that the functions contained in the Collection will meet your requirements, or that the operation of the CD or the Collection will be uninterrupted or error-free, or that any defects in the CD or the Collection will be corrected. In no event shall Licensor or its suppliers or distributors be liable for any direct, indirect, special, incidental, or consequential damages arising out of the use of or inability to use the Collection or the CD, even if Licensor or its suppliers or distributors have been advised of the likelihood of such damages occurring. Licensor and its suppliers and distributors shall not be liable for any loss, damages, or costs arising out of, but not limited to, lost profits or revenue; loss of use of the Collection or the CD; loss of data or equipment; cost of recovering software, data, or materials in the Collection; the cost of substitute software, data, or materials in the Collection; claims by third parties; or other similar costs. (B) In no event shall Licensor or its suppliers' or distributors' total liability to you for all damages, losses, and causes of action (whether in contract, tort or otherwise) exceed the amount paid by you for the Collection. (C) Some states do not allow exclusion or limitation of implied warranties or limitation of liability for incidental or consequential damages, so the above limitations or exclusions may not apply to you.

4. U.S. Government Restricted Rights. The Collection is licensed subject to RESTRICTED RIGHTS. Use, duplication, or disclosure by the U.S. Government or any person or entity acting on its behalf is subject to restrictions as set forth in subdivision (c)(1)(ii) of the Rights in Technical Data and Computer Software Clause at DFARS (48 CFR 252.227-7013) for DoD contracts, in paragraphs (c)(1) and (2) of the Commercial Computer Software Restricted Rights clause in the FAR (48 CFR 52.227-19) for civilian agencies, or, in the case of NASA, in clause 18-52.227-86(d) of the NASA Supplement to the FAR, or in other comparable agency clauses. The contractor/manufacturer is No Starch Press, 555 De Haro Street, Suite 250, San Francisco, CA 94107.

5. General Provisions. Nothing in this Agreement constitutes a waiver of Licensor's, or its suppliers' or licensors' rights under U.S. copyright laws or any other federal, state, local, or foreign law. You are responsible for installation, management, and operation of the Collection. This Agreement shall be construed, interpreted, and governed under California law. Copyright (c) 2000 No Starch Press. All rights reserved. Reproduction in whole or in part without permission is prohibited.